Best of
FamilyFun
Crafts & Boredom Busters

This book is dedicated to
the readers of *FamilyFun* magazine

Printed in the United States of America. For information, address Disney Editions, 114 Fifth Avenue, New York, NY 10011-5690.

All of the crafts and photographs in this book were previously published in *FamilyFun* Crafts and *FamilyFun* Boredom Busters.

FamilyFun magazine is a division of the Walt Disney Publishing Group.
To order a subscription, call 800-289-4849.

The Best of FamilyFun Crafts and Boredom Busters

BOOK EDITORS: Rani M. Arbo, Deanna F. Cook, Ann Hallock, Alexandra Kennedy, Cindy A. Littlefield, and Catherine Newman
CONTRIBUTING EDITORS: Jonathan Adolph, Dawn Chipman, Barbara Findlen, Priscilla Totten, and Katherine Whittemore
ART DIRECTORS: Ginger Barr Heafey, David Kendrick, and Mark Mantegna
CRAFT DEVELOPERS: Janet Street and Maryellen Sullivan
COPY EDITORS: Laura MacKay, Paula Noonan, and Mike Trotman
EDITORIAL ASSISTANTS: Grace Ganssle, Jean Graham, Julia Lynch, Susan Roberts, and Ellen Harter Wall
ART ASSISTANTS: Lynn Carrier, Sage Dillon, and Catherine McGrady
PRODUCTION EDITORS: Martha Jenkins, Jennifer Mayer, and Dana Stiepock
EDITORIAL INTERNS: Debra Liebson, Danielle Zerbonne
TECHNOLOGY COORDINATOR: Luke Jaeger and Tom Lepper

Impress, Inc.

DESIGNERS: Howard Klein, Hans Teensma, Carolyn Eckert
PROJECTS DIRECTOR: Lisa Newman
ART ASSOCIATES: Jen Darcy and Katie Winger

The staffs of **FamilyFun** and **Impress, Inc.**
conceived and produced *The Best of FamilyFun Crafts and Boredom Busters* at
244 Main Street, Northampton, MA 01060

In collaboration with
Disney Editions, 114 Fifth Avenue, New York, NY 10011

Library of Congress Cataloging-in-Publication Data on file

ISBN 0-7868-5901-6
First Edition

Special thanks to all the *FamilyFun* writers and readers for their wonderful recipes and party ideas from *FamilyFun Crafts* and *FamilyFun Boredom Busters*. With gratitude to all the staff of *FamilyFun*'s art and editorial departments, who directed much of the original work. Special thanks to all the photographers, stylists, and models for their excellent work.

FamilyFun
Crafts
Creative Activities for You and Your Kids **5**

FamilyFun
Boredom Busters
Games, Crafts, and Activities for Every Day of the Year **165**

Thumbs Up,
page 87

FamilyFun Crafts

EDITED BY **DEANNA F. COOK**

AND THE EXPERTS AT FamilyFun MAGAZINE

Contents

Milk Jug Dollhouse, page 34

Spooky Spiders, page 152

Farm Animal
Puppets,
page 140

Splatter Shirts,
page 103

Chapter One

Setting Up

O F ALL THE activities we publish in *FamilyFun* magazine, our crafts generate the most mail from readers. Every day, our mailbox offers up handwritten letters with snapshots of kids proudly displaying craft projects from the magazine's pages: clay bead necklaces, clothespin Christmas ornaments, or homemade finger puppets. Seeing these photos and reading the letters remind us what crafting is all about — the chance to spend time together as a family and, in the process, create lasting memories for our children.

Since we started *FamilyFun* in 1991, readers have turned to us for craft ideas to help make the most of a rainy afternoon, a Scouting event, a birthday party, or a holiday celebration. They have clipped and saved and spilled glue all over our directions — and some have even organized their own filing systems for favorite projects. So we decided it was time to gather our crafts in one book.

That way, our readers would no longer have to rustle through back issues to find that paper wind sock or those Thanksgiving decorations they want to make *right now.*

We've hit upon a tried-and-true method for developing crafts: we look to our families, to our regular contributors, and to our readers for inspiration. What crafts have been the most impressive? The most fun for the kids? The answers, which lie in the pages of this book, range from easy drawing games to homemade play doughs to holiday keepsakes. Some are as simple as a paper chain; others are as grand as a giant playhouse. But they all have one thing in common: they have been tested by families like yours — and are proven winners with both parents and kids.

For every craft in this book, we've kept the directions as straightforward as possible. For almost all of them, we've used materials that are readily available and inexpensive (an entire chapter, in fact, is devoted to art made from recyclables). Most importantly, every project passes the kid test: children must be able to complete

Matisse Cutouts, page 57

A Child's Craft Corner

A special craft area in the basement, garage, or in a corner of your child's room can make art sessions positively habit-forming. Here are a few helpful hints for setting up.

Work surface: Start with a comfortable seat, good lighting, and an uncluttered surface, such as a table, desk, low closet shelf, easel, or even a breakfast tray.

Storage and supplies: A small bookcase keeps supplies out of the way yet accessible. The following ideas will help you organize:
- Shoe boxes and plastic containers filled with crayons, paints, and glue.
- Markers, pencils, scissors, and paintbrushes can stand upright in coffee cans or plastic jars or lie flat in plastic silverware trays.
- Egg cartons are just right for holding buttons, stickers, glitter, and odds and ends.
- A cardboard box can become a "collage container" for storing feathers, fabric, yarn, pinecones, shells, and other treasures.
- Stow paper supplies (newsprint pads, a roll of butcher block paper) on a shelf, along with a large envelope that holds loose sheets of paper, doilies, and old magazines.

the craft with only a little help from a patient adult — and have room to add their own embellishments to the design.

Doing crafts with kids does take time, but it's worth the effort. Hands-on activities hold a child's attention and develop creativity, dexterity, problem-solving skills, and confidence. With art budgets dwindling in many American schools, it's becoming more important than ever for parents to encourage and participate in art at home. Maybe that's one reason why arts and crafts are on the rise — ninety percent of all U.S. households now have at least one crafter.

So the next time you are looking for a quick activity, just open this book. Don't worry about getting a little paint on the pages. You may discover, as many of our readers have, that even if the craft turns out slightly lopsided or the tail is in the wrong place, your child will be pleased with his creation. And if you happen to take a photo of him holding up his project,

by all means send it along — your pictures are a continuing inspiration to us.

Planning a Craft Project

If you wonder what parent has the time and energy to choose a craft project, set it up, help the kids complete it, and clean up, take heart: you and your children can pull it off like pros. Here are tips to get you started, and a promise that the more you do it, the easier it gets.

Set up a work space. Since craft projects do make somewhat of a mess, set yours up in an easy-to-clean place, such as a utility room, a back porch or garage, or a corner of the kitchen. Ideally, the room should be well ventilated, especially if you are working with spray paints and sealers. Even better, reserve a spot exclusively for crafting, where art materials can be stored within arm's reach (see A Child's Craft Corner, at left, for ideas).

Choose age-appropriate projects. Try to pick crafts your children have the motor skills for — and set aside

time enough to complete the task. For a kindergartner, choose a project with very few steps or be prepared to take over when he loses interest. Older kids should be able to handle a larger-scale endeavor (say, the little red barn on page 44). Let them go for it, but you can also encourage them to spread it out over a week of after-school time or over two weekend days.

Gather materials before you begin. There's nothing worse than realizing halfway through a project that you're out of tempera paint or construction paper. In this book, we've pulled the art materials into recipe-style lists so you can plan ahead and stock up on supplies.

Put on smocks. Before you launch into any messy craft, you're smart to dress your child in a smock. You don't need to buy an expensive one — instead, try an oversize oxford, a big T-shirt, an old apron, or anything else that's loose enough to let your child move freely yet still keep him relatively clean.

Make cleanup part of the project. Cleaning up as you go will help preserve order in your work space, and it may also save art supplies from an early demise (uncapped markers and open containers of paint or glue, for example). Start this habit early, and it will become a part of your child's regular craft ritual. For Cleanup Tips, see page 14.

Encouraging Creativity

As you approach any craft project, be sure to give your children creative license. The more room you give them, the more their art will reflect their personalities and experiences. To help them enjoy the creative process — and feel good about their artwork when it's complete — follow the tips below.

Steer toward a finished product, but emphasize the process. It's fine to have an end result in mind — older kids, particularly, like closure and are proud of finished projects. But make sure you aren't so determined to follow directions that your child can't add her own flair. The end result, after all, is no more important than the steps that lead up to it. So when you're

Setting Up

The Rules of Crafting

Safety First

trying a new project, always ask yourself, "Can my child be creative with what we're doing here, or am I running an arts and crafts assembly line?"

Offer help, but not too much of it. To make your crafting time a bit more efficient, you may be tempted to lay out precut pieces of fabric or construction paper for your child to assemble. But be careful of doing too much. All that organizing, measuring, folding, cutting, and shaping can be part of the fun for your kids — and it teaches valuable lessons.

Set ground rules. Contrary to what Jackson Pollock's mother might have thought, childhood creativity rarely thrives when paint is being strewn with abandon. As in most pleasurable situations with children, an adult needs to create an environment where kids feel free because they understand the limits. After all, they don't instinctively know that the blue paintbrush goes back in the blue paint pot or that markers shouldn't be pounded down on paper. Laying down a few guidelines won't squelch your child's imagination, and it will put you more at

ease. Just be sure you limit disorder, not creativity. See The Rules of Crafting, left, for some basic guidelines.

Don't rush your child. Encourage your kids to take their time when working with scissors, markers, crayons, and other art tools that require fine motor skills. These skills are not developed overnight, so try not to get impatient just because you'd like to move on to more interesting projects. The fun of making things withers if the learner is held to impossible standards of maturity. Let your kids proceed at their own pace; they will let you know when they're ready for something more complicated.

Expose kids to art. Take your kids to arts and crafts museums, check out books from the library, and look in your local paper for special exhibits or art classes in your area to inspire your crafters to be more creative.

Choosing Good Materials

All of us have felt the irritation of working with unresponsive materials (wallpapering comes to mind). Imagine, then, how frustrating it is for a child to use

paper that rips when wet, scissors that chew rather than cut, or crayons that crumble. Good materials are worth the investment. Consider stocking up on the following basics — and if you are unfamiliar with any of them, visit your local craft store.

Paint. Although liquid tempera is handy to have, we recommend buying the bottles of tempera powder, available at most office or school supply stores, because they last for ages. Mix the powder with a little water in a clear jar, put the lid on, and shake. Add more powder or water if the paint is too thick or runny. Add 1 teaspoon of dish detergent for every ½ cup of paint and it will wash out of clothes more readily. You will also need acrylic paint, a longer-lasting paint that's available at art stores, for some of the finer crafts in this book, and fabric paint, for jazzing up T-shirts, sneakers, and other wearables in Chapter Eight.

Paper. For drawing with markers or crayons, buy copier paper or pads of watercolor, construction, or drawing paper. Or, try a roll of white butch-

er paper, available inexpensively at paper or food service supply stores. Cheaper paper, such as newsprint, is okay for scribbling with pens and pencils, but it soaks up markers and paints in a most unsatisfying way. Some projects in this book also call for tissue paper, card stock, and poster board. And of course, you can never have too much scrap paper on hand.

Paintbrushes. Stockpile a few easy-to-hold brushes. Inexpensive 1-inch or ¾-inch ones, available at hardware stores, make good brushes for glue or paint. Avoid the truly cheap ones because their bristles fall out, and always rinse the brushes to prolong their lives.

Glue. White glue goes further and is neater when kids apply it with brushes. If you buy a big tub of white glue, pour it into jars that can be capped for storage. Glue sticks are ideal for kids, especially young ones. Superglue and some brands of rubber cement are toxic, so use them with caution. A hot glue gun is suggested for several activities in this book, but it should be used by parents

How to Respond to a Child's Artwork

Instead of interpreting your child's artwork, ask questions or talk about the effort that's gone into the art. Some good phrases to try are:
"What bright colors you used here!"
"Look at all the different kinds of lines you drew."
"I can see you've been working very hard on this picture."
"Can you tell me what is going on here?"
"This picture makes me feel happy."
  Or, write down your child's own description of their art on the bottom or back of the paper.

Setting Up

only and should be stored out of kids' reach.

Crayons and colored pencils. For young kids, invest in good crayons; cheap ones leave weak colors and snap easily. We recommend the large Crayola box with the built-in sharpener. For older kids, use sharpened colored pencils.

Markers. Art teacher and *FamilyFun* contributor Elise Webb especially loves Mr. Sketch markers; they are broad-tipped, come in nice colors, and last. They, and other good (and more washable) markers, can be found in toy, art supply, and discount stores. Avoid cheap no-name markers, and avoid permanent markers altogether for young kids.

Scissors. A good pair of scissors is an indispensable craft tool. Fabric scissors, pinking shears, and other specialty scissors (such as crazy scissors) are recommended for a few of the projects in this book. You'll also need a craft knife (with a screw-in, replaceable blade) or a utility knife (with a retractable blade) — both of which

should be used by parents only.

Recyclables. From empty boxes to milk jugs to egg cartons, many activities in this book call for household recyclables. See page 30 for an extensive list of potential art supplies.

Tape. Scotch tape, double-stick tape, masking tape, and duct tape are all worth having in your supply closet. When tape is an outwardly visible part of the finished craft, you might opt for brightly colored electrical tape.

Tools. Desk tools, such as a hole punch (single hole is best), a ruler, and a stapler, will be necessary for some crafts. Kitchen supplies (cookie cutters, straws, toothpicks, rolling pins, forks) are useful for clay projects. A hammer, nails, and other carpentry tools will come in handy for the wooden crafts in this book.

Sewing supplies. For hand-sewn projects, make up a small sewing box for your child, including needles, thread of various colors, ribbon, buttons, fabric scraps, and felt (see the Perfect Sewing Box on page 125 for more ideas). A few of the projects in this book require a sewing machine.

Extras. You should examine each project's list of materials to see what you need, but here are a few things to keep an eye out for at craft supply shops: googly eyes, pipe cleaners, self-adhesive Velcro fasteners, glitter, paper fasteners, wooden dowels, Fome-Cor board, string, and twine.

Organizing Kids' Artwork

Most kids are prolific enough to fill a minivan with their artwork. So there's a good chance you have a fast-growing pile in your home of paintings, a cardboard tube castle, and a complete flour-and-salt zoo. Throwing it all away may break your heart (and your child's, too), but saving all of it could drive you out of house and home. The following tips will help you eliminate the clutter — and appreciate the crafts you treasure the most.

Save some and toss some. If a piece of artwork is simply stunning, save it. If it doesn't knock your socks off, take a deep breath and throw it out. (We're talking about at least a four-to-one ratio of chuck-to-save in the early years.) But beauty is not the only reason to save a piece of art. Consider saving anything that shows a developmental jump: the first scribbles, then shapes, the first sun, the first people and objects, and any self-portraits.

Stow the masterpieces. Professional artists store artwork in flat files (shallow chests of drawers) and in portfolios. Even secondhand flat files are expensive, so try a cardboard portfolio; for about $16, you can buy a 20- by 26-inch version that fits behind the couch or under the bed. Artists who work in three dimensions photograph their work and save photos in a book — not a bad idea for kids' sculptures.

Label each piece of art. Write in pencil at the bottom your child's name, age, and the subject, as told by the artist (*Shark Eating Monster* or *Paris in Spring*). If you want it to look professional, jot down the type of media.

Give some art away. If you run out of wall space, encourage your kids to think of their grandparents' houses (or anywhere else their art might be cherished) as museums for their work.

Displaying Kids' Art

Make a big to-do of your kids' artwork by putting it up around the house and rotating the displays periodically.

✂ The refrigerator door is a good first stop. Use as many heavy-duty magnets as you can find to make sure the stuff stays put.

✂ Inexpensive frames (either the glass clip kind or the inch-thick clear plastic boxes) are perfect for a rotating gallery of special drawings.

✂ Mat artwork on construction paper (which conveniently fades in the sun, letting you know when it's time to change the art).

✂ Hang artwork on a clothesline with clothespins (see page 21).

✂ Display small 3-D pieces and freestanding framed artwork on a shallow set of shelves. To keep frames from sliding off, you can nail a thin dowel along the edge of the shelf. You can use a regular bookshelf, but it helps if the shelves have adjustable heights so you can accommodate Popsicle stick sculptures or papier-mâché figures of any shape and size.

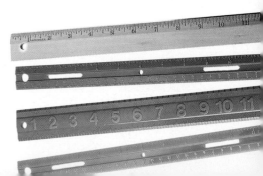

Setting Up

Chapter Two

Let's Color!

ONE WINTER DAY when *FamilyFun* editor Deanna Cook was seven years old, her mother had an inspired idea. She took out paints, brushes, crayons, and markers and invited all six of her children to scribble on the walls in the front hallway. The kids thought she was joking. Paint on the walls? And not get in trouble? You bet — the room was going to be freshly wallpapered in a week. So the Cooks went to town, covering every inch of the walls with stick figures, animals, houses, and squiggles. They admired their homemade gallery for more than a week before the new wallpaper went up, and their handiwork disappeared. A few days later, Deanna's mother was shocked to find her youngest daughter, two-year-old Tobye, armed with a fistful of crayons, eagerly decorating the newly papered walls.

Like the Cook kids, children are natural scribblers. Just as crawling and toddling are the first stages of learning to walk, so scribbling is a prerequisite for learning to draw. What's more, fine motor skills, such as drawing, take a long time to develop, which means that kids need to be given a lot of unrushed and agreeable practice time with paint, markers, crayons, and other art supplies.

Contrary to what some parents remember from their childhood art sessions, there is no wrong or right way to do art. So what if your child chooses a black crayon for black paper or wants to mix blue and orange paint only to get a big brown blob? What really matters is that she has creative license to experiment. You don't have to go as far as letting your kid paint on the walls —

Watercolor Butterflies, page 20

Scribblers' Supplies

In addition to the paint supplies detailed below, you'll want to keep a few other things on hand for your scribblers: crayons, markers, regular and colored pencils, erasers, sharpeners, and colored chalk (make sure it's not "for chalkboards only").

Paint: Tempera paints are nontoxic, washable, and easy to manage (most acrylics are nontoxic but they do stain, while watercolor paints and brushes are delicate and harder to control). Liquid tempera is conveniently ready-mixed, but the powdered form is preferable if you'll be adding in dishwashing liquid or glitter.

Paintbrushes: Any art store can help you pick out the right brush; for little kids using tempera, thicker, shorter brushes are ideal.

Paint containers: No-spill paint containers are handy, but expensive; try yogurt containers, baby food jars, or a foil-lined muffin tin.

Paper: Have scrap paper on hand (for doodling), as well as a roll of newsprint (for coloring) or a stack of copy paper (for painting and marker projects).

newsprint or copy paper will suffice — as long you make her feel her artwork is worth looking at.

Stick to nonpermanent scribbler supplies. Before you buy crayons, markers, paints, or other coloring supplies, read the back of the box and be sure they are washable and nontoxic. Instead of acrylic paints, which do stain, mix liquid tempera with 1 teaspoon of dishwashing liquid for easy cleanup. If a little color spills on your kids' clothes, spray with a stain remover and toss in the washing machine — and next time, be sure your child is draped in a smock (a big T-shirt, an old apron, or a garbage bag with holes cut out for head and arms).

Cover floors and furniture within paint-flinging range. For paint projects, it's a good idea to cover your work area with a plastic tablecloth or trash bag; for crayon and other nonliquid art projects, newspaper works fine.

Hand out art supplies one at a time. To keep from overwhelming your child, especially if he is under five years old, introduce coloring supplies one at a time (crayons, then markers, then paint, for example) and let him use each one for as long as he wants.

Work with your child. The best way to help a child learn the joy of painting and drawing is to experience it yourself. If that brings up old fears about the right and wrong way to paint, just think of your sessions as doodling. Or, try working with your left hand (if you're right-handed) to get a little more freedom from worries about mistakes.

Take care of supplies. You want them to last as long as possible, so when your child is done with a project, make sure markers and paint jars are capped, brushes are washed, and crayons are back in the box. For storage ideas, see A Child's Craft Corner, page 10.

Window Art, page 19

Paint

Window Art

Don't like what you see outside? Then change it! Mix up a batch of this washable paint and let your kids bring some color to a gray day. Or, follow the example of *FamilyFun* reader Darlene Mihaloew of Springfield, Virginia, who waits for a sunny day to let her kids paint her glass deck doors from the outside — while she snaps photos of them from the living room.

Materials

- ½ tablespoon powdered tempera paint
- 1 tablespoon clear dishwashing liquid
- Aluminum foil–lined muffin tin

Mix the powdered tempera with the dishwashing liquid until the mixture acquires the creamy consistency of house paint. (If you don't have powdered tempera, mix ½ cup liquid tempera with 1 teaspoon of dishwashing liquid.) Use the muffin tin to mix and preserve colors. Then, pick a window: picture windows are ideal for large scenes, while smaller panes can be filled either with a series of pictures that tells a story or with a single motif, such as a spring bouquet or a rainbow.

Line the window sash with masking tape, spread newspaper to safeguard the surrounding area, and your window artists can get under way. To remove dried paint or to make corrections while decorating, simply rub off the designs with a dry paper towel.

Let's Color!

Marble Painting

Marble Painting

It's easy to get on a creative roll with this project — after all, kids can hardly resist playing with marbles and generating masterpieces at the same time.

Materials

- Paper
- Paper plate
- Aluminum foil–lined muffin tin
- Tempera paints
- Marbles
- Spoon

Trim a sheet of paper to fit on a sturdy paper plate. Then, fill the muffin tin cups with different colors of paint. Have your child drop a marble into one cup and roll it around with the spoon. When the marble is coated with paint, transfer it by spoon to the plate. Use a gentle wrist action to swirl the marble around until the paint wears off. Or, try using two or three marbles simultaneously. To preserve the hues, use a different marble for each color. Lift the artwork from the paper plate to dry.

Spin Art

Emily Larson of Battle Lake, Minnesota, lets her kids use her old salad spinner to create paintings. The kids put a paper plate at the bottom of the spinner and squirt different colors of paint around the plate. Then, they cover the spinner, churn away, and hang their finished paintings up to dry.

Squirt Painting

Watercolor Butterflies

This terrific idea came from *FamilyFun* contributor Jodi Picoult, who discovered it at her son Jake's preschool in Hanover, New Hampshire. After she saw his classroom ceiling alive with these butterflies, she and Jake made a slew of their own, which they clipped to curtains, hung from the kitchen chandelier, and even fastened to the telephone cord.

Materials

> Paper coffee filters (the round variety)
> Watercolors and paintbrushes
> Markers
> Glue and glitter (optional)
> Clothespins
> Colored paper

To color the filters, dab on watercolor paint with a brush or draw on designs with markers — or both. For a shimmery effect, add glitter-and-glue designs. Once the filter is dry, pinch it in the middle like a bow tie. Slide or clip the clothespin onto it and fan out each side of the filter to resemble a butterfly's wings. Cut two strips of construction paper, about the size of matchsticks, and glue them onto the clothespin for antennae.

make into a mobile

Squirt Painting

Kids get pumped up about this abstract painting technique: instead of applying careful brushstrokes, they get to squirt color onto a giant canvas. Liquid tempera works best for this project, but food coloring will do in a pinch.

Materials

> Old bedsheet or large piece of newspaper
> Clothesline and clothespins
> Squirt gun or empty plastic pump bottle (do not use bottles from toxic household cleaners)
> Tempera paint

First, use clothespins to hang your canvas from the clothesline. Then, fill the pump bottle three quarters full of water. Add just enough paint to color the water — too much will clog the spray nozzle. Tighten the cap and shake well. Have your child stand a few feet from the sheet, adjust the nozzle to shoot a thin stream, and squirt away. (If more than one child paints, have kids stand on the same side of the canvas.)

Roll-on Paints

FamilyFun reader Joellen Pisarczyk of Cozad, Nebraska, found a creative way to reuse roll-on deodorant bottles. With a screwdriver, she pried off each ball. Then, she washed the bottles, filled them with slightly diluted tempera paint, and replaced the balls. Her three-year-old, Carrie, and six-year-old, Greta, had a blast making roller paintings at the table, and Joellen didn't have to worry about messy drips. After the fun, she replaced the caps, and the paint stayed fresh for next week's art session.

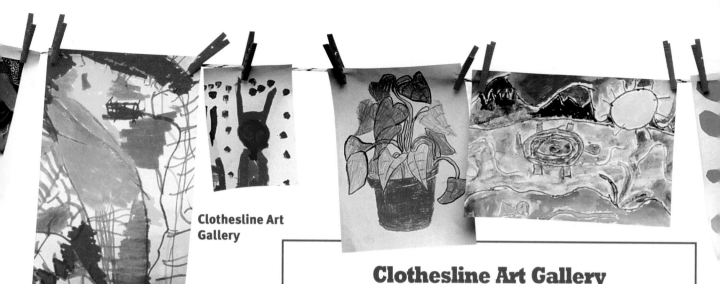

Clothesline Art Gallery

Clothesline Art Gallery

To make a big to-do of your kids' artwork, string it up for all to see. Set up a clothesline and let your child clip on finished works, as well as projects still wet with paint or glue. Not only is it an easily movable gallery, but it's one that makes rotating in new artwork a cinch.

Bubble Prints

After reading about our bubble prints, *FamilyFun* reader Terry Wright of Scottsdale, Arizona, said that her kids, Bryan, age six, and Danielle, age four, had just as much fun blowing the colored bubbles as they did making the prints.

Materials

> 2 tablespoons tempera paint
> 1 tablespoon clear dishwashing liquid
> 1 cup water
> Pie plate
> Straw

After covering your work surface with newspaper, measure all of the ingredients into an empty jar, cover tightly, and shake. Pour the mixture into a pie plate. Stick one end of a plastic drinking straw into the paint and blow through the other end (remind your child not to suck on the straw). When a large billow of bubbles forms, remove the straw and gently lay a sheet of white paper on top. As the bubbles break, they'll leave vivid impressions. Once the imprints dry, use markers to outline interesting shapes.

Let's Color!

Bubble Prints

Rain Painting

Rain Painting

This activity, from the If-You-Can't-Beat-'Em-Join-'Em Department, makes the most of rainy weather.

Materials

Paper plate (Chinet or other uncoated plate)
Food coloring
White crayon (optional)

After sprinkling a few drops of food coloring on a paper plate, your child can don her rain gear and walk outdoors with the plate for about a minute. For a batik effect, try drawing a white crayon design on the plate before adding the food coloring.

MIX YOUR OWN

Shiny paint: Add white glue to liquid or powdered tempera paint.
Crystalline paint: Mix salt into liquid or powdered tempera paint.
Bubbly paint: Stir shampoo into liquid or powdered tempera paint.
Sweet-smelling paint: Add lemon extract to yellow tempera paint, peppermint extract to green paint, and vanilla extract to white paint.
Puffy 3-D paint: Mix together 2 tablespoons all-purpose flour, 2 tablespoons salt, and 2 tablespoons water. Add several drops of food coloring and stir until you get the desired shade. Pour the mixture into a plastic squeeze bottle. Your kids then can squirt designs onto paper, cardboard, or wood. As the paint dries, it will become puffy and textured.

Tub Art

Homemade Finger Paints

With a batch of this quick and easy paint (which keeps in airtight containers), you can turn your young artist loose on newsprint or in the bathtub at a moment's notice.

Materials

2 tablespoons sugar
⅓ cup cornstarch
2 cups cold water
¼ cup clear dishwashing liquid
Food coloring (for vibrant colors, use food coloring paste)

Mix the sugar and cornstarch in a small pan, then slowly add the water. Cook over low heat, stirring until the mixture becomes a smooth, almost clear gel (about 5 minutes). When the mixture is cool, stir in the dishwashing liquid. Scoop equal amounts into containers and stir in the food coloring.

Tub Art: This paint contains dish soap, so it dissolves in water — which makes it perfect for bathtub finger painting. (Test to be sure bright paints won't leave a residue; most come clean with a powdered cleanser.)

Waxed Paper Painting

If you don't have time to mix up a batch of finger paint, try this tempera paint alternative, which is just right for little hands. Cover a tray with a sheet of waxed paper and have your child spoon tempera paint over it in different colors. Cover with another sheet of waxed paper. Your child can press down on the colors and watch them blend and move. If you wish, peel off the top layer to make a paper print of his design.

Let's Color!

Markers

Faux Fishbowl

MARKER MAGIC

Just when your kids are about to whine that there's nothing to do, put a tin of markers and white paper on the kitchen table and watch them gravitate toward it. Markers offer versatility and precision to artists who crave a line that isn't fuzzy and waxy. Here are several other marker projects:

✂ Draw a face with washable markers on a balloon.

✂ Decorate shoelaces with fabric markers.

✂ Sketch a fruit bowl with scented markers.

✂ Brighten up a window with dry erase markers (from an office supply store) and wipe away with a dry cloth.

Faux Fishbowl

For this tankful of tropical swimmers, you don't need aerators or fancy temperature controls — just a bunch of permanent markers and other household supplies. And if your kids overfeed them? Not to worry — unlike the real thing, these critters live forever.

Materials

Clean Styrofoam meat tray
Permanent markers
Thread or fishing line
Rocks and seashells
Glass container, such as a fishbowl or large mayonnaise jar
Sand

On the Styrofoam tray, have your child draw and color in several fish with permanent markers. Cut the fish out with scissors, then punch a hole at the bottom center of each one. Run a long piece of thread or fishing line through each hole and tie each end to a rock or seashell.

Cover the bottom of a glass container with a few inches of sand, then place the rocks and shells on the sand. Add the weighted fish carefully, so that the threads don't get tangled. Slowly pour water into the container and watch the fish float.

Foil Masks

FamilyFun contributor Jodi Picoult agrees with her kids that having one measly day a year for wearing costumes is not nearly enough. So, with these shiny masks, Kyle and Jake can celebrate Halloween any day of the week. Using permanent markers, the boys jazz up the shiny foil surface, making freckles, warts, and tattoos, so that they'll be sufficiently terrifying by the time Dad arrives home from work.

Materials

24- by 12-inch piece of heavy-duty aluminum foil
Permanent markers

To make a mask, double up the foil into a 12-inch square. Press the foil onto your child's face, making sure to mold it over his cheekbones, nose, eye sockets, and lips. (It won't actually resemble your child that much, but the process is fun.) Pull the mask away, taking care not to bend it. With scissors, your child can cut strips of hair at the top; eye, nose, and mouth holes; and even eyelashes that can be curled on a pencil. Then, using permanent markers and pressing down gently, he can add in all kinds of colorful details.

Foil Mask

Draw Out
the Plot

elp her seven-year-
daughter remember
acters and story
ence in chapter
ks, Betsy B. Gengras
von, Connecticut,
s a sheet of butcher
er to the wall in her
d's room. She then
des the paper into
ares for each chap-
and Lindsay draws
cture to illustrate
content. The next
she reads the
k, she looks at her
wings and tells her
her what has hap-
ed so far.

Shadow Silhouettes

They say it's impossible to catch your shadow — but if you can make it stay still long enough, your kids can trace it onto the wall to create a large-scale portrait.

Materials
- Desk lamp
- Blank wall
- Chair
- Crayons, markers, or colored pencils

Place the lamp on a table about 5 to 8 feet away from a blank wall. The subject sits, facing sideways, in a chair between the lamp and the wall. The artist turns on and aims the light so that the subject's shadow shows up on the wall, then tapes up a large sheet of paper so that the shadow is cast upon it. The shadow size can be decreased or increased by moving the subject nearer to or farther from the lamp. Now, the artist uses a crayon (or anything else that won't bleed through the paper) to trace the shadow. When the tracing is done, the artist continues decorating the profile with details such as hair-style, jewelry, and clothing.

Tinted Photo

Tinted Photos

Coloring takes on a whole new dimension when your kids are trying to stay within the lines of a photocopy of their pets or best friends. Your artists can add neon purple stripes to a shirt, color their dog's ears hot pink, or draw a fort onto the top of a tree.

Materials
- Family photos (for best results, choose ones with sharp contrast)
- Photocopy machine
- Crayons, markers, or colored pencils

To start, make copies of the photos you've chosen (experiment with the copy machine settings to get the clearest image). Then, let your kids hand-color the photo using anything from markers to crayons to colored pencils (even watercolors). There are no rules, and you should encourage the whimsical: how about coloring Uncle Steve, sleeping in a lawn chair with a three-headed alien lurking nearby?

ow Silhouettes

Crayons

Crayon Batik

Batik is a process commonly used in the design of cloth; here, it adds a neat texture to a crayon design on paper.

Materials

- Crayons
- Heavy piece of paper
- Paintbrush
- Watercolors, tempera paints, or ink
- Paper towel
- Iron

Have your child draw a thick crayon design on heavy paper, then crumple the paper into a ball and smooth it out again. Over the crumpled picture, she can paint a wash of watercolor, tempera paint, or ink. Dab the wash with a paper towel so it doesn't seep under the crayon. The wash will color wherever the crayon is not, including the cracks made by crumpling the page.

An adult can iron the artwork flat again by turning it over onto another sheet of paper (with a rag underneath that) and applying a warm iron for a few seconds. Be careful not to let it burn. Wipe the iron clean afterward and test it on a white rag before using it on clothes.

Crayon Batik

Birthday Boards

FamilyFun reader Ivy Delon Lee of Littleton, Colorado, came up with a great idea for her daughter Hanna's mermaid birthday party. Together, Ivy and Hanna used crayons to color a life-size (well, five-year-old-size) mermaid on a piece of Fome-Cor. Then, they cut out a circle for the face. At the party, Hanna's friends posed behind the board for a snapshot, which they later received with their thank-you notes. The project was such a hit that they repeated it for Ivy's brother's clown-themed birthday party a few months later.

Rainbow Crayons

Wondering what to do with that mountain of stubby crayons in your kid's room? You can show your child how to create new crayons out of old ones — a recycling lesson and art project all in one. The crayons will actually draw different colors as they are used.

Materials

    Old crayons
    Empty tuna cans or a muffin tin
    Aluminum foil

First, remove the paper wrappers from lots of brightly colored broken crayon pieces (to remove wrappers from crayons, soak them overnight). Then, fill each tuna can (or a muffin tin lined with aluminum foil) about halfway with contrasting crayon pieces, each about ½ inch in size. Bake the crayons in a preheated 300° oven for about 5 to 7 minutes. Watch them

closely, because they melt quickly. Melt them just enough to blend the colors, but not so much that they completely liquefy and meld into one color.

Carefully remove the cans from the oven and let the crayons cool for about 30 minutes. When the rainbow crayons are completely cool, remove them. The new crayons should pop out easily when you tap the cans with a knife. If you used the muffin tin method, remove them from the tin and peel off the foil. The crayons should be more colorful on the foil side.

Solid Color Crayons: Use the same method as for rainbow crayons, but use only one color of crayons. This makes wonderful, easy-to-handle crayons suited for very small children.

Shaped Crayons: To make fish, stars, trees, and other simple shapes, follow the same directions but use cookie cutters for molds. Cover the bottom of a cookie cutter with a few layers of foil (let it bend up to cover part of the inside edges as well), making certain there are no holes in the foil. Fill the molds halfway with crayon pieces and use the same method to bake on a cookie sheet.

Crayon Hunt

For her son Mark's third birthday party, *FamilyFun* reader Alice Giarrusso of Amherst, New Hampshire, sent him and his eleven guests on a scavenger hunt. Since Mark was into art and drawing, they held a crayon hunt. Mom Alice bought several boxes of crayons and hid individual crayons around the yard. Mark and his guests went out armed with envelopes to collect as many as they could find. Because she had hidden so many, every child found quite a few. At the end of the hunt, all the kids received coloring books.

Color Me Mauvelous

The first box of Crayolas sold in 1903 for a nickel and contained only eight colors: black, blue, brown, green, orange, red, violet, and yellow. Today, with 112 hues to choose from, simply matching a color to its name is an art in itself. Give it a try with these.

1. timber wolf
2. wisteria
3. cornflower
4. tumbleweed
5. mauvelous
6. macaroni and cheese
7. thistle
8. bittersweet
9. cerulean
10. asparagus
11. periwinkle
12. razzmatazz
13. denim
14. dandelion
15. tropical rain forest

Answers: A-8, B-6, C-1, D-9, E-7, F-10, G-11, H-14, I-12, J-2, K-3, L-5, M-15, N-4, O-13

Chapter Three

Likable Recyclables

T O PARENTS, an empty cardboard box has two possible fates: fill it with stuff and shove it in the attic — or recycle it. But to kids, it belongs in the same category as mud and dirt and sand: it is one of the raw materials of play. Along with jelly jars, milk jugs, egg cartons, and pretty much anything else you might toss in the recycling bin, a cardboard box is a blank slate for a kid's imagination. With a scrap of felt and a layer of cotton batting, it is ready for a sleepy baby doll. With ample application of markers and paint, it's a moon-bound rocket. Additionally, in the process of transforming trash into treasure, kids reveal a bit about themselves — who they'd like to be, what they'd like to do, things they'd like to know.

Craft projects that use household recyclables have always been favorites with *FamilyFun* readers, mainly because the materials can be found right under the kitchen sink — and they're free. Which means, of course, that it doesn't cost you a cent to go wild. You and your kids can follow our directions to the letter, alter them to suit your whimsy, or use them as a springboard to a brand-new vision of fun. Whatever you do, you really can't go wrong. After all, your mistakes are completely recyclable.

Start a junk box. You don't need to comb through your kitchen garbage to extract every ounce of recyclable waste, but you do need to keep an eye out for interesting trash — and salvage it for a "junk box." Into the box (perhaps a large cardboard one or a sealable plastic bin) goes anything with art potential — see the list on page 30 for good green candidates.

Give your recyclables a good scrub. Before launching into any of the crafts in this chapter, make sure the containers

Egg Carton Critters, page 37

Simple Dollhouse Furnishings, page 38

are clean (a few drops of leftover milk can spoil an afternoon project). If you're using glass jars or milk jugs, fill your kitchen sink with soapy water and let your kids "do the dishes." They'll love playing in the water and peeling off the labels. One *FamilyFun* reader uses this trick to get her kids involved in the recycling process — the clean jars go straight into her recycling bin.

Let the kids invent their own toys from the trash. Offer your kids a refrigerator box, empty milk carton, or egg carton and see what happens. They can enhance it with any household junk they please, as long as they give you a report of their creation when it's complete. You may discover some serious pretending going on.

Be a green consumer. Think twice before you buy products made from materials you can't recycle (and yes, we count using them for an art project as one way to recycle). Once you get the hang of it, you may find yourself buying a special brand of crackers so your kids can use the box for the dollhouse on page 38 or purchasing a special color of egg carton for the silly disguises on page 36.

Recycle the end results. After your kids have enjoyed their toys from the trash, don't throw them away. Separate out the recyclables — plastic milk jugs, tin cans, and so on — and toss them in the recycling bin. Not everything will be recyclable in your community, so find out what qualifies at your local recycling center.

Cans & Bottles

Coffee Can Stilts

Kids are forever wishing they could be bigger and taller. One way they can reach new heights is with these home-made stilts. Coffee cans and 28-ounce fruit cans work best for this activity.

Materials

  2 large, matching tin cans
    (opened at one end only)
  Hammer
  Ruler
  Nail
  Phillips head
    screwdriver
  About 10 feet of
    ⅜-inch cotton rope

First, lay each can on its side on a hard work surface. Use a hammer to flatten any jagged edges along the inner rim (parents only). If you're using coffee cans, replace the plastic covers.

On the side of one of the cans, make a mark an inch from one end (either the open or closed end; either can be the bottom of the stilt). Make a similar mark on the opposite side of the can. Do the same with the second can. Use the hammer and the nail to punch holes through the cans where marked. With the screwdriver, widen the holes to about ½ inch. Try to tap down any rough edges with the hammer.

Cut two pieces of rope that measure three times the length from your child's knee to the floor. Attach a rope to each can by threading the ends through the holes from the outside. Tie overhand knots in the rope ends. Then, pull the

rope so the knots rest against the insides of the can.

When using her stilts, your child should wear rubber-soled shoes to avoid slipping off. At first, she may need help stepping up onto the cans and balancing. Once she's comfortable, she can grip the ropes as she would two bucket handles, straighten her legs, and start walking tall.

FunFact

In Padova, Italy, a scale model of the Basilica di Sant'Antonio di Padova was built from 3,245,000 empty cans. It took 20,000 hours to construct.

Coffee Can Stilts

Likable Recyclables

Tin Can Lantern

In Colonial times these lanterns were a popular way for children to carry around candles safely. This project takes some planning, but the result is well worth it — whether you parade your lamps outside or use them to give a spooky feel to a nighttime picnic.

Materials

    Large tin can, label removed
    Markers
    Towel
    Hammer
    Nails of different sizes
    Small screw-in hook
    20-inch wooden dowel
    Coat hanger or thin wire for
      hanging loop
    Votive candle
    Dried spaghetti noodle for lighting
      the candle

On the outside of the can, have your child draw a pattern for the lantern holes. Fill the can with water and freeze it for two days. (The ice keeps the sides from collapsing when you hammer them.) When the water in the can is frozen solid, place the can on its side on top of a towel and use the nail tips to hammer in holes according to the design. Make two holes near the top, on opposite sides, for stringing a handle.

Remove any chunks of ice from inside the can (a parent's job, since the hammered-in holes have sharp edges). Help your child screw the hook into one end of the wood dowel, then string the length of wire through the hook. Wind the ends of the wire through the hanging holes on the can until they are secure. Use a bit of melted wax to affix the votive candle to the bottom of the can. The dried spaghetti noodle is a handy way to light the lantern; it burns steadily and lessens the likelihood of scorching your fingers.

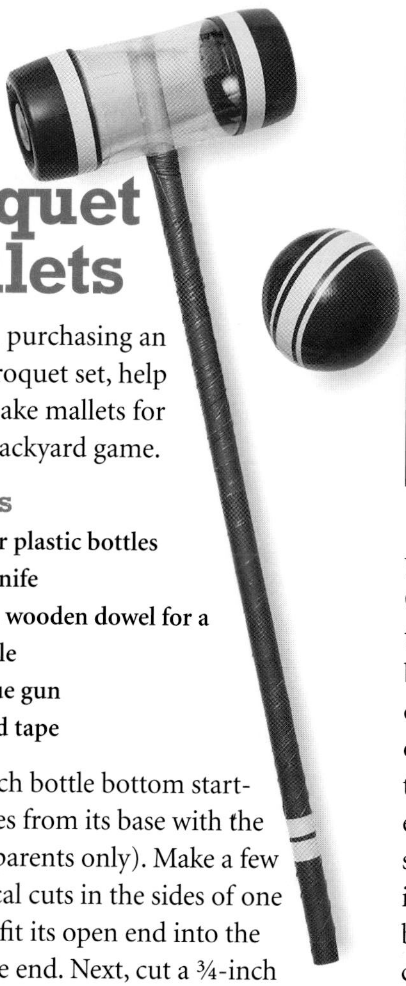

Croquet Mallets

Rather than purchasing an expensive croquet set, help your kids make mallets for the classic backyard game.

Materials

- 2 1-liter plastic bottles
- Craft knife
- ¾-inch wooden dowel for a handle
- Hot glue gun
- Colored tape

Cut off each bottle bottom starting 5½ inches from its base with the craft knife (parents only). Make a few 3-inch vertical cuts in the sides of one bottom and fit its open end into the second bottle end. Next, cut a ¾-inch hole in two sides of the joined bottles. Fit the dowel through the holes so the end is flush with the side of the bottle. Glue your dowel in place with a glue gun (parents only) and wrap the handle with colored tape.

Piggy Bank

Pigs are good for all sorts of storage. Here are two you can create, inspired by "McCall's Creates" booklet 14215, using empty plastic bottles: a piggy bank for a kid's savings and a swinish pencil holder.

Materials

- 4 thread spools
- Pink paint
- Plastic soda bottle and cap
- Hot glue gun (Krazy Glue will work, too)
- Pink felt
- 2 matching buttons
- Craft knife
- Pink pipe cleaner

Likable Recyclables

Backyard Croquet

Want to turn your backyard into a croquet course? Start by choosing a series of obstacles that players must hit the ball over, in, under, or around — say a hose, a bucket, or a wagon. Next, make wickets by snipping coat hangers (parents only) into 21-inch lengths. Bend the hangers into U shapes with pliers and set one in the ground near each obstacle. Finally, order the course by taping a numbered index card to the top of each wicket. At tee time, players should start 20 feet from the first wicket and should alternate turns, tallying one point for each mallet stroke. The player who finishes with the lowest score wins.

To assemble the pig, begin by having your child paint the thread spools pink. Once they're dry, he can glue them to the bottle, positioning them as shown below for legs. Make the ears next, cutting a pair of 3-inch-wide triangles out of the felt. Fold the base of each triangle in half and glue the lower edges together. Use paper clips to secure them while drying. Trim the felt into ear shapes and glue them to the bottle. Glue on the button eyes. Use the craft knife (parents only) to poke a small hole in the bottle for the pipe cleaner tail. Cut a slot in the top through which your child can feed coins to the pig.

Piggy Pencil Holder: Follow the instructions for the Piggy Bank, but instead of a slot for coins, use the craft knife (or a wood-burning tool, if you have one) to make holes in its back for pencils.

FunFact

Believe it or not, the pig has been a popular bank shape for almost three hundred years. It dates back to the Middle Ages, when a dense, orange clay known as pygg was used throughout western Europe in the making of pots and jars, which frugal people used to save their money.

Piggy Bank

Piggy Pencil Holder

Milk Jugs

Dollhouse Dinners

When *FamilyFun* reader Robin Taplitsky made a milk jug house with her daughter, three-year-old Bayley came up with her own idea for decorating. She cut out magazine pictures of food and glued them to the miniature tables — creating a ready-made dinner for her dolls.

Milk Jug Garage

Milk isn't the only thing that packages well by the gallon. With a little help, your child can turn an empty plastic jug into a portable hot-rod garage or dollhouse, one of the many recycling crafts featured in *EcoArt!* (Williamson Publishing).

Materials

- Plastic gallon milk jug
- Craft knife
- Construction paper
- Black marker
- Toothpick
- Cardboard
- Thread spool

First, cut a 3½-inch-square garage door opening in one of the container's flat sides with a craft knife (parents only). Glue construction paper roof shingles around the top of the jug. Next, add a business sign, made of construction paper and hung on a toothpick. Poke the toothpick into the jug just above the garage door.

To make a floor, set the jug on a piece of cardboard and trace around the base. Trim the edges so it will slide easily through the doorway. Decorate by gluing on construction paper tiles.

Glue on a construction paper fuel pump and air hose by poking a hole in the side of the jug and tying on a piece of string. A thread-spool car lift finishes off the interior.

Milk Jug Dollhouse: For this variation on the Milk Jug Garage, cut a

Milk Jug Garage

Whale of a Water Scoop

As dismal as water seems to kids when it's streaking down the windows, it's a blast to pour, splash, and play with indoors. Some days, when *FamilyFun* contributor Jodi Picoult's kitchen sink gets a little cramped, she moves to larger seas — the bathtub. Her two boys, Kyle and Jake, like to sneak up on their rubber duckies with this great whale scoop (it also makes washing one's hair much more fun). For added adventure, they dot the seas with a few shaving cream icebergs.

Materials

> Plastic gallon milk jug
> Permanent marker

Turn the gallon jug onto its side so that the handle is at the top. With the marker, draw a mouth shape on the base of the jug and extending partway up the sides, as shown. Cut along the lines with scissors, creating a widemouthed scoop (a parent's job). Using the marker, outline the edge of the mouth and add eyes and a blowhole.

Blast Off

During the week, *Family Fun* reader Annette Hayes of Dalton, Georgia, watches two little boys in addition to her son. One afternoon, they all invented this costume idea: they cut up plastic gallon milk jugs and decorated them with crayons to make NASA space helmets. The children turned over a table, draped it with a blanket, and they were off to the moon for the afternoon.

3½-inch-square door opening in one of the container's flat sides with a craft knife (a parent's job). Cut out windows, if desired. Glue construction paper roof shingles around the top of the jug. For a chimney, use a black marker to draw a few rows of bricks on a strip of red construction paper. Wrap the paper around the jug spout and glue it in place. Stuff a puff of cotton "smoke" into the spout. Then, add paper window boxes on the dollhouse.

To make a floor that fits inside the jug, set the jug on a piece of cardboard and trace around the base. Trim the edges of the floor so it will slide easily through the doorway. Decorate the floor by gluing on paper rugs.

Dollhouse Furniture:

• Mold a sofa out of modeling clay and add pom-pom throw pillows.

• Use an alphabet block for an end table.

• To make a table lamp, start with a round wooden bead. Bend up the lower end of a pipe cleaner and push it into the bead. Shape the upper end into a frame for a shade. Wrap a strip of paper around the frame and glue.

• For a houseplant, fill a thimble with short snips of a green pipe cleaner.

Likable Recyclables

Whale of a Water Scoop

Egg Cartons

Nosy Disguises

Nosy Disguises

Does your child need a quick disguise for the school play? Start scrambling eggs — and use the empty carton to create stylish animal snouts and ears.

Materials

- Cardboard egg carton
- Hole punch
- Stapler
- Sewing elastic
- Light-gauge craft wire
- Headband
- Acrylic paints and paintbrushes
- Colored markers

For a basic pattern, cut out an individual egg cup, make breathing holes in the bottom, and staple the ends of sewing elastic (cut to fit around your child's head) to the sides. Cut ears out of the carton top (the corners or the flat part, depending on the shape you want), punch holes in the bases, and use wire to attach them to a headband.

TRASHY COSTUMES

Let your kids get a last laugh out of old, worn-out clothes by recycling them into outlandish costumes. They might dress up an old pair of sneakers with pom-poms and paint, add plastic dinosaurs and sequins to a floppy summer hat, or make giant buttons for one of Dad's old shirts by decorating colorful milk jug caps. When they've got a boxful of duds all fixed up, let them invite friends over for a "trashy fashion" show.

White Rabbit: Paint the nose white and glue on a pink pom-pom. Draw on a mouth with a marker. Poke holes in both sides of the nose, then feed white pipe cleaner whiskers through the holes (push the centers of the pipe cleaners into the bottom of the egg cup to make room for your child's nose). Paint the backs of the ears white and the insides pink.

Tiger Cat: Paint the nose orange (or black for Halloween) and add whiskers. In place of the pom-pom, glue on a small paper triangle. Make the ears short and pointed.

Little Piggy: Onto a pink snout, draw large nostrils. Cut broad pig ears from the flat portion of the egg carton lid. Fold the base of one ear so that it flops forward.

Hound Dog: Paint a nose brown, black, or white with black spots. Glue a paper triangle to the front and use a marker to draw on a mouth. Add ears.

Egg Carton Critters

When *FamilyFun* editors brought the materials for these egg carton critters into a local fifth grade classroom, the kids made a slew of the six-legged bugs with many clever adaptations. We swear your kids won't stop after making one.

Materials

- Cardboard egg carton
- Tempera paints and paintbrushes
- Glue
- 12 pairs googly eyes
- Hole punch
- 12 pipe cleaners, assorted colors and thicknesses

Cut the twelve cups out of the egg carton bottom and trim them. Paint the outside green or another bug color and let them dry. Glue on the eyes and punch a hole for the mouth, positioning the hole at the edge. Add three leg holes on each side with the hole punch. Cut all the pipe cleaners into 4-inch sections for the legs and antennae. Poke two holes above the eyes for the antennae (you will need to use a push-pin or pencil or snip with scissors). For the legs, insert one pipe cleaner piece through one side hole and out the other side. Bend it up inside the shell and into shape for the legs and feet. To make the antennae, push the pipe cleaner through one hole and out the other, bending it into shape. Now let the critters crawl.

Buggy Buggy

Christine Silveira of Plainfield, Connecticut, found that a box full of sprightly egg carton creatures really sparked the imaginations of her two kids, two-year-old Nicole and three-year-old Jimmy. After having a ball making the critters, the kids have played "buggy buggy" (as Jimmy dubbed the game) time and time again. The game has no particular rules — rather, each time the kids play, the little critters have different names and different things to do.

A Bug House

To house a colony of egg carton critters, open an egg carton and press the five center dividers down flat to make room for the bugs. Make grass out of paper and glue it onto the carton, bending the blades upright. The house is now ready for your litter of critters.

Egg Carton Critters

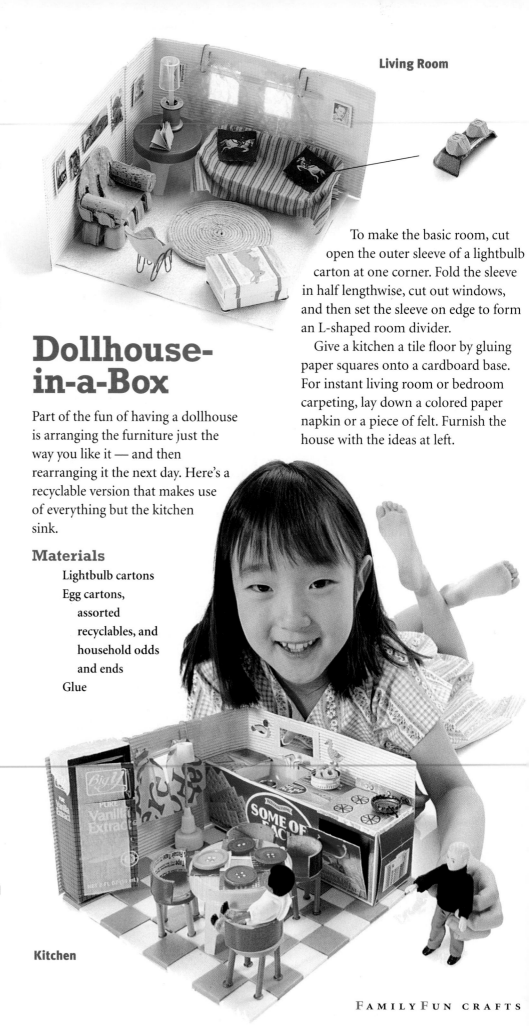

Simple Dollhouse Furnishings

Sofa: Cut one end from a Styrofoam meat tray. On the bottom, glue two cups from a cardboard egg carton (see model at right). Turn upright and drape on a cloth cover.

Easy chair: Attach paper clip legs to an egg carton cup.

Curtains: Fold down the top ½ inch of a fabric square and glue the edge of the flap down. Insert a straw or toothpick and hang with paper clips.

Lamp: Use a spool or bottle cap base to support a toothpick or straw; use a bottle cap for a shade.

Pictures: Glue postage stamps to the walls.

Kitchen counter: Cover one end of a cracker box with a square of aluminum foil and draw on burners. Cut an oven door.

Sink: Glue the bottom of a plastic cup to a fitted opening in the countertop. For faucets, glue on the tops of flexible drinking straws.

Kitchen table: Invert a plastic cup and draw four legs on the sides. Cut away the sections between the legs.

Kitchen chairs: Glue short sections from a drinking straw to the bottom of a milk jug cap. Use a section of a cardboard tube for a chair back.

Plates: Set out a few colored buttons.

Frying pan: Attach a paper clip handle to a bottle cap.

Living Room

Dollhouse-in-a-Box

Part of the fun of having a dollhouse is arranging the furniture just the way you like it — and then rearranging it the next day. Here's a recyclable version that makes use of everything but the kitchen sink.

Materials

Lightbulb cartons
Egg cartons,
   assorted
   recyclables, and
   household odds
   and ends
Glue

To make the basic room, cut open the outer sleeve of a lightbulb carton at one corner. Fold the sleeve in half lengthwise, cut out windows, and then set the sleeve on edge to form an L-shaped room divider.

Give a kitchen a tile floor by gluing paper squares onto a cardboard base. For instant living room or bedroom carpeting, lay down a colored paper napkin or a piece of felt. Furnish the house with the ideas at left.

Kitchen

Cardboard Tubes & Paper Bags

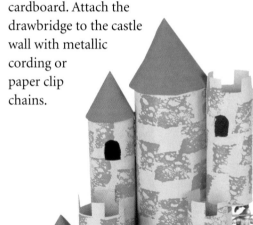

Cardboard Castle

With tall spires, stone walls, and a wooden drawbridge, this castle has the makings for an afternoon of adventure. The project is adapted from *Crafts from Recyclables* (Bell Books).

Materials

Assorted cardboard tubes
Gold and other poster paints
Small sponge square
Craft knife
Black marker
Construction paper
Popsicle sticks
Metallic cording or paper clips

Color the toilet tissue and paper towel rolls with a coat of gold poster paint. Once they are dry, you can create the appearance of cut stone by applying a contrasting color with a small sponge square. Using a craft knife (parents only), cut windows in the tube towers or just draw them on with a black marker. Cut notches around the tops of several turrets.

When assembling the castle, start from the center. Glue together two or three taller tubes for the main towers. Then, stack smaller rolls around them, interlocking the towers with tabs cut in the tube bottoms (as shown). Create the castle's front wall using a 4-inch square of construction paper. Draw on an ornate door frame and sandwich the wall between the front two towers.

For roofing, cut a circle out of construction paper. Make a single snip into the center and form a cone by overlapping and gluing together the cut edges. Glue the roofs in place on top of the towers. For a drawbridge, glue Popsicle stick planks side by side onto a piece of cardboard. Attach the drawbridge to the castle wall with metallic cording or paper clip chains.

Cardboard Castle

Likable Recyclables

Marble Maze

All it takes is a little ingenuity and some Rube Goldberg styling to create this runway made just for marbles. Half miniature golf game, half physics experiment, this project is delightfully flexible. Your kids can construct a simple runway one day, then add other twists and turns as they collect more cardboard tubes.

Materials

Assorted cardboard tubes
Tape (masking tape is fine, but colored electrical tape will give the chute a cheerful look)
Marbles — the bigger the better
Scissors
Stacks of books, cereal boxes, toys, blocks, wastebaskets, and other objects for supports

Offer your kids a bunch of paper tubes — as varied a selection as you can find. Long wrapping-paper tubes are the most efficient for covering distance, paper towel tubes are good for the shorter runs, and toilet tissue tubes make great corner pieces. Then let the kids tape the tubes together to form a runway. You may need to cut some tubes into shorter lengths for corner sections before taping them together.

Help the kids set up a platform for the start of their run. A stool or the back of a chair or sofa works well. Then, arrange several stacks of books, toys, and other objects for supports, so the marble run will slope down toward the floor.

Marble Rolling Tips:

• If you slip one tube inside another, be sure the larger tube is on the downward side of the run.

• Make sure the end of the run is at floor level. Flying marbles can be dangerous.

• A combination of closed tunnels and open sections (where kids can see the marbles moving) makes everything a lot more interesting. To make an open section, simply cut a tube in half, lengthwise, or cut a narrow window in its top.

• Larger marbles tend to roll better than smaller ones. Small rubber balls can travel well, too.

Marble Maze

Paper Bag, U.S.A.

Once you introduce your children to paper bag architecture, you'll find yourself setting aside a store of lunch bags earmarked for enthusiastic city planners. This is a wonderful activity for a group of kids — each child can make a building, then add it to the growing bag town.

Materials

- Paper lunch bags
- Crayons or markers
- Colored paper
- Newspaper
- Cotton balls

For each building, your child will need two lunch bags. Have her draw or color a building on one of the bags that is positioned either horizontally or vertically. She may want to color bricks or clapboards, then sketch in doors and windows, complete with shutters. A window box filled with flowers or a vine growing up one side of the building is a nice finishing touch.

Next, stuff the second bag with crumpled newspaper and slip the decorated bag on top.

Help your builder cut out signs and awnings from colored paper, then glue them onto the buildings. Fashion roofs out of paper rectangles and top them with paper chimneys; use cotton balls for smoke. Doors can be made by folding construction paper into a small card, decorating the front, and gluing the back to the bag. Help your child set up the city on the floor or on a table, add a few little cars and dolls — and you've got your own boomtown.

FunFact

Before Charles Stilwell invented the grocery bag as we know it today, these paper bags were hand-glued and V-shaped.

Paper Bag Hometown

Lisa Burmester and her kids, Joshua and Amy, were so inspired by *FamilyFun*'s "Paper Bag, U.S.A." project that they decided to build a paper bag replica of their hometown of Roscommon, Michigan. In three evenings of steady work, the young architects constructed Roscommon's school, gas station, doughnut shop, and firehouse — not to mention their Gramma's house and the Burmesters' own home.

Paper Bag, U.S.A.

Likable Recyclables

41

Fabric

Pocket Purses

With a few easy snips and stitches, your children can turn an old pair of hip-huggers into over-the-shoulder purses.

Materials

> Old pair of blue jeans
> Fabric scissors
> Needle and thread
> Ribbon, an old belt, or braided rope about 1 yard long
> Decorations (iron-on transfers, fabric paint, patches, embroidery thread)
> Velcro, buttons, or snaps

Begin by cutting out a back pocket of an old (but not threadbare) pair of jeans, being careful to cut outside the seams so the pocket stays intact.

If your child is old enough to use a needle and thread, have her sew a long piece of ribbon, an old belt, or braided rope to the sides of the pocket to make a shoulder strap. This should be about a yard in length, but you'll want to adjust it to suit her height. You can also make a handbag by using a smaller, thicker piece of ribbon for a handle.

Next, let the outside of the purse become a canvas for ornaments. Decorate with iron-on transfers, fabric paint, beads, patches, appliqués, or whatever you can dig up in your junk drawers. More ambitious kids might even like to embroider their initials or other designs on the denim for an authentic seventies look.

To hold the purse shut, sew strips of Velcro, buttons, or snaps to the inside of the pocket. Finished purses will add a retro edge to any wardrobe, and your child can bump, hustle, and keep on truckin' through summer.

Pocket Pals

On a rainy day in Carbondale, Colorado, *FamilyFun* reader Katie Leto and her kids, Alicia, six, and Ryan, four, delved into the scrap bag to make a pair of pocket purses. The kids picked out their own appliqués and decorative buttons and then added finishing touches to their "pockets" with fabric paint. With his mom's help, Ryan modified his purse into a fanny pack, complete with a belt made from a pet collar. At day's end (as you can see from the smiles) the kids were proud of their pockets, which they use to carry sunscreen and sunglasses wherever they go.

Pocket Purses

Book Jackets

It's never easy for a kid to relinquish a favorite old shirt to the rag bag. One way you can soften the blow is to help her turn the treasured gear into the latest in back-to-school fashion — denim, flannel, and buffalo plaid book jackets.

Materials

- Measuring tape
- Old shirt, jacket, or piece of fabric
- Fabric scissors
- Double-sided, iron-on seam binding
- Thread and needle
- Buttons and patches

First, you'll need to calculate the book jacket dimensions. Determine the width by measuring from the right edge of the book's closed cover, around its spine and across the back, and then adding 2 to 3 inches for each jacket flap.

The height of the book jacket will depend on the type of material you're using. Fabric that won't fray (like flannel or T-shirt cotton) can be trimmed to the same height as the book. Denim and other materials prone to fraying should be cut with an

Likable Recyclables

inch allowance, top and bottom. This lets you hem the edges by folding them over a strip of seam binding and pressing them with a hot iron.

Have your child spread the cloth jacket right-side down on a flat surface and center the book on top of it. Fold the right flap around the book's back cover. Stitch the corners of the flap to the upper and lower edges of the jacket (as shown below). Fold the left flap around the front cover, pulling the jacket taut for a snug fit before stitching the corners.

Your child can accessorize the jacket by adding colorful buttons, embroidered patches, or a pocket she can fill with pens, erasers, and other school supplies.

A Keeping Quilt

In Patricia Polacco's storybook *The Keeping Quilt*, a family of immigrants sews a special quilt from the clothing of their relatives in Russia and uses it to teach new generations of children the story of their ancestry. When they read the story, *FamilyFun* contributor Janet Goldstein and her three children were inspired to create their own "keeping quilt." Along with the kids' first baseball jerseys and favorite, worn-out dresses, they patched together shirts and fabric scraps donated by aunts, uncles, cousins, and grandparents. Piecing and sewing the quilt provided hours of fun family time — and now that it's done, it's a storehouse of Goldstein family lore.

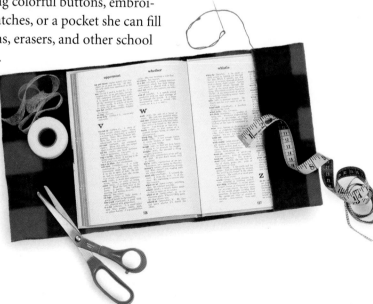

Cardboard Boxes

Little Red Barn

Since age five, *FamilyFun* reader Jade Littlefield has been collecting Breyer Horses, plastic figurines that come in nearly every breed and color. Her horses had been living in a wicker basket — until Jade made them a new stable. After all, every precious possession needs a home, even if it is just a cardboard box.

Materials

- Utility knife
- 15- by 18- by 21-inch corrugated cardboard box
- Ruler and pencil
- Packing tape
- Extra cardboard
- Small paint roller
- Acrylic paints and paintbrushes
- 8- by 8- by 13-inch box
- Paper fasteners

Cut a 4-inch slit down each corner of the larger box. Fold the two 18-inch sides in toward each other so that they form a peak (to make them fold easily, score the folds). Holding the peak in place (figure 1), raise the other two flaps to meet the peak. Trace the peak shape on each side flap, then cut away the excess. To make the ridgepole, cut out a 1½- by 21-inch strip of cardboard.

Cut a small notch in the top center of each side flap. Set one end of the ridge-

pole in each notch, then fold up the roof so it meets the ridgepole. Tape all the roof edges in place.

To make the left Dutch door (figure 2), mark off a 6- by 10-inch rectangle (position it about ½ inch from the bottom and top of the front panel and 1 inch from its left edge). Cut along the top, right edge, and bottom of the rectangle and also cut the door in half. Repeat, reversing the directions, for the right door, and make two more doors on the opposite side. Score down the hinged edges so that the doors open easily. Cut a 2- by 3-inch, four-pane window about ½ inch down from the roof peak on each side of the barn.

For the stalls, cut a 4½- by 18-inch and a 4½- by 14-inch piece of cardboard. Make a 2-inch notch in the center of each strip, then interlock them to form a cross. Slip the cross shape inside the barn.

Use the roller to paint the barn red and the roof gray; when dry, use the brush to paint on the white trim.

To make the tack room, fold in the peak of the small box. Measure and cut the side flaps as for the barn. Tape in place — minus a ridgepole this time. Cut a front door and windows. To attach the tack room to the barn, poke four matching holes through one side wall of the tack room and one side wall of the barn. Slip a paper fastener through each hole and bend into place.

Easy Storage Boxes

Looking for an inexpensive way to round up your kids' books and CDs? Here's one, courtesy of your empty laundry detergent box, that needs only a few touches to beautifully organize a bookshelf or desk.

Materials

- Empty laundry detergent box
- Colored paper
- Glue
- Felt

Cut off the top half of the box and recycle it. Then, cut the bottom portion of the box in half vertically to create two open-face cases with rounded edges. Use a pencil to trace around the sides and back of each case onto a piece of colored paper. Cut out the paper tracings and glue them onto the outside of the cases. Then, cut out felt pieces to cover the undersides of the cases and glue them on. Now, your kids can decorate the cases to suit their tastes with stickers, colored tape, glitter glue, or original drawings.

Easy Storage Boxes

Likable Recyclables

A Recycled Castle

Everyone knows that cardboard box playhouses are a blast to make, but few discover that playhouse-building can be downright educational. Ask the eleven-year-old twins of *FamilyFun* readers Maureen O'Meara and Bill Hursh. The twins got a good dose of history when their baby-sitter Andy Turner helped them build a cardboard castle with appliance boxes from their local recycling center in Bethlehem, Pennsylvania. While they were building, Andy talked about the history of castles — so that when the kids showed Mom and Dad their palace, they made up an amazing story of famous figures, including King Arthur and Galileo, who had once lived in it.

Airplane-in-a-Box

Recycle your cardboard boxes into this winning costume, which was inspired by the book *Build It With Boxes* by Joan Irvine (Morrow Junior Books). Once you've made the costume, hand the pilot a pair of swimming goggles and a winter hat with earflaps, and he'll be ready for takeoff in your backyard or at a local park.

Materials

Large cardboard box
Scissors or utility knife
Metallic spray paint
Cardboard scraps
Aluminum foil
Long paper fastener
Plastic wrap
Masking tape

Start with a large box that is big enough to cover half your child's body. Cut off the bottom flaps of the box with scissors or a utility knife (a job for parents). Cut out rectangular wing flaps on the sides, making sure that they are a little longer than your child's arms and directly across from each other. When cutting, leave the tops of the wings attached to the box at the shoulder line.

For the head hole, cut out a rectangle on the top of the box that's big enough

for your child's head but not too close to the edges of the box. You should make the opening for the head on the smaller side to prevent the costume from slipping off your child's shoulders.

Paint the entire box with the spray paint (regular tempera works fine, too). For the propeller, cut two strips out of cardboard and cover them with aluminum foil.

Fasten the strips to the front of the plane with a long paper fastener and give the propeller a trial spin.

For the windshield, cut a frame out of cardboard. Tape a piece of plastic wrap inside the frame to make it look like glass and attach it to the box with masking tape. Finish the plane by adding a cardboard tail fin to the back.

Airplane-in-a-Box

Chicken-in-a-Box

With scissors, cut the flaps off the large cardboard box. Turn the box bottom up. Then, make an opening for your child's legs by drawing an arch on one of the longer sides and cutting it out using a utility knife (parents only). Using the cutout as a pattern, cut an identical shape from the opposite side of the box. Discard both pieces.

Next, cut the tops from all of the food boxes. Attach the deeper boxes to the sides of the desk with short pieces of tape. Then, wrap longer pieces of tape all the way around the desk and side pockets to firmly secure them.

For pencil holders and other desktop compartments, arrange smaller cartons and canisters along the back edge of the box and secure them by gluing the bottoms to the top of the desk. Lastly, make the working surface spillproof by covering it with clear Con-Tact paper.

Homework Helpers

It's not easy to make a stack of homework look inviting, but you can start by encouraging your child to jazz up his collection of schoolwork equipment. Here are a few craft ideas to try.

Box Office, below

Book Jackets, page 43

Easy Storage Boxes, page 45

Piggy Pencil Holder, page 33

Homemade Books, page 61

Chicken-in-a-Box:

Use the same construction as for the airplane but leave off the paint, propeller, and windshield. Help your child cut feathers out of yellow construction paper. Using masking tape, attach one row of feathers to the bottom of the box, then overlap it with a second row; continue until the box is completely covered. Fashion a tail out of a piece of cardboard and layer it with feathers as well. Make a mask by taping a construction paper beak and feather to a store-bought mask.

Box Office

Kids on the go will appreciate the portability of this lightweight cardboard desk, not to mention all the nooks and crannies for storing stuff.

Materials

Large cardboard box
Utility knife
Pencil
Cereal, cookie, and pasta boxes
Colored tape
Glue
Clear Con-Tact paper

Likable Recyclables

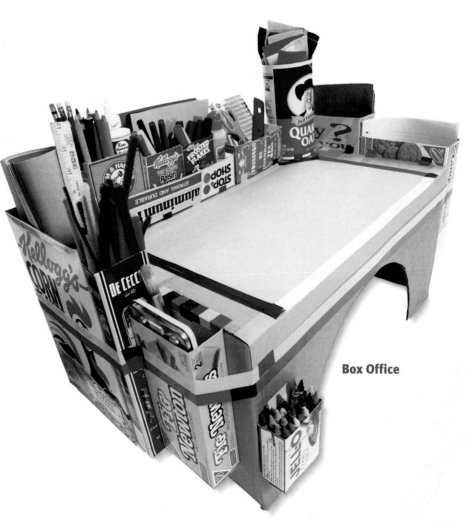

Box Office

A Winter Wonderland

When your family comes down with cabin fever, build a replica of your cabin and add it to this Lilliputian landscape to make a twinkling decoration for the winter holidays.

Materials

- Pint-size cardboard milk cartons and assorted cracker boxes
- Craft knife
- Construction paper
- Glue
- Colored markers
- Large sheet of poster board
- Masking tape
- Mini Christmas lights (optional)
- Nonflammable batting (available at craft stores)

Using the craft knife (adults only), remove the bottoms from the cartons and boxes. Then, make siding for each building by tracing around the sides onto a sheet of construction paper. With scissors, cut out the individual pieces and glue them onto the carton. For the roof, cut a paper rectangle from a contrasting color. Fold the roof over the top of the carton, as shown, and glue it in place.

Next, draw on windows, doors, and corner boards with the colored markers. Then, cut out the window openings with the craft knife. Finally, decorate the doors by gluing on tiny wreaths cut out of colored paper.

Arrange the finished buildings side by side on top of the poster board and lay the unplugged string of lights behind them. Fit a few bulbs into each building through the bottom and tape

the wires to the inside so that the bulbs are in the center of the carton. Then, if necessary, use tape to secure the bottom edges of the buildings to the poster board.

For snow, spread the batting around the buildings, being sure to cover the electrical wire running between them. Then, your kids can add small figures, paper trees, and toy cars. You can even use a small mirror for a skating rink.

Back to Schoolhouse

When older brothers and sisters head off to school, younger siblings need not feel left behind. They can attend a special class of their own — in a miniature schoolhouse made out of boxes, an egg carton, and thread spools.

Materials
Empty cereal box, tea box, and cardboard egg carton
Craft knife
Glue
Paper
Drinking straw
Pipe cleaners
7 thread spools
Felt
Permanent markers

To make the schoolroom, use a craft knife (adults only) to cut a large flap in the front of the cereal box. Pull the flap down to serve as the classroom fioor. Next, cut a small tea box in half diagonally and glue one of the halves onto the top of the classroom for a peaked roof.

Top off the roof by drawing a miniature flag on a piece of paper. Cut out the flag and glue it to the side of a drinking straw.

Cut a small *X* in the side of the roof and push the bottom of the flagpole through it.

To make desks, remove the front row of cups from the egg carton and recycle them. Then, cut out the remaining six cups individually, leaving a portion of the egg carton cover attached to each one for a desktop (see photo). Glue the desks to the schoolhouse floor.

Now it's time to round up some pupils and a teacher. To make each figure, push the ends of a pipe cleaner through the holes in the top and bottom of a thread spool and then bend the tips (this forms the torso, legs, and feet). For arms, sandwich the thread spool between two short pipe cleaners. Then twist together the ends of the pipe cleaners. Glue on felt clothes and hair. Finally, use permanent markers to draw on faces.

Likable Recyclables

Back to Schoolhouse

49

Chapter Four

Paper Play

WHEN WE asked craft expert Susan Milord to contribute a paper project to *FamilyFun*, she offered up the beautiful paper boxes on page 60 — and along with them, a surprising story. Apparently, as soon as she had taught her son, Angus, how to fold the paper squares, he began to fill the house with them. He made little boxes to hold tiny treasures and larger ones to store everything from school supplies to letters from his grandparents. Once Angus got on a roll, he couldn't stop. Of course, Susan had seen this before. It's what happens, she reminded us, when a child meets just the right kind of craft project. No matter how simple it is, he'll take it to the hilt and turn it into something extravagant.

Paper is one of the most basic craft materials there is. Around the house, it has a host of mundane uses (like grocery lists, cat toys, and homework). But as a craft material, it's irresistible. Kids can fold, tear, or cut it into shapes. In a pinch, it can become a toy, such as a paper airplane, a wildlife menagerie, or a dress-up costume. It comes in vibrant colors and all different weights and sizes. Best of all, you can even make it yourself.

In this chapter, we'll show you and your kids a few of the grander uses for a piece of paper. It won't take your child long to get the hang of the origami pinwheels on page 58 or the homemade envelopes on page 70. Perhaps she'll want to try her hand at Angus's famous boxes. But you'd better be prepared — if your child discovers a favorite project, as Angus did, you should have a good stock of supplies on hand.

Keep a paper bin. Scraps of white paper — as well as magazines, envelopes, bags, newspapers, gum wrappers, and junk mail

Rain Forest Vines, page 56

Paper Players

Aside from the papers you ordinarily have around the house (such as newspaper, tissue paper, and copy paper), here are others you may want to have on hand.

Construction paper comes in many colors; a generous supply will satisfy any kid's passion for cutting and pasting. Its downside: it fades quickly.

Butcher paper (also called craft paper) is lightweight brown paper available in rolls at art and craft stores. It's suited to large-scale projects, such as body tracings, and murals.

Card stock is about twice as thick as regular paper. It comes in many colors and is available at art stores or copy shops. It's great for — yep — cards.

Drawing paper is sturdy white paper available in large sketch pads. It's more expensive than computer paper, so save it for special projects.

Newsprint is lightweight, inexpensive paper available at art supply stores in large pads perfect for scribbling.

Poster board is heavy, colored paper. It comes in 22- by 28-inch sheets and can be found at craft and stationery stores.

Instant Dresses, page 64

— all can find new life in crafts. Tuck a scrap box by your recycling bin, so you're always reminded to save anything that might work for a project.

Use a portfolio for storage. To keep large or especially nice pieces of paper flat, you can store them in a paper artist's portfolio. These are available at art supply stores for about $7 to $13, and they fit well under a bed.

Buy in bulk. Butcher paper and newsprint, in particular, are worth buying in bulk. Also, stock up on colored tissue paper, wrapping paper, ribbons, and greeting cards when they go on sale after the holiday season. Wallpaper scraps for decorative projects can be salvaged from unwanted sample books at home improvement stores.

Cut carefully. Scissors are the tool of choice for most paper projects. However, if there's a need for a paper cutter or craft knife, that's a job for parents only. Kids should be cautioned not to use those tools unsupervised.

Glue it all together. Paper has a way of buckling and bending when it interacts with glue, especially regular white glue. While white glue, a glue stick, or rubber cement suffices for most projects, Sobo glue (from an art store) works better for delicate projects that use thin paper, such as books or collages.

Try making paper. Making paper at home is a science lesson and art project in one. For fun, learn how to turn old sheets of paper into pulp and create new paper.

Take a trip to the art supply store. For a special treat, let your children purchase a few sheets of specialty paper at an art store. Colored paper comes in vibrant hues and is usually "lightfast," which means it won't fade. In addition, the store may stock stamp-printed papers, fragile Japanese papers, and recycled papers with woven-in fibers, dried flower petals, or glitter. These varieties aren't cheap, but they do make crafts look terrific.

Colored Paper

Pop-up Neighborhood

This neighborhood rivals Mister Rogers's hometown for entertainment — and it folds right up to fit under a bed or dresser.

Materials

> 24- by 18-inch piece of green poster board
> Heavyweight colored paper
> Glue

Fold up the top of the poster board 6 inches from the edge to form a backdrop. For sky, cut out an 18- by 3-inch strip of blue paper. Scallop one long edge to create a hilly horizon. Glue the sky to the top of the poster board flap, so that the edges of the paper and the board are flush. Cut out a sun, clouds, and trees (pinking shears create a leafy look) and stick them to the backdrop. Next, glue on a winding paper road that runs from the lower edge of the poster board to the edge of the backdrop. To create the illusion that the road continues, it should get progressively narrower.

For houses, cut out paper rectangles — large ones for the foreground and smaller ones for the background. Glue on paper windows, roofs, shutters, and chimneys. Fold back the completed houses ½ inch from their lower edges and glue the bottom edges to the poster board. Use the same method to add Stop signs, shrubs, and picket fences. Then, your child can populate the neighborhood with little toy people and pets.

Pop-up Neighborhood

Paper Play

Fold-up Animals

With a collection of these exotic beasts, your kids can host a living room safari. Set out pillows for boulders and a plush towel for grassland — and let the wildlife roam.

A Menagerie of Crafts

If your child is an animal-lover, be sure to check out these other projects:

Materials

Heavyweight colored paper
Glue

Crocodile: This is the easiest animal to make. Fold a single sheet of paper in half. With the crease serving as its backbone and the top of its head, sketch a rounded body, legs, and a lower jaw. Cut out the shape. Create teeth by using pinking shears to trim along the mouth opening.

Hippopotamus: To make this water dweller (*hippopotamus* means river horse), use the same method as for the crocodile, except make short, straight cuts for teeth. Glue on small rounded ears and a tail.

Lion: This mighty beast needs a mane and a tufted tail. For a shaggy effect, use a butter knife to score an outline of the mane, then tear out the shape. Cut into the center of the mane and slip it around the lion's neck. Glue a torn-out tip onto the tail.

Elephant: For floppy ears that reach the tops of his legs, sketch a large angel-wings shape. Make a snip near the back of the elephant's head and slip the ears into the groove.

Giraffe and Baboon: For long-necked animals such as these, start by drawing an outline of the legs and belly, but not the head, neck, and tail. Next, unfold the paper and spread it flat. Draw the rest of the animal's body above the crease. Cut around the head, neck, and tail. Then, refold the paper and cut out the remaining parts.

Fold-up Animals

Curlicue Critters

These cheerful habitats, made from rolled strips of paper, are a project for an older child to curl up with on a quiet afternoon. Once she's shaped a few animals, she can use them to design a greeting card or turn them into a decorative pin to wear on a favorite jacket.

Materials

- Several ⅛-inch-wide strips of construction paper
- Round wooden toothpicks
- Glue

Moisten an end of one strip of construction paper and press it against the middle of a round wooden toothpick. Hold an end of the toothpick in one hand and, using your thumb and index finger, roll the paper around the toothpick to form a loose coil. Slide the paper off the toothpick. Secure the free end using clear-drying white glue applied with the tip of a second toothpick.

Once you've made a coil, you can turn it into a teardrop by pinching one side. Squeeze the opposite side, too, and you get an oval.

Or, space the creases closer together to form a semicircle. Glue these shapes together and you can create the animals described here or make up your own.

Caterpillar: Coil seven 4-inch strips and glue them side by side to form the insect's body. Add a round head made from a 6-inch strip and fold a ½-inch strip into V-shaped antennae.

Rabbit: Use a 12-inch strip, a 4-inch strip, and a 3-inch strip to roll circles for the bunny's body, head, and tail. Make oval ears out of 3-inch strips and loop a ¾-inch strip to form a long rabbit's foot.

Duck: With a 12-inch strip, make a teardrop to use for the bird's body. Use a 4-inch strip to make a round head and a V-shaped snip for a bill.

Turtle: For the turtle's shell, shape a semicircle out of a 12-inch strip. Use 3-inch strips to make two smaller semicircles for feet. Glue them flat side up to the bottom of the shell. With another 3-inch strip, make a teardrop head. Add a short curled tail.

GO FISH

For a quick game, let your kids cut out paper fish from construction paper — while they're at it, they can also cut out a deep blue sea. Poke paper clips through the mouths of the paper fish. Then tie a magnet to a string on a pole and send your kids fishing on the floor.

Curlicue Critters

Paper Play

Wind Sock

This sprightly wind sock can catch the breeze outside your house any day — or you can save it for a special day, as *FamilyFun* reader Judi Ensler did. With these directions, she made a bright pink clown-face wind sock to decorate the porch for her daughter Lindsey's second birthday party.

Materials

6- by 18-inch strip of construction paper
Markers, paint, crayons, glitter, or sequins
White glue
9 26-inch-long crepe paper streamers
Stapler
30-inch piece of string

Have your child begin by decorating the strip of construction paper with markers, paint, crayons, glitter, or sequins. She can make stars, flowers, or birthday candles or give the wind sock a face by gluing on paper cutouts of eyes, ears, a nose, and a mouth.

Next, glue the paper streamer strips to the back of the bottom edge of the construction paper. Then, staple the ends of the paper to form a tube. Finally, knot the string at each end and staple the knots to the tube sides to make a handle. Hang the wind sock on a porch or patio where it will be protected from strong winds and watch it ride the gentle breezes.

Wind Sock

Rain Forest Vines

When *FamilyFun* contributor Jodi Picoult noticed that a spell of damp weather was making her house feel like a rain forest, she ran with the idea and made these vines. Her kids were transfixed by this activity, and the fruits of their labors stayed wound around their hallway railings for months.

Materials

Construction paper
White glue
Twine or yarn
Glitter, markers, and scraps of felt

First, cut out lots of matching pairs of construction paper leaves (cut and trace a leaf template, if you wish). While you're at it, make matching pairs of paper flowers. On a long table or on the floor, set out all the pairs in a long line.

Flip over half of the flowers and leaves so that their "wrong" side is facing up, then spread glue on each one. Cut a length of twine or yarn and drape it over the middle of each glued flower or leaf. Press down each matching flower or leaf on top of its glued mate (in short, you're making a yarn sandwich), until you have a connected line of double-sided flowers and leaves. When dry, your kids can decorate the vine with glitter, markers, and felt or add construction paper details, such as petals and curlicue vine tendrils.

Rain Forest Vines

Matisse Cutouts

When Henri Matisse developed arthritis and could no longer paint, he began creating paper collages, known as cutouts. In this project, which is best for kids ages six and up, kids use scissors to cut paper shapes and arrange them into dynamic designs.

Materials

 Colored paper
 White or black paper
 Black or dark blue construction
  paper
 Glue

Before your child begins creating her design, look together for a book from your library that shows Matisse's collages. Notice how he used geometric shapes and organic ones (those found in nature) in his compositions. Geometric shapes, such as triangles, circles, and squares, are symmetrical. This is not the case with many organic shapes, which include squiggles and blobs.

Set out the colored paper and a pair of scissors and let your child begin cutting out shapes (younger kids may need help with the scissor work). You don't need to give her much direction in this activity, but if you like, you might encourage her to vary sizes and colors. Resist the urge to "tidy up" your child's cutouts. Her stars may not be perfectly symmetrical, but they will look beautiful when joined with the other shapes in the final collage.

Once she has amassed a collection of shapes, she can arrange them on a sheet of white or black paper. When she has settled on an arrangement, she can glue the cutouts in place. If the collage was done on white paper, mount the work onto black or dark blue construction paper to create a striking contrast or mount it against a dominant color within the collage.

Paper Play

Paper Blossoms

These paper flowers are beautiful, quick to make, and, unlike the real things, guaranteed to last.

Materials

 Colored tissue paper
 Crayons
 Pipe cleaners

For each flower, cut eight 3 1/2-inch squares out of the tissue paper. Using the side of a crayon, color along two opposite edges of each square. Place one of the squares on a flat surface with the uncolored edges at the top and bottom. Starting at the top, fold the square as you would a paper fan. The pleats should be about 1/2 inch wide. Fold the remaining squares using the same method.

For a stem, bend a pipe cleaner 1 1/2 inches from an end to form a hook. Stack the pleated squares (without unfolding them). Place the stack inside the hook and twist the hook end around the stem. Now, to open up the flower to full bloom, twist the petals a half turn near the stem.

1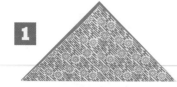

2

3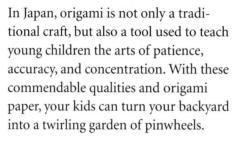

4

5

6

Origami

Paper Pinwheels

In Japan, origami is not only a traditional craft, but also a tool used to teach young children the arts of patience, accuracy, and concentration. With these commendable qualities and origami paper, your kids can turn your backyard into a twirling garden of pinwheels.

Materials

> 4 sheets of origami paper
> Glue (a glue stick works well)
> Pushpin
> Thin wooden dowel or pencil

1. Place one sheet of paper on a table, with the plain side up, and position it in a diamond shape. Fold the bottom point up so it is even with the top point and make a light crease. (The less you flatten your creases and the less glue you use later on, the more freely your pinwheel will turn.) Fold the left corner across to the right corner, make a light crease, and unfold.

2. Fold one layer of the top point down to the fold and secure with a spot of glue. Take three more squares of paper and repeat steps 1 and 2; you will need four of these units for each pinwheel.

3. Position one unit so the unfolded plain corner points toward you. Slip the printed point of a second unit into the first unit as shown, aligning the fold with the center crease. Secure it with a spot of glue.

4. Tuck the printed point of a third unit into the second unit, aligning the fold with the center crease. Glue it in place.

5. Hold the fourth unit so the unfolded plain corner points to the left and tuck the downward point into the third unit (make sure that the plain corner slides behind the first unit).

6. Secure the last corner with a dab of glue. To complete, use a pushpin to attach the paper wheel to a wooden dowel or to the eraser of a pencil.

Rainbow Flier

Rainbow Flier

Like the real thing, this rainbow flier from *Hands Around the World* (Williamson Publishing) can brighten a rainy day. Have your kids stockpile a handful of them, then hold a throwing contest when the sun comes out — they soar just like Frisbees.

Materials

8 3½-inch squares of origami paper
Glue

1. To make a flier, fold one square in half so that the crease is at the top (see diagram below).
2. Then, fold down the upper left corner to form a triangular pocket.
3. Fold up the lower right corner. This will create a parallelogram. Repeat the process with the other squares.

To assemble the flier, fit the open triangle of one parallelogram into the triangular pocket of the next, working clockwise to complete a circle. Dab glue between the pieces to secure them. Once dry, the ring is ready to fly.

Gum Wrapper Chain

The classic gum chain, a playground favorite, is really a version of origami — with teeny-weeny pieces of paper. A word of warning, though: once your children figure out the simple technique, they will be working their choppers day in and day out to generate the raw materials for a record-breaking chain.

Materials

Lots and lots of gum wrappers
(from long sticks of gum)

To start, tear a gum wrapper in half the long way. Fold the long sides of one strip in so they line up in the center, then fold it in half on the line. Now, you should have a long skinny piece. Fold the ends in so they meet in the center and fold the strip in half where they meet.

Make a second link and slide it into the first as shown (the two ends of one link slip into the folds of the two ends of another). Presto! You're on your way.

PERFECT FOLDING PAPER

Origami paper, which often is printed on one side and plain on the other, is available in craft supplies stores, but kids also can cut their own squares from writing paper, wrapping paper, Sunday comics, scraps of wallpaper, or any other thin paper. Typically, origami squares are 6 by 6 inches.

Gum Wrapper Chain

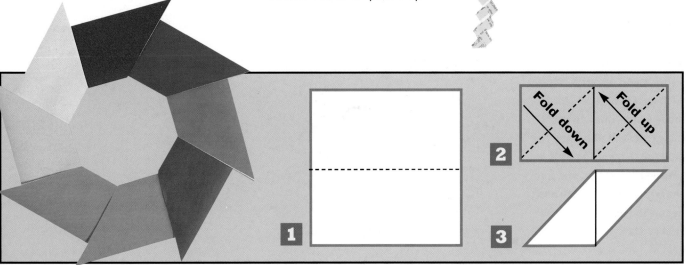

1

2 Fold down / Fold up

3

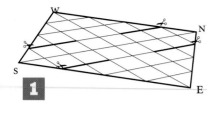

1

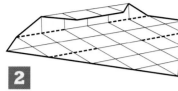

2

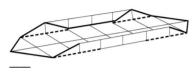

3

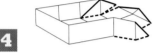

4

A Generation of Boxes

When *FamilyFun* reader Anne D. Driskill of Knoxville, Tennessee, saw our article on paper boxes, she wrote to tell us a story. When Anne was a child, a Japanese visitor stayed with her family and taught them how to make paper boxes similar to the ones featured in *FamilyFun*. Anne's mother regularly recycled their junk mail into boxes to use them as place cards for special occasions. Anne herself made boxes for Valentine's Day, rubber-stamped them with hearts, and filled them with chocolate bars. She made them from old greeting cards — if she liked the design, she would put it on the outside; if not, she put the white side outside and decorated her box with her rubber stamps.

Paper Boxes

With this simple technique, your kids can turn out a cache of colorful boxes to decorate and fill with treasures. Our sample measures 4 inches across and 2 inches deep, but your child can vary the dimensions by changing the size of the two paper squares she starts with.

Materials

> Heavyweight drawing paper, cut into one 10⅝-inch square and one 11-inch square
> Crayons, markers, stickers, or paints

To make the bottom, fold the smaller paper square in half diagonally, first one way and then the other, creasing the folds well before unfolding them. Next, fold in all four corners so they meet in the center; crease them well and unfold.

Fold one of the corners so that it meets the farthest crease line opposite

that corner, crease, and unfold it; repeat with the three other corners. Finally, fold each corner to its closest crease line. Unfold all the corners to reveal an overall pattern of creased squares.

1. Make two cuts in the paper at one corner, two squares deep and two squares apart. Make identical cuts on the opposite corner.

2 and 3. Orient the paper with the cuts facing north and south. Fold in the east and west corners along the crease lines two times, finally bringing the two sides up vertically.

4. Bend the pointed ends of the east and west sides toward one another, crossing them. Bring the tongue-shaped portion of the paper (the one facing south) up and over the crossed ends, folding it down over the ends and tucking it so that it stays put. Do the same with the north end of the paper. This completes the bottom of the box.

To make the lid, fold the larger sheet of paper the same way you did the bottom of the box. Before you cut and assemble the lid, decorate the paper using crayons, markers, stickers, or paints.

Paper Boxes

Homemade Books

Accordion Book

Even if your kids can't read or write yet, they can help create a versatile accordion-style book and dictate their tales to a parent or older sibling to record. Folded books are fun to make and to read — they can be spread out for a panoramic effect or closed up and read by turning the pages as you would with an ordinary book. When they are flipped over, there is room for a second story.

Materials

    9 8½- by 14-inch sheets of colored
      paper
    Ruler
    Double-sided tape or glue
    Cardboard
    Ribbon or string

1. Fold nine 8½- by 14-inch sheets of colored paper in half so they each are 7 by 8½ inches, then unfold. Overlap the right half of the first piece with the left half of the next piece and so on. Attach the overlapping pages with double-sided tape or glue.

2. Fold up the pages accordion style. Attach the front and back pages to pieces of cardboard that are just a bit bigger than your pages.

Accordion Book

3. As a finishing touch, attach a piece of ribbon or string to the front and back covers for tying the book closed.

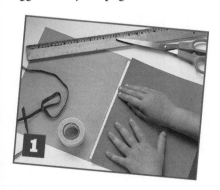

Paper Play

Hand-sewn Blank Book

1. Determine the finished size of your book and, using the ruler and craft knife, help your child cut sheets double the final size from the paper and the card stock. (If you want the final book to be 4 by 6 inches, for example, start with sheets that measure 8 by 6 inches.) Fold all the sheets in half vertically, sandwiching the pages between the front and back covers. Mark a row of evenly spaced dots about ½ inch in from the folded spine. As shown, punch holes in all the sheets where marked. Cut a piece of yarn or embroidery thread that is about four times the length of the book.

2. Thread the needle and, starting at the top of the book (leave a loose end of a few inches), sew it together with a running stitch: up through the first hole, down through the second, up through the third, down through the fourth, and so on.

3. After sewing down through the last hole, loop the yarn around the bottom of the book as shown and insert the needle in that hole again. Pull the thread tight, then insert the needle in that hole once more, this time looping the yarn around the spine of the book. Work your way back up the spine, sewing through each hole two times — once to complete the running stitch and the second time to loop the yarn around the spine. Tie the two loose ends together at the top with a small bow.

Gently score a vertical line (do not cut all the way through!) on the front cover near the lacing to make the book easier to open. Your child can decorate the cover any way she likes.

BOOKS UNDER COVER

Fancy coverings for school notebooks make a backpack of homework seem more inviting. Here are a few ideas to start with.

✂ Use bold wrapping paper, with shiny, floral, or polka-dot designs.

✂ Cover a piece of your child's art or a favorite greeting card with clear Con-Tact paper and trim it to fit.

✂ Cut covers out of the Sunday comics. Or use the black and white daily strips and have your kids hand-color them first.

✂ Recycle a favorite old shirt into a fabric cover (see page 43 for specific instructions).

Hand-sewn Blank Book

This adaptation of the traditional Japanese sewn binding can be used to create books of any size. The punched holes make it easy for even young kids to have the satisfaction of assembly.

Materials

White or colored paper
Card stock or construction paper
Pencil
Ruler
Craft knife
Hole punch
Yarn or embroidery thread
Blunt tapestry needle

Creative Bookmarks

Kids who are hooked on chapter books can mark their reading progress with personalized bookmarks, which are easy to make, sturdy, and even may speed up the page turning.

Materials

Construction paper or poster board
Pinking shears or crazy scissors
Clear Con-Tact paper (optional)
Hole punch
Ribbon

For each bookmark, begin with a piece of construction paper or poster board 6 inches long and 2 inches wide. Let your kids decorate it however they like (see suggestions below). For a glossy finish, cover the bookmark with clear Con-Tact paper. If you're using pinking shears (or one of Fiskars's line of crazy scissors) to make jagged edges, cover the bookmark before you trim it to size. Lastly, punch a hole in the top and tie on a festive ribbon.

Stickers Galore: Kids can show off their sticker collections on their bookmarks. Put one large seal on the bottom of the paper or line several smaller ones in a row.

Paper Play

Rubber Stamps: Print colorful figures or shapes onto the paper. If you track down alphabet stamps, your kids can print their names or the book's title. For a homemade rubber stamp, see page 137.

Magazine Collage: Cut out bright pictures from magazines or travel brochures. Overlap the images and lightly glue them onto the bookmark.

Geometric Designs: Cut a strip of graph paper to the same size as the bookmark and glue them together. Working from the center out, use fine-tip markers or colored pencils to create geometric designs in the squares. Try diagonal stripes, symmetrical patterns, or random designs.

Photo Collage: Gather snapshots of family members, friends, or pets. Cut out figures and lightly glue them onto the paper. Then, jazz up the images with funny bubble captions.

Glitter: Sprinkle the bookmark with glitter, then cover it with a piece of clear Con-Tact paper. Trim the paper, leaving a ¼-inch border.

Keepsake Scrapbook

To practice and enjoy writing, drawing, and photography over school vacation, help your kids create a summer scrapbook. Begin with a large blank or lined book, a glue stick or white glue, and photo corners or clear tape. Divide the pages into categories — ticket stubs, photos, nature finds, family stories, jokes, dreams, or a tally of ice-cream cone flavors and sports scores. Enter the headings on different pages throughout the scrapbook. If it's kept in an accessible place, your child's journal will become a summer catchall, organized around the principle that anything goes.

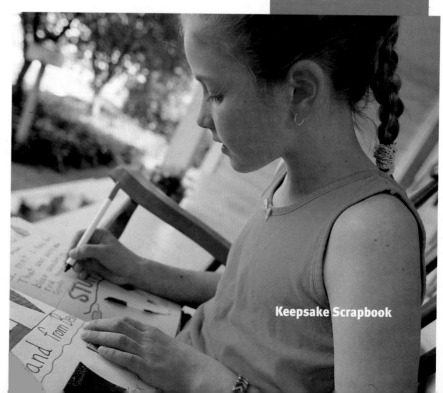

Keepsake Scrapbook

Newspaper & Butcher Paper

Instant Dresses

Not only are these disposable dress designs a snap to make, but they also cost little more than the price of paper and tape.

Materials

> Sheet of newspaper
> Butcher paper
> Tape
> Paint or colored tape
> Sponges

First, make a basic shift-style dress pattern. Spread open the newspaper sheet and refold it in half horizontally. Turn the sheet so the fold is on the right, then cut a U-shaped armhole in the upper left corner. Spread the sheet open again and cut out a U- or V-shaped neckline in the center of the top edge. (This will form shoulder straps between the armholes.) Hold up the pattern in front of your child and trim the paper where necessary for a better fit.

Next, trace around the pattern onto two pieces of heavyweight butcher paper. Extend the length to suit your child's height. Cut out both pieces and tape together the shoulder and side seams. Decorate the dress with sponge-painted designs, colored-tape stripes, and paper buttons.

Cabin Fever

Sometimes, all it takes to lift a kid's spirits is a change of scenery. With this paper log construction technique from *Kids Create!* (Williamson Publishing), your child can build a frontier cabin without ever leaving home.

Materials

- 3- by 2-inch strips of butcher or construction paper
- Pencil
- Ruler
- 3½-inch cardboard square (for house base)
- Glue
- 3½- by 5-inch paper rectangle (for the roof)
- 5-inch paper square (for the chimney)

Make logs out of the strips of craft paper by wrapping each one around the pencil, taping down the open edge, and sliding the cylinder off the pencil. Make twenty-four 3-inch logs: seventeen to use as is and seven to trim into shorter lengths as called for.

Assemble the cabin on top of the cardboard square. Glue 3-inch logs along three edges of the square, staggering the log ends, as shown. On the fourth side, create a front door opening by gluing a 1-inch log and a ¾-inch log to either corner. Glue on two more rows of logs, alternating the shorter lengths on the sides of the door. Add another two rows of 3-inch logs all around. For the last four rows, build onto the front and back only, using progressively shorter logs. Taper the ends to create an A-shaped roofline.

For a roof, fold the paper rectangle in half and glue it in place atop the cabin. To make a chimney, loosely roll up the 5-inch paper square and glue down the open edge. Then, glue the cylinder to the rear of the cabin.

Cabin Fever

Chapter Five

Back to Nature

ONE THING we learn early on as parents is that if you're planning to take your kids on a hike through the woods, along a beach, or even across a meadow, you'll need to allot plenty of time. It's not that our children can't keep up with us, but rather that they lag behind on purpose — to watch a ladybug climb to the top of a blade of grass, to marvel at the intricacy of a spiderweb glistening in the dew, or to pocket an unusual stone (if they can resist skipping it across a stream). For kids, the natural world is instantly and totally fascinating, even rivaling a store-bought toy or the latest video game.

That's what this chapter is all about. It's filled with ideas that let your kids take their favorite outdoor experiences a step further, by turning natural finds into lasting treasures. For example, they can build a toy raft out of sticks (page 69), fashion a frog out of a rock (page 71), or sculpt a giant rabbit out of snow (page 78). And that's just for starters. With a little imagination and seasons full of opportunities, the possibilities are endless.

Craft with the seasons in mind. Once you have read this chapter, pick out a few seasonal projects your family would like to try. Go on an autumn leaf hunt and make leaf-print greeting cards. Plant a house of sunflowers in your garden in the spring, or build a backyard bird feeder on a winter day.

Think with your senses. When choosing a project, take your clues from the natural world. If you love the smell of pine needles or eucalyptus leaves, mix your

Homemade Potpourri, page 73

Shell Painting, page 76

own potpourri. If a certain rock looks like a bullfrog or a turtle, make a painted doorstop.

Work outside whenever practical. Make the environment part of your kids' crafting experience. Set up the supplies you'll need on a backyard picnic table, under a shady tree, or even on the beach, if it makes sense.

Seize the opportunity to learn. While nature crafts are a blast in and of themselves, don't stop there. Are you planning to look for animal tracks and cast them in plaster? Pick up a guidebook at the library so you'll be able to read up on the creatures that left their distinctive mark.

You don't need a backyard to try nature crafts. Just because you live in the city doesn't mean the crafts are off-limits. Take your family on an outing to a park or beach to collect pinecones, leaves, or shells for your craft projects.

Show respect for wildlife and their habitats. Above all, follow the lead of true conservationists and make it a family policy to have as little impact on the natural world as possible. If you need sticks for a particular project, search the ground for fallen branches instead of cutting them from trees. If you discover a salamander under a rock, remind your kids that it belongs in the wild.

Sticks & Stones

Wooden Raft

Huck Finn knew how to ride out the dog days of summer: drifting down-river on a homemade raft. Your kids can follow suit (on a much smaller scale) by building a miniature craft out of sticks to launch in a stream or a wading pool.

Materials

- Dry sticks
- Hedge clippers
- Glue
- Fishing line
- Small piece of cloth
- String

For the raft base, use the clippers to cut two foot-long lengths from the thickest stick (a parent's job). Lay them on a flat working surface, 6 inches apart and parallel to one another.

Cut the remaining sticks into 10-inch lengths to use for flooring (you'll need about two dozen). Lay the flooring across the base, one stick at a time. Start in the center and work your way toward the sides, gluing the pieces in place as you go.

To make sure the raft holds (the wood will swell when it's wet), lash the flooring ends to the base with fishing line. Tie a piece of line to an end of one of the base sticks. Then, weave the line over and between the flooring boards and around the base, working your way to the other end. Tie off the line. Use the same method to lash the opposite side of the raft.

For a sail, cut a triangle (8 inches tall and 7 inches across the base) from the piece of cloth. Apply glue along the

Wooden Raft

8-inch edge of the sail, then wrap the glued portion around a slender stick. Wedge the lower end of the stick between the flooring and use string to tie the top of the mast to both sides of the raft base.

Finally, tie a long piece of string to the back of the raft for launching the craft and then pulling it back to shore.

Back to Nature

Pine Needle Nannies

Stick Figures

Children have a knack for imagining entire worlds in the crook of a tree or a patch of meadow grass. This autumn craft lets them bring those musings to life by turning acorns and sticks into a village of woodsy elves.

Materials

Unshelled acorns
Fine-tipped marker
Craft knife
Twigs
Leaves
Glue
Meadow grass and other nature finds

Straw Man

Babes in the Woods:
Draw eyes and a mouth on the bottom of an unshelled acorn — the pointed tip of the shell will serve as a nose. Next, use a craft knife (a parent's job) to bore a small neck hole into the side of the shell at the base of the cap. For a body, fit the end of a short, forked twig into the neck opening. Then, glue on a leaf shawl or cape. Or, wrap a colorful leaf dress around the twig body and belt it with a blade of grass.

Pine Needle Nannies:
Make acorn heads following the method given above. For the nannies' wispy bodies, just fit the stemmed end of a clump of pine needles into each neck opening

Babes in the Woods

and use a drop of glue to secure it, if necessary.

Mr. & Mrs. A. Corn: For each figure, make a body by gluing together the ends of two forked twigs — one fork should resemble outstretched arms; the other should look like legs. Attach acorn heads, as previously described. For Mrs. Corn's grass skirt, tie the top of a bunch of pine needles around her trunk with a piece of grass. To make Mr. Corn's pants, glue a smaller bunch of needles around each leg. Then, glue a leaf sweater around his arms and trunk. Finally, glue on a pair of pumpkin seed shoes.

Pinecone Pony: To make the pony's body, glue the ends of four straight twig legs to a medium-size pinecone. For a head and neck, glue a small pinecone to the end of a pine needle–covered twig and trim the needles to create a spiky mane. Then, glue the base of the neck to the body. Lastly, glue a thick bunch of pine needles to the back of the body for a flowing tail.

Straw Man: Cut twenty 5-inch lengths of dry meadow grass with scissors. Tie them together in a bunch, an inch from the top, with another piece of grass or string to create a head and body. Divide the body to form legs and bind each one with grass a half inch from the bottom. For arms, slip a single 4-inch shaft of grass through the center of the body. Finally, use a fine-tipped marker to draw on a face.

Pinecone Pony

Mr. A. Corn

Cookpot and Stand

Rock Group

With some paint and a little imagination, your child can turn a pocketful of stones into a family of rock stars or an entourage of stony-faced creatures.

Materials

Assorted pebbles and stones
Glue
Acrylic paints and paintbrushes

First, wipe off any sand or dirt and then study each stone to see what its shape or composition suggests. A rough, chunky rock may resemble a crouching cat, a toad, or an owl. Tiny, smooth pebbles can make great ladybugs or bumblebees. A flat, round stone can be used for a snail shell or a face; long, thin ones make natural arms, legs, and tails.

To make an animal, start with a larger stone as a base for the body. Then, use glue to attach smaller stones for eyes, ears, wings, antennae, and feet. For stone people, glue arms, legs, and heads to rock bodies or leave the limbs unattached for future mixing and matching.

Use acrylics to highlight the facial features and paint on hair. Dress the figures any way you want — in stripes or checks, ties or dresses, tutus or Stetsons.

More Fun with Stones

Play games with stones: Hunt for ten coin-size pebbles and paint half of them one color and the rest another. Use them for tic-tac-toe markers (just draw a grid in the dirt) or as a substitute for jacks.

Write in stone: Paint individual letters on a bunch of stones and use them to spell out messages on a windowsill or along the edge of a garden. Or, print a favorite slogan or your family's motto on a heavier rock for a paperweight or bookend.

Build a stone town: Turn larger stones into houses and shops by painting on windows and doors. Then, use small rocks to outline roadways between them for a fleet of toy cars.

Rock Group

Back to Nature

Flowers

Sunflower House

Sunflower House

You don't need a hammer and nails, or even wood, to build this pretty little house — just sunflower seeds for planting the walls and a little TLC to help them grow.

Materials

    Gardening tools
    Mammoth sunflower seeds
    Teddy Bear or Dwarf sunflower
      seeds

The best time to start planting will of course depend on your location, but generally any time after the last frost should be okay. Choose a sunny spot where the soil is dry and drains well — sunflowers can take the heat but will suffer from overwatering. Keep in mind that the taller sunflower varieties will also need moderately rich soil, although the shorter ones will grow in poor soil conditions.

Before planting, loosen the soil with the gardening tools. Then, sow the seeds (according to the package directions) in a horseshoe shape, alternating Mammoth sunflower seeds (for height) and Teddy Bear or Dwarf sunflower seeds (to fill in the walls).

While waiting for the seeds to sprout (it takes 2 to 3 weeks in warm temperatures), your child can spruce up the grounds around her house site — laying a stepping-stone walk-way to its door or making a welcome sign.

Flower Pounding

At a craft fair two years ago, *FamilyFun* reader Fredda Parish Lake of Doylestown, Pennsylvania, saw a woman make prints by hammering on a leaf between two pieces of fabric. Fascinated, Fredda wondered if you could make prints with flowers. She went home and tried with husband Larry and daughters Laura and Julia (ages eleven and seven) as willing partners. They found that pansies didn't work, and that blue lobelia printed well; red impatiens were too bright, but pink ones left a delicate color. "You just need to play with it," Fredda says. The girls have since used the technique to make stationery, a table runner, and quilt pieces. One of Laura's designs even won her first place at the Middletown Grange Fair.

Materials

- Paper bags
- Unbleached muslin cloth
- Fresh leaves and flowers
- Hammer
- Butter knife
- Paper

Cover a smooth, hard surface with paper bags and spread out the fabric. Arrange a leaf and flower design on one half of the fabric, then fold the other half over the design. Using a hammer, pound on top of the leaves or flowers, being sure to go all the way to the edges. When the color has bled through the fabric, open it up and scrape off the plant residue with the butter knife. You'll have a mirror image of the leaves and flowers. The fabric pieces make great pillow fronts or quilt

Back to Nature

Flower Pounding

squares, though they will fade after repeated washings (use cold water).

For an alternative to the mirror image method, simply place the flowers on the fabric, cover with a sheet of waxed paper, and pound away. You can also use the same method to pound leaves and flowers onto paper to make floral stationery or gift tags.

HOMEMADE POTPOURRI

Throughout history, fragrant flowers and herbs have been mixed together to freshen the air and add a little spice to life. Here's how your kids can custom-mix a colorful blend of potpourri to use in their rooms or to give as a gift.

When a bouquet starts to fade, remove the petals and spread them out to dry. Later, place them in a bowl or basket. For extra color and texture, blend in natural objects, such as bark, pine needles, seashells, or eucalyptus leaves. Or liven up the mixture by adding cinnamon sticks and citrus peels, dried rosemary or basil, or even a quick spray of your favorite cologne.

Sand & Shells

An Octopus Built of Sand

Sculptor Dale Zarrella, who lives on Maui with his eight-year-old daughter, Shala, has carved a menagerie of animal likenesses from ice, wood, stone, wax, and even chocolate. When *FamilyFun* invited him to try his hand in sand, molding a giant octopus that would inspire our beachgoing readers to try sand-sculpting themselves, his 25-foot creation surpassed our expectations. Zarrella, it turns out, is savvy about octopi. Studying them in the island's tide pools, he has witnessed them change color instantaneously and peered into their eerily humanlike eyes. He has also watched native Hawaiians carry them from the surf, bound for the dinner table. His impression of the new medium? "It's amazing what detail you can create in sand," says the artist. "My wheels are turning." And from what we've seen, the beach is his limit.

Materials

Cornstarch
Plastic spray bottle
Stick or piece of driftwood
Sand
Trowel or large spoon

1. Dissolve a bit of cornstarch in fresh or salt water and pour the mixture into the plastic spray bottle.

Then, use the stick or driftwood to make a simple sketch on the beach. Draw a bulbous body from which eight arms extend and intertwine. Pile and pat down sand atop the outline.

2. Use your hands to shape two rows

of sand domes on a tentacle's underside to resemble the suckers octopi use to trap fish and shrimp. Scoop out the centers of the domes with a trowel or a large spoon.

3. Mist the sculpture frequently with the cornstarch solution to keep it from drying out and crumbling during the process.

4. Finally, bask in the company of your octopus!

An Octopus Built of Sand

with acrylic paints (bright colors will be easier to spot against the sand). Finally, seal the comb with a few coats of clear acrylic gloss.

Shell Painting

With rounded frames and smooth, chalklike surfaces that soak up paint, seashells make good palm-size canvases for your children's seascapes.

Materials

- Seashells (chalkier, white shells work best)
- Jar of freshwater (for rinsing shells and mixing paint)
- Watercolor or acrylic paints and paintbrushes

To start, rinse a few shells with freshwater and let them dry in the sun. Your child can paint pictures on the inside of each shell, being careful to let each color dry before adding the next for a crisp picture, or letting the colors blend for an abstract splash of color. Set out in the sun until dry.

Shell Painting

Sculpt a Dune Buggy

Here's a beach craft your kids will really get into — a two-seater dune buggy that comes with all the options (sand dollar headlights, a Frisbee steering wheel, a driftwood windshield, and a pebble license plate). To get your assembly line rolling, help your kids pile up a big mound of sand and pack it down firm. Working from the top down, sculpt the car's body, rounding the hood and trunk, carving fat tires into the sides, and digging out a seat for the driver and passenger. Then, add a shell hood ornament and a beach grass antenna, or whatever else your kids dream up.

Beach Comb

Whether your child sculpts his palace on the beach or in a backyard sandbox, this giant cardboard comb can come in handy for clearing and leveling a building site or for swirling designs on or around castle walls. This nifty tool is inspired by *Wacky Cakes and Water Snakes* (Penguin Books), a season-by-season collection of crafts and activities for kids.

Materials

- Corrugated cardboard
- Glue
- Craft knife
- Acrylic paints and paintbrushes
- Acrylic gloss

To fashion the comb, first cut four 6- by 15-inch pieces of corrugated cardboard and glue them one on top of another. Once the glue dries, use a craft knife (parents only) to cut out seven 1- by 3-inch notches along one long edge. Your child can decorate the comb

Sea Creatures

Just as a day at the beach seems to fit the bill for various ages and temperaments, so does the following project. The procedure is simple enough: to create a decorative, plaster-cast mask using beachcombed objects. The outcome is another story. Each mask, created facedown in the sand, hides its identity until unmolded and washed in the sea.

Materials

> Beach stuff, such as shells, driftwood, sea glass, or feathers
> Plaster of Paris
> Water buckets for mixing and cleaning up
> Stirring tool for the squeamish (a bare hand works best!)
> String, about 4 inches per mask

An ideal spot to cast your molds is the moist, hard-packed strip of beach just above the wet tidal sand — but not too close to the water lest the incoming waves wash over your setting plaster.

1. Collect elements for facial features.

2. Dig an oval hole in the sand that measures about 5 to 8 inches tall and 2 inches deep (the sides of deeper molds may crumble while you are putting in your objects).

3. Arrange your beach finds in the hole. Remind your kids to think in reverse since you are seeing the mask from the inside out. Open eyes and mouths, teeth, and hair look great but require engineering, and firm sand, if you want them to hold in place. If you bury feathers, seaweed, or rope in the bottom of the mold so that enough projects up for the plaster to grip, they will dangle or stick out from the mask without being completely embedded.

Next, mix the plaster in your bucket — you can use seawater. (A standard box will make three to six masks, depending on the amount used for each.) Usually, a thick cream consistency works well — too runny, and your plaster can seep beneath objects, so that they are hidden when you uncover the masks; too thick, and the plaster dislodges objects and messes up the mask's shape.

4. As soon as the plaster is ready, slowly pour it over your hand, held just an inch or two above the impression, to break its fall. Keep the plaster layer about an inch thick.

For a hanger, tie a knot about a half inch from each end of the string. When the plaster begins to thicken, push the knots into the back of the mask to harden in place as the plaster dries.

5. Before the plaster becomes too firm, dig the sand away from the mask (rather than yanking the mask out). Then, use ocean water to gently wash away any flaws — you will have a few moments to manipulate the plaster's surface (cleaning off, digging in, rubbing away excess sand) before the plaster hardens completely.

Back to Nature

Sea Creatures

Snow

Neighborhood Snow Bunny

Once they've formed the basic shape, have them carve legs, arms, and faces using the sticks, sand shovels, kitchen tools, or mitten-covered hands.

Ice Castle

When the temperature drops below freezing, you can add a little shimmer to the backyard by building your own ice hideaway.

Materials
> Household containers, such as
>   buckets, pans, and ice cube trays
> Food coloring (optional)
> Large pail
> Spray bottle

To make the building blocks, just fill household containers with water and set them outdoors to freeze. (You can even stir in food coloring for a special effect.) When you're ready to unmold the frozen blocks, fill the large pail with warm water and briefly dip the containers in it. The ice should then slip out easily. Be sure to wear gloves to protect your skin.

To raise the walls of your castle, just spray water on the surfaces to be joined and hold the blocks in place for several seconds until they freeze together.

Ice Lantern

Add a little warmth to a cold snap with a glistening outdoor candleholder. Fill the bottom of a bucket with a few inches of water and set it outside to freeze. Next, cut the top off a 2-liter plastic bottle and set the bottom in the bucket, on top of the ice. Place a heavy object in the bottle to weigh it down. Then, fill the bucket (but not the bottle) with more water and let it freeze solid. Pour warm water on the outside of the bucket and slide the ice out. Finally, fill the bottle with warm water to loosen it. Remove the bottle and insert a votive candle.

Neighborhood Snow Zoo

After a snowstorm, the first thing most kids want to do is build a snowman. To expand on this popular winter pastime, try making a zoo full of animals in your backyard.

Materials
> Snow
> Sticks
> Shovels or large spoons

Have the kids begin by rolling together and stacking balls of snow from which they can carve their favorite animals — a bear standing on its hind legs, a sitting bunny, or even an alligator creeping along the ground.

Ice Castle

Sugar Cube Igloo

Sugar Cube Igloo

Who says you need snow to make an igloo? The polar landscape shown here, inspired by *Wim Kros's Fun Foods* (Sterling), is made from sugar cubes.

Materials

Cardboard
Sugar cubes
2 egg whites
3 cups confectioners' sugar

Cut out a cardboard circle with a 7-inch diameter. Then, lay a base row of sugar cubes around the circle, leaving space for the igloo entrance.

Next, make mortar by mixing together the egg whites and confectioners' sugar. Add subsequent layers of cubes, applying the mortar to the bottom of the new cubes, not to those already in place. Work alternately left and right from the entrance toward the back of the igloo, staggering the cubes the way a builder lays bricks. Gradually decrease the circumference of the igloo with each new row by setting the cubes a little closer to the center each time.

Build a total of ten layers, stopping halfway through the construction to let the igloo dry.

Make the doorway arch and roof separately, working on a flat surface. When they are dry, glue them in place. Allow the igloo to dry completely, then sprinkle with a blizzard of sugar.

SNOW SPRAY PAINT

During winter, the most vibrant sight out your window could just be your kids' handiwork — neon blue snowballs, orange snowdrifts, and rainbow snow people. All they need is some snow paint.

First, make several pitchers of colored water with half a dozen drops of food coloring per container. Experiment to get hot pinks, bright purples, and gaudy greens — the bolder the colors, the better. Choose a variety of applicators for the kids to take outside. Anything with a nozzle will do, including a turkey baster and a watering can. The dye will harmlessly melt away with the next thaw.

Back to Nature

Chapter Six

The Toy Factory

WHEN *FAMILY FUN* associate editor Cindy Littlefield was clearing her kids' school papers from the table before dinner one night, she came upon a tiny man made of paper. A touch of her fingertip set it cartwheeling across the tabletop. "Isn't it cute?" asked her twelve-year-old daughter, Jade. "Ian made it at school." The thought made Cindy smile. Even with the hefty competition of high-tech store-bought toys, a simple handmade gadget could still amuse her fourteen-year-old son.

That fact is proven over and over again in the Littlefield household, where many of the toys featured in the Family Almanac section of *FamilyFun* magazine are conceived and tested. Ian's acrobatic character turned into the tumbling tots on page 96, while Jade's furry pipe cleaner ponies and woolly poodles became the sculptures on page 85.

"The best part about homemade toys," says Cindy, "is that the excitement begins the instant you and your kids come up with an idea — and it continues throughout the crafting process. That's all before your kids even start playing with the toy."

The next time you're looking for a way to entertain your family — on a rainy weekend or during school vacation — take a tip from the Littlefields and embark on a toy-making adventure. Start by check-

Nadia (Siberia)   **Suki (Japan)**   **Duncan (Scotland)**

Worry Dolls, page 86

Rain Stick, page 97

ing out the ideas in this chapter and see where your imaginations take you.

Let your kids call the shots as often as possible. As a parent, you'll want to be in charge of certain toy-making tools (handsaws, drills, and craft knives), but resist the temptation to step in and do the whole project yourself. Remember, if your child has a hand in making his toy, he'll like it more.

Enjoy the toy-making process. There's no need to rush to the finish. Making the toy can be as much fun as playing with it.

Remember, beauty is in the eye of the beholder. If your child is happy with a hairless doll, so be it. On the other hand, if she's determined to fash-

ion a wig out of yarn and can't manage it on her own, offer to help. You can still let her add the finishing touch, cutting the bangs or, say, tying on a ribbon bow.

Turn toy-making into a learning opportunity. If the toy you decide to make has a functional part, such as the marble inside the tumble tots (see page 96), discuss, in simple terms, how the toy is engineered. Encourage your child to use his newfound knowledge to invent a new toy altogether.

Give a homemade toy as a gift. Your child can surprise a friend on her birthday with a unique gift, such as a set of homemade finger puppets (see pages 87 and 88) or a handcrafted puddleboat (see page 93).

Juice Can Puppets, page 87

Dolls

Life-size Doll

Older kids tend to like their dolls small, but for the younger set, the bigger the better. Even more so if it's one that bears an uncanny resemblance to its owner.

Materials

- Large sheet of paper and chalk
- White bedsheet
- Straight pins and fabric scissors
- Fabric glue or sewing needle and thread
- Polyester filling (available at most craft stores)
- Broom handle
- Yarn and buttons

Ask your child to lie down on the paper, with her arms and legs outstretched. Use chalk to trace around her entire body. Keep the outline loose, sketching around both hands as if they were mittens. Cut out the pattern and pin it on top of a bedsheet that's been folded in half lengthwise.

Trace around the paper, leaving a 2-inch margin near the head and body and a 1-inch margin for the arms, legs, and feet. Draw a bit closer to the hands. Using fabric scissors, cut through the doubled sheet, 1 inch outside of the chalk line.

The easiest way to attach the doll's front and back is to stick the edges together with fabric glue, but stitching them (allow a ½-inch seam) will produce a sturdier doll. Either way, leave an opening at the top of the head. Turn the figure inside out and stuff with polyester filling. Use a broom handle to push the filling into the arms and legs. Now, stitch the opening closed. Glue on strands of yarn hair and button eyes, and your doll is ready to dress — right from your child's closet.

Life-size Dolls

A Dolls' Hammock

If you're looking for a place for your child's dolls to bunk, here's a tip from *FamilyFun* reader Mireille Church from Kanata, Ontario. When her son Jean-Francois turned four years old, she painted a life-size tree on the wall in one corner of his room. Next, she screwed hooks into the painted bark on the adjoining walls and hung up a hammock, where Jean-Francois's entire stuffed animal collection roosts.

The Toy Factory

1

2

3

4

Meet the
Beadles

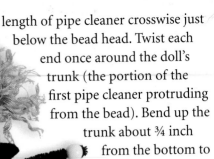

Meet the Beadles

Of all the dolls we've crafted at *FamilyFun*, twelve-year-old Jade Littlefield, a frequent visitor around the office, claims these futuristic figures with their posable bodies and wigged-out hair are the best. They can sit on a windowsill — just bend their knees and straighten their torsos — or move into your child's dollhouse.

Materials

Embroidery floss
Tape measure
Pipe cleaners
¾-inch round wooden bead (with a 5-millimeter center hole)
Felt scraps
4 smaller wooden beads (with center holes you can fit a pipe cleaner through)
fine-tipped colored markers

1. First, create the doll's hair by cutting the embroidery floss into 20 pieces that measure twice the length you want. Fold a 6-inch pipe cleaner in half over the midpoint of the collective strands, as shown. Feed both ends of the pipe cleaner through the center of the large bead. Slide the bead up the pipe cleaner until the fold is hidden in the bead center. Separate each strand of embroidery floss to fashion a thick shock of hair. For curls, dampen the strands with a few drops of water, wind them around a pencil, and let them dry.

2. For the doll's arms, place a 5-inch length of pipe cleaner crosswise just below the bead head. Twist each end once around the doll's trunk (the portion of the first pipe cleaner protruding from the bead). Bend up the trunk about ¾ inch from the bottom to form a hook. For legs, fold a 5-inch pipe cleaner in half and hang it on the hook, as shown. Secure the legs by twisting the ¾-inch trunk ends around them.

3. To make a pair of pants, fold a 6- by 1½-inch piece of felt in half, so that the shorter edges meet. Starting from the fold, make a 2-inch cut up the middle, stopping 1 inch from the open end. Make a ¼-inch waist hole ½ inch from one end. For foot openings, make a small slit through the felt fold at the bottom of each pant leg.

4. Slip both legs through the waist opening from the front. Then, push the pipe cleaner tips through the foot openings and match up the short felt edges behind the doll's waist.

For a skirt, cut a 4-inch-long hourglass shape out of felt. Make a waist hole in the center to slide the doll's feet through.

For a shirt, use a 2-inch felt square. Cut two small armholes ½ inch apart and ¼ inch from the upper edge. Wrap the shirt around the doll's chest and over the top of its pants or skirt.

Wind a 3-inch pipe cleaner belt around the doll's waist to secure the clothes. To keep the pants' side seams closed, twist a 2-inch piece of pipe cleaner around each knee.

For hands and feet, slip a smaller bead onto the end of each limb. Bend the pipe cleaner tips to keep the beads in place. Draw on a face with fine-tipped markers, testing the colors on a spare bead first.

Yarn Dolls

On a rainy day, invite your kids to spin yarns — into these cuddly palm-size dolls.

Materials

Skeins of yarn
Book

To form a yarn doll's body, loosely wrap yarn around a book, about seventy times, to create a thick hank. Slip a 6-inch piece of yarn between the hank and the book spine and use it to tie the strands together. Slide the hank off the book.

Create the doll's head by tightly tying another piece of yarn around the bundle an inch from the top. Add eyes and a mouth by tying contrasting yarn around single strands in the face and clipping the ends close to the knot. Next, cut the loop at the bottom of the hank.

1. For arms, pull one quarter of the strands to each side and tie them at the wrists, as shown. Trim the yarn ½ inch below the wrists. Then, tie a strand of yarn around the doll's waist, leaving the yarn loose to resemble a skirt. Or, make pants by dividing the strands into two bunches and tying them at the ankles.

2. For a wig, wind another hank of yarn. Tie together one end and snip the other. Feed a piece of yarn through the doll's head and use it to tie on the wig. Then, you can cut bangs, make ponytails, or add a hair ribbon.

The Toy Factory

Pipe Cleaner Sculpture

Pipe cleaners and twist ties have saved many a parent's sanity on long car trips. Kids can fashion these quiet building tools into endless designs, from stick figures to animals to furniture. Just twist, but don't shout.

85

Worry Dolls

In Guatemala, kids tell their troubles to worry dolls — toothpick-size colorful figures that they tuck under their pillows at night. Your kids can take this tradition worldwide with a multicultural collection of clothespin dolls.

Materials

- Craft stick
- Craft knife
- Straight wooden clothespin
- Glue
- Colored markers
- Yarn
- Toothpick
- Fabric scraps
- Sewing notions

Nadia (Russia)

First, make the doll's arms (a parent's job) by using a craft knife to score the stick 1½ inches from each end and then snapping the ends off against a countertop edge. Smooth jagged edges by rubbing them against a hard, level surface. Position the arms, curved ends down, just below the clothespin head and glue in place.

Style worry doll hair just by drawing on a "do" with a marker or crown your creations with yarn tresses. Cut a bunch of strands that measure twice the desired length, tie them together around the middle, and glue the wig on the doll. Once the glue dries, unravel individual strands for a frizzy look or make ringlets by wrapping wet yarn around a toothpick and allowing the yarn to dry.

You can fashion an outfit for your doll out of fabric scraps and notions from the sewing basket. For inspiration, refer to a cultural guidebook, such as *Children Just Like Me* (Dorling Kindersley Publishing). Create shirts, slacks, and kimonos by wrapping the clothespin with cotton yarn and gluing the ends in place. For robes, kilts, dresses, and ponchos, use bright cloth swatches belted with an embroidery floss sash.

Make a wide-brimmed hat by cutting an *X* in the center of a small felt circle. To wrap a tall turban, make a thimble-shaped dome out of a pipe cleaner and glue it onto the doll's head. Wind and glue a strip of fabric around it.

For jewelry, coil bracelets and necklaces out of craft wire or metallic pipe cleaners. Finally, draw facial features on these tiny confidants with colored markers — the cheerier the better for easing fretful minds.

Rosita (Spain) **Chinda (Thailand)** **Kate (U.S.A.)** **Sesi (Ghana)** **Meena (India)**

Puppets

Thumbs Up

With a set of these mini puppets at her fingertips, your child can act out a favorite nursery rhyme or make up an incredible tale of her own.

Materials

- Felt scraps
- White glue
- Googly eyes
- Permanent colored markers
- Sewing notions

For each puppet, first cut out a pair of 1¾- by 3-inch felt rectangles to serve as the front and back of the animal. Join the front to the back by gluing together the side and top edges. Leave the bottom edges open for a finger opening. Once the glue dries, use scissors to round the top of the puppet's head. Glue on googly eyes. Now it's time to add distinguishing animal traits.

Woolly Lamb: Attach ears horizontally to the front of the lamb. Glue a bit of cotton "wool" to the top of its head and draw on the face.

Pig Pal: For floppy pig ears, use 2-inch felt circles. Fold them in half lengthwise and glue together the lower edges. Glue the bases of the ears to the back of the puppet. For pig cheeks and a snout, glue on ¾-inch felt circles.

Mr. Horse: For ears, cut out a pair of felt ovals (about 1½ inches long). Attach them as previously described. Add a fringed forelock, white blaze, and rounded muzzle. Use a marker to draw jawlines and nostrils.

Birds of a Feather: Cut out a triangular felt bird beak and glue it in place. Add plumage.

Spotted Heifer: Make cow ears following the same steps used for the pig. Glue on a pink muzzle. Color bold black spots on the ears and face.

Frog Friend: Position googly eyes at the top of the head. Glue webbed frog feet to the front of the puppet.

JUICE CAN PUPPETS

The best part about making a juice can puppet like the ones on page 82 is that your child can let his imagination run wild. Start by wrapping and gluing felt around an empty juice can, then place the can open-end down on a table. Glue on felt arms and legs. Then, set out fabric scraps, buttons, feathers, and googly eyes and watch your kids get creative.

Thumbs Up

The Toy Factory

A Paper Bag Puppet

Turn a brown lunch bag into a stage character in minutes. Just invert the bag and draw or paint on a face. Then, pinch and twist two corners of the bag bottom to form ears.

Farm Animal Puppets

If your kids are looking for a way to liven up a quiet afternoon, turn things zooey by shaping up a menagerie of animal finger puppets. For the creatures shown here, use the directions below or adapt them to create characters of your own.

Materials

Construction paper

Glue

Masking tape

Googly eyes, pom-poms, string, waxed paper, and twist ties

To make a basic body, use scissors to shape the puppet's midsection from a 3-inch square of construction paper — perhaps a round potbelly for a pig or a rectangular body for an alligator. For legs, roll and glue four 1½- by 3-inch paper strips into cylinders. Make them wide enough to fit your child's fingers, so she can walk the puppet around. Attach each leg to the midsection with a piece of masking tape, pressing one end inside the cylinder and the other onto the back of the body.

Dog, Lion, Bug, or Deer: Draw a suitable head and ears on a piece of craft paper. Then, cut out the shape and glue it onto the body. Glue on googly eyes and distinguishing details, such as a pom-pom nose, a mane fashioned from snips of string, waxed-paper wings, or twist-tie antlers.

Piglet: With a small half circle, form and glue a paper cone. Flatten the tip of the cone with your thumb to create a pig snout. Glue on big floppy ears and attach the head to the body with tape.

Alligator: Match up a pair of 2½- by 1½-inch rectangles with the shorter edges at the top and bottom. Glue together the very tops, then fold back the glued portion and make a crease. With pinking shears, trim the sides and bottoms of the rectangles to create a tapered, toothy jaw. Glue the folded edge to the back of the body. Finally, glue on a pair of googly-eye stalks.

Farm Animal Puppets

Duck Walk

spread the prongs. (The fastener should be loose enough for the lid to turn.) Then, insert the dowel between the body pieces and tape it in place. Glue the top edges of the body together.

Next, glue together the head circles, except for the lower edges. Slip the head onto the body and glue it in place. Glue on the feathers and bill. To set the duck in motion, grasp the dowel and push.

Duck Walk

Ducks are great swimmers, but these freewheeling drakes, adapted from *Look What I Made!* (TAB Books), are more at home on dry land than water.

Materials

5 9-inch paper plates
Paints and paintbrushes
Clear plastic coffee can lid
Craft knife
Metal paper fastener
12-inch wooden dowel
Tape and glue

Cut a 4-inch circle from the center of one of the paper plates. Draw on rotating duck feet, as shown above, and paint them orange. Once dry, trim along the outer edge of the connected feet. Glue the cutout onto the plastic lid. Then, use a craft knife (parents only) to cut a small hole in the center of the lid.

From the remaining plates, cut two 5-inch circles for the front and back of the duck's body and two 3½-inch circles for its head. Cut wings, tail feathers, and a beak from the plate rims and paint all of the pieces.

To assemble the duck, cut a small hole 1 inch from the bottom of both body pieces. Sandwich the plastic lid between the body, lining up the three holes. Push the paper fastener through the holes and

Sir Frog

He may not be a prince, but this paper frog is charming — and your kids will get a kick out of his flicking tongue.

Materials

Dessert-size paper plate
Green paint and paintbrush
Craft knife
Construction paper (green, white, black, and red)
Tape and glue

Paint both sides of the paper plate green. When it is dry, fold the plate in half and use the craft knife (parents only) to make a 1-inch slit (for the frog's tongue) in the center of the fold. Create a fingerhold on the underside of the body using a 2- by 3-inch piece of green construction paper. Center it on the bottom of the folded plate and tape the shorter edges in place.

For eyes, cut out a pair of 1- by 2-inch green rectangles and round the upper edges. Fold each rectangle in half and glue the lower portion to the top of the body. Glue on white and black paper circles, as shown.

Cut frog legs out of construction paper, a shorter set for the front and a long, bent pair for the back. Tape the tops of the legs to the underside of the body. Cut out a ¾- by 7-inch tongue from red construction paper. Round one end and slip it through the slit. To wag the tongue, jiggle the straight end.

Sir Frog

The Toy Factory

Super Sam

Fast Finger Puppets

If your child draws faces on the tips of his fingers, he'll be the hit of your house. Add one of these winning wardrobes, and he'll be ready to costar with Kermit.

Materials

- Felt or fabric scraps
- Tape
- Pipe cleaners
- Glue
- Paper clips
- Needle-nose pliers
- Cotton balls
- Yarn

Super Sam: Wrap a blue felt rectangle into a tube, secure with tape, and slip it on your finger. For a cape, trim the sides of a red felt rectangle, cut a hole in the narrow end, label the back with an S to complete the costume.

Blue Gene: Dress him in a denim tube and make a crepe paper baseball cap. For his red hair, tie 1-inch lengths of yarn together with one piece of yarn.

Piper the Dog: Coil a pipe cleaner around your finger, leaving a tail at the end. Bend a second piece into ears — and don't forget a nose.

Mrs. Pearl: Dress her in a tube of pink felt. Coil a red pipe cleaner into a hat and slip on a string of tiny beads.

Professor Acorn: Bend a paper clip into wire glasses (use needle-nose pliers) and top with an acorn cap.

Ted E. Bear: Make your bear by shaping two ears in the middle of a brown pipe cleaner. Coil the ends into a big circle and shape into a hat.

His Majesty: Craft a purple cape like Super Sam's. Bend a pipe cleaner into a crown; rub with glue and add glitter. Then, glue on a white cotton mustache and beard.

Bikini Bev: Fashion the bikini top and bottom out of ribbons. For a beach hat, cut a doughnut-shaped brim out of felt and tape on a felt top. For sunglasses, add clear tape to the wire glasses and color with markers.

Chill Bill: Wrap masking tape around your finger, sticky-side out, and apply yarn to make a sweater. Make a scarf out of felt and a cap with a red ribbon base and red tape bill.

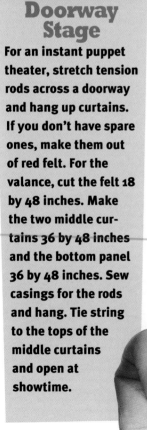

Doorway Stage

For an instant puppet theater, stretch tension rods across a doorway and hang up curtains. If you don't have spare ones, make them out of red felt. For the valance, cut the felt 18 by 48 inches. Make the two middle curtains 36 by 48 inches and the bottom panel 36 by 48 inches. Sew casings for the rods and hang. Tie string to the tops of the middle curtains and open at showtime.

Blue Gene

Piper the Dog

Professor Acorn

Mrs. Pearl

Boats

Cardboard Canoe

Like the birch bark canoes built centuries ago by the Native American tribes in New England, this lightweight toy craft cuts quickly and smoothly through water. It's adapted from *The Kids' Summer Handbook* (Ticknor & Fields/Books for Young Readers), which features a host of warm weather crafts and activities.

Materials

- Cardboard
- Pushpin
- Large-eye needle and string
- Acrylic paints and paintbrushes
- Box of paraffin wax
- Tall tin can
- Pot holder and newspaper
- Metal tongs

Cut out a 6- by 12-inch piece of cardboard and fold it in half so that the long ends match up. Draw a side view of a canoe on one side of the cardboard, using the fold for the bottom of the boat. Cut through both layers along the sides and top of the canoe, but not the bottom. With a pushpin, make a series of holes in the curved ends, as shown. Then, use the needle and string to sew them together.

For seats, cut two 3½- by 1½-inch strips out of cardboard scraps. Fold in the sides of each strip 1 inch from the short edges and wedge the seats inside the boat. Next, paint the canoe and let it dry thoroughly.

To waterproof the canoe, put the wax in the can and set the can in a saucepan filled with a couple inches of water. Heat slowly until the wax melts (parents only). Use a pot holder to set the can on newspaper. With tongs, dip the boat, an end at a time, into the wax. (You may have to tilt the can.) When the wax hardens, place a few pebbles in the hull to prevent tipping, and the boat is ready to float.

Cardboard Canoe

Bobbing Buoy

To warn boaters of shallow or rocky spots, the channel markers used by the Coast Guard must stay upright in the roughest waves. You can show your child how a little extra weight can keep a marker from tipping over by helping him fashion a toy buoy.

Materials

Ping-Pong ball
Craft knife
Modeling clay
White glue
Drinking straw
Paper triangle

Use the craft knife to slice the top off the Ping-Pong ball (adults only). Next, cut a hole (big enough for the straw) in the center of the top while your child fills the bottom of the ball with clay. Glue the top of the ball back in place.

Make a slit in the top of the straw and insert the long edge of the paper triangle flag. Push the bottom of the straw through the hole in the ball.

Now test the buoy in a sink full of water. Encourage your child to try tipping over the buoy by making waves. Explain that the weight of the clay (called ballast) pulls downward into the water, keeping the buoy upright.

Iceboats

Iceboats

The rules for racing one of these miniature ice block boats are simple. Instead of crossing the finish line first, the object is to outlast the competition.

Materials

Empty pint-size juice carton
Food coloring
Duct tape
Craft knife
12-inch-long wooden dowel
Cellophane triangle, 6 by 8 by 10 inches
Stapler

Fill the juice carton with 1½ cups of water and several drops of food coloring. Seal the top with duct tape and shake gently. Lay the sealed carton on its side and use a craft knife (parents only) to cut an X through the center of the side facing up. Push the wooden dowel through the opening and set the carton in the freezer overnight.

Next, fold the cellophane triangle along the 8-inch side ¾ inch in from the edge and staple to hold. Cut the carton away from the frozen boat, slip the sail onto the mast, and launch the boat in a wading pool or bathtub.

FunFact

Compartments in the bottoms of large boats are also filled with ballast, such as lead or even water, to help keep them stable at sea.

Bobbing Buoy

Puddle Boat

Spring showers bring more than flowers. They set the stage for the type of adventure you can find only in a big mud puddle — like setting afloat a toy boat. The paddleboat shown here is adapted from *Adventures in Art* (Williamson Publishing).

Materials

> ½-inch Fome-Cor (available at craft
> stores)
> Utility knife
> Glue
> Acrylic paints and gloss
> Paintbrushes
> A few small nails
> Rubber band

Use the utility knife (parents only) to cut a 10- by 5-inch rectangle out of Fome-Cor. Contour one of the shorter ends so that it resembles the bow of a boat. Starting 1½ inches in from the

The Toy Factory

opposite end, cut a 4- by 3-inch opening for the paddle wheel. Use the removed material to make a cabin. Cut out a half circle 3 inches long at the flat end and glue it to the top of the bow, as shown.

To make the paddle wheel, cut two 3½- by 2-inch rectangles from Fome-Cor and make a notch (1 by ¼ inch) in from the center of each of them. Fit the two pieces together to form a cross.

Paint the boat and the wheel and then seal them (top, bottom, and sides) with a coat of acrylic gloss. Tap a small nail partway into the Fome-Cor on both sides of the wheel opening.

Tie an overhand knot at both ends of a rubber band to form two small loops. Slip a loop around each nail. Fit the middle of the band around the center of the paddle wheel. To launch your boat, rotate the wheel until the rubber band is tightly twisted, set the boat in the puddle, and release.

Build a Boat in a Nutshell

If you're not in the mood for heavy construction, try making a fast fleet of little walnut boats instead. Using walnut shell halves, hot-glue a matchstick mast into the bottom of each. Cut out triangular paper sails and use a glue stick to attach one sail around each matchstick. You'll be surprised at how well these boats hold their own on the water. They also do well in private bathtub ponds.

Toys & Games

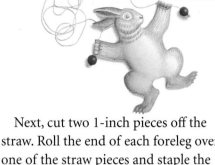

Turtle Shells

FamilyFun reader Angie Ball, of Palo Alto, California, came up with a recycling project that turned out to be a snap — making turtles out of paper bowls. They were easy enough, in fact, for her sons Benjamin and Andrew (ages five and three) to make almost entirely on their own. For each turtle, the boys cut four feet and a head from green construction paper and glued them to the rim of an inverted paper bowl. Then, the kids decorated the turtle's shell with markers, glitter, and paint. Their distinctive turtles became well-behaved centerpieces on the Balls' dinner table.

The Tortoise and the Hare

Your kids can stage a rematch between the tortoise and the hare with this pair of string-climbing critters — or they can break new ground by facing off with the animals of their choice.

Materials

Crayons or colored markers
Paper plate
Drinking straw
Stapler
Paper towel tube
String
Two wooden beads

Use the crayons to draw an animal on the paper plate. It can be as simple or fancy as your kids like. Cut out the drawing with scissors and then color the flip side.

Next, cut two 1-inch pieces off the straw. Roll the end of each foreleg over one of the straw pieces and staple the edge of the paper in place.

Next, cut two 4-foot lengths of string and tie them around the ends of the paper towel tube. Thread the strings through the straw pieces. Then, tie a bead to the end of each string.

To make the animal climb, first use a short piece of string to hang the tube overhead — from a cupboard knob, perhaps. Then, slide the cutout to the bottom of the strings. Using the beads as handles, pull the strings gently, alternating from side to side, and the animal will scoot to the top.

The Tortoise and the Hare

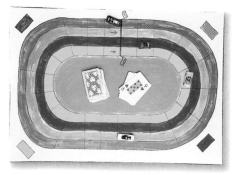

Start Your Engines

If your kids are all revved up with no place to go, let them use their toy dragsters in this grand prix of card games.

Materials

> Large sheet of cardboard or
>   poster board
> Colored markers or crayons
> Ruler

Draw a four-lane track on the cardboard sheet or poster board and shade the individual lanes with colored markers or crayons. Measure and mark 3-inch increments along the inner edge of the inside lane. From each mark, draw a straight line that extends to the far edge of the outside lane. Add a start/finish line across one of the straightaways. Place the card deck in the center of the track.

Before the race, ask players to choose a card suit — drivers can even tape a mini heart, club, diamond, or spade on the hoods of their cars. The game starts with one player turning over the top card of the deck. If the suit on the card matches his own, he gets to move his car ahead one space. If not, he stays put. Play continues with drivers alternating turns and moving ahead only when they draw a card with the right suit. The first one to cross the finish line wins.

The Toy Factory

Audio Bingo

Start off your family's game of bingo with a bang by using noisy symbols instead of numbers.

Materials

> Tape recorder and tape
> Old magazines
> Colored markers
> Paper or poster board
> Glue
> Buttons

First, record eighteen different sounds, such as a dog barking or a door slamming. Then, clip out two magazine photos (or make two drawings) that represent each sound you've recorded. With these depictions you'll be able to make four playing cards. For each card, use a colored marker to divide an 8-inch paper square into nine blocks. Glue a different photo in each block. Be sure no two cards are exactly alike.

To play, give each child a card and nine buttons and turn on the recording. Now, players place buttons on the pictures that match the sounds. The first kid to fill his card wins. For each new game, fast forward or rewind a bit between sounds so that they are played in a different order.

Audio Bingo

SINGING GAME BOARD

To entertain the preschoolers in her day-care center, *FamilyFun* reader Arlene Mayer, from Calgary, Canada, came up with a singing game board. She glued an $8\frac{1}{2}$- by 11-inch piece of plain white paper to a piece of cardboard and then divided the sheet into eight pie-shaped wedges. In each wedge, she drew a nursery rhyme picture (a spider for "Little Miss Muffet," a lamb for "Mary Had a Little Lamb," Barney the dinosaur for his famous "I Love You," and so on). For a spinner, she nailed a cardboard arrow to the game board with a brad. To play, the kids take turns spinning the arrow and guessing the title they land on. Then, everyone gets to sing the song.

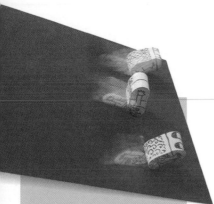

Tumble Tots

These paper dolls put on a good show — jumping and cartwheeling along. To make one, cut out a 5- by ³/₄-inch paper rectangle

and form an oval band by bringing together and gluing the short ends with a ³/₄-inch overlap. For the tumbler's sides, cut out a pair of 1 ³/₄- by ³/₄-inch paper rectangles and round the corners. Glue one of the sides onto the oval band and allow the glue to dry thoroughly. Drop a marble into the tumbler and then glue on the second side. Trim the glued edges so they are flush. Use colored markers to draw on a face, arms and legs. To set the tumbler in motion, simply place it on a slightly inclined cloth-covered surface and give him a gentle poke.

Felt Storytelling Board

Spinning a tale comes naturally for many children, especially when inspired by a storytelling board with movable characters and props.

Materials

Felt or flannel material in assorted colors
Shoe box
Craft glue

First, cut one piece of felt or flannel to fit on the inside of the box lid and glue it in place (sky blue is a good, neutral color for this background).

Next, cut the scraps of felt into figures, which will naturally stick to the storyboard. Try making trees, fish, birds, flowers, stars, and even letters. People and animals can be made up of several shapes, so be sure to cut out circles for faces and eyes, as well as rectangles for arms and legs.

Once you have a variety of characters and props, your child can use them to tell an imaginary story or retell a tradi-

tional fairy tale. When the story is finished, clear the board and let your child start a new one. When he's done, pack up the felt figures and store them in the shoe box.

Photo Cutouts Storyboard:

You can also clip magazine pictures, coloring book characters, and real photos to stick on a storytelling board. Glue the cutouts onto cardboard and then trim around them. Glue a strip of sandpaper to the back so they will adhere to the fabric.

Felt Storytelling Board

Rain Stick

If you make only one instrument with your children, a rain stick is the one to try. Not only is it immensely satisfying for kids to hammer nails into a mailing tube, but it also will make your children want to dance up a storm.

When choosing a mailing tube, keep in mind that the sound it produces will vary depending on its diameter. A tube with a 1½-inch diameter works well because the filling (rice or beans) will trickle slowly down through the tube and sound like falling rain.

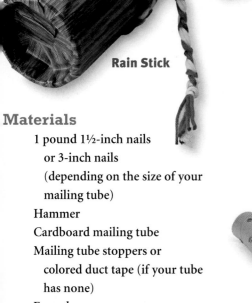

Rain Stick

Materials

1 pound 1½-inch nails or 3-inch nails (depending on the size of your mailing tube)

Hammer

Cardboard mailing tube

Mailing tube stoppers or colored duct tape (if your tube has none)

Funnel

Rice, lentils, popcorn, or dried beans

Con-Tact paper or colored paper and tape

Colored string or embroidery floss

First, let your kids hammer all of the nails into the tube to make an inner maze. Advise them to drive the nails

straight through, because the ends will poke out if they are driven at an angle (if this happens, you can simply push the nails back out and adjust their angle by hand).

Seal up one end of each tube, either with a stopper sold with the tube or with duct tape. Then, let your kids experiment with the different choices you've provided for the filling. To minimize spilling, they can use a funnel to pour a test amount of rice or beans (start with about 1 cup) into the tube. Then, they can seal the open end with one hand while they try out the sounds. Once they decide what the contents of the tube will be, seal both ends securely, so that it doesn't rain beans all over your kitchen floor.

To decorate the rain stick, wrap it with Con-Tact paper or use colored paper and tape (this also ensures that the nails will stay in place). Lastly, tie a colorful tassel, made from braided string or embroidery floss, onto one end of the rain stick.

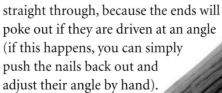

Strike Up a Band

To spark your child's interest in music, you don't need to buy a shiny new instrument. In fact, he'll learn a lot about musical sounds if he makes one of his own. Rhythm can spring from anything, such as a popcorn-filled can shaker to a pair of spoons you click against your knee. Here are two music-making projects that come right from the recycling bin:

Backyard music station: String a series of gongs from a tree or clothesline. Use old hubcaps and sturdy, clay flowerpots, both of which already have holes to thread string through. For strikers, use wooden spoons or chopsticks with rubber bands wrapped around the ends. Get your kids to experiment by hitting different parts of each gong.

Trash can drum: Lay a piece of canvas across the top of a trash can and tape down the edges, pulling the drumhead tight as you do so. Tie string around the can just below the rim for reinforcement. To tighten the drumhead, spray the canvas with water and then let it dry. Play the drum with wooden spoons, sticks, or with your hands.

The Toy Factory

Chapter Seven

Ready to Wear

FOR CENTURIES, Americans have left their mark on fashion. In the 1800s, it was stovepipe hats and laced corsets, and in the early 1900s, flapper dresses and zoot suits. But possibly the most expressive trends of all came from the 1960s when many of us tie-dyed our shirts and embroidered our blue jeans. What freedom we felt back then, tossing our father's staid old white T-shirts into the dye bin or chopping our frayed blue jeans into skirts and pocketbooks. Even if we were only in grammar school, we got to be groovy.

Now our children, growing up three decades later, can express themselves by turning their clothes into works of art. Much to his delight, a preschooler can experience the exhilaration of pressing potato stamps on a jersey (page 101). ("This is okay? I can put paint on my shirt!?") Older kids will be thrilled, and plenty skillful enough, to apply dyes or sew decorations on their clothes. After all, the processes of stamping, gluing, and stenciling make a child's wardrobe truly his own.

The projects in this chapter are largely free of the socio-political commentary of the 1960s — they're mostly just fun. Your child can use them to recycle old T-shirts into fabulous new summer clothes (page 103), turn plain socks into slippers for a slumber party (page 104), or color up a picture and use it to create artful earrings and other wearable masterpieces (page 108). Above all, they can use them to celebrate their own creativity.

Prep your garments for decorating.
Prewash new T-shirts and garments before

Slipper Socks, page 104

String Stamp Shirt, page 102

Clothes-decorating Supplies

Don't throw away old clothes — save them for a rainy day when your kids can transform them into brand-new styles. Here's a checklist of supplies that will come in handy for decorating shirts, socks, sneakers, or even shoelaces.

✂ **Fabric crayons and markers, fabric paints, and dyes** (just be sure they're designed for fabric use and won't wash out in the laundry).

✂ **Disposable containers** (for paints and dyes), paintbrushes, stencil brush, and sponges.

✂ **Measuring tape, fabric scissors, sewing and embroidery needles and floss, thread, sewing elastic, fabric glue, and a hot glue gun.**

✂ **Fabric scraps, felt, ribbon, rickrack, pom-poms, and pipe cleaners.**

✂ **Sequins, beads, buttons, trinkets, and glitter glue.**

✂ **Cardboard, tracing paper, and masking tape.**

applying fabric paints or dyes. In all cases, refer to the manufacturer's instructions for setting color, as well as washing, drying, or ironing the decorated garment. And afterward, never wash them with your whites!

Keep fabric paints on hand. Plan a trip with your kids to your local art supply store to stock up on fabric pens, paints that puff, permanent glitter markers, or other supplies your kids can use to leave their stamp on their clothes.

When in doubt, practice first. When printing with potato stamps or using a medium you've never tried before, experiment first on paper, a handkerchief, or a scrap of fabric.

Dress in old clothes while you work. Fabric markers and paints do stain, so before you set them out to use, be sure your kids are wearing smocks or old clothes you don't care about. When using fabric dyes, it also is a good idea to wear rubber gloves.

Defer to your kids' tastes. Try not to flinch if your kids sew flashy beads or rows of sequins on a garment you think looks good already. Fashion is in the eye of the designer — and we were in our kids' shoes once, if without the sequins.

Have a party! Most of the projects in this chapter lend themselves to festive group activities. Plan a birthday party — or a Scout meeting — around T-shirt decorating or jewelry-making.

Cool Clothes

Stamped T-shirt

For kids, a colorful design, particularly one they come up with on their own, can turn an ordinary T-shirt into a favorite article of clothing. This simple potato-printing technique lets your child stamp a plain shirt or jersey with a variety of bright, bold shapes.

Materials

- Cardboard
- Prewashed T-shirt
- Masking tape
- Paring knife
- Potatoes
- Pencil
- Nontoxic fabric paints and paintbrushes
- Pie plates or flat bowls
- Scrap paper

To begin, place the cardboard inside the shirt and tape the arms together in back (this provides a flat printing surface and prevents paint from seeping through).

For a printing block, cut a potato in half (a parent's job). Have your child use a pencil to lightly etch interesting shapes on the flat surfaces of the two halves. Then, help her cut away the parts of the potato around her design and blot it with a paper towel.

Pour a shallow layer of paint into the pie plates or bowls and have your child practice printing the designs on scrap paper. Show her how to apply the paint by evenly pressing the potato into the paint dish or by dipping a brush into the color and painting it onto the potato. She then can stamp a pattern of random or repeated images on the shirt.

When your child's design is complete, let the paint dry thoroughly, then heat-set it according to the manufacturer's directions. This usually involves running a very hot iron over each area for about 30 seconds. You may want to iron from the reverse side of the shirt with a rag underneath to protect both the iron and the board. Then, the shirt is ready to wear.

Fruit Stamps

Instead of potatoes, stamp the beautiful shapes of other vegetables and fruits. Cut open the fruits and vegetables and blot the cut surfaces with a paper towel. Your kids can pick their favorite shapes, press them into some fabric paint and then onto a T-shirt. Onions, peppers, and pears work especially well, and an apple cut in half lengthwise will print heart shapes. Remind them not to squeeze the fruits or the paint will bleed. After the shirt is decorated, hang it up to dry before heat-setting the paint.

Ready to Wear

101

String Stamps

If squiggly lines and wacky spirals strike your child's fancy, these home-made stamps are just the ticket for sprucing up a cotton top or sweatshirt.

Materials

- Corrugated cardboard
- Pencil and ruler
- Glue
- Thick twine
- Prewashed T-shirt or sweatshirt
- Thin cardboard
- Fabric paint
- Plastic dish

1. Cut the corrugated cardboard into several 3-inch squares and have your child draw a design on each one. Next, help him trace the design with an even line of glue.

2. Press a single strand of twine directly on top of the glue. Then, let the glue dry thoroughly so that the twine is secure before stamping.

3. Stretch the T-shirt or sweatshirt flat (but not too tightly) by fitting thin cardboard inside the shirt. Pour some fabric paint in a paper or plastic dish. Place the stamp, twine-side down, in the dish and push it around in the paint until it is evenly covered. Then, press the stamp onto the shirt, applying equal pressure on the stamp before lifting it. One coat of paint should last for two or three stampings.

Your child may choose to cover every inch of the shirt or to print just one row of the design. If he wishes to print a single string shape in a variety of colors, either he can wait for the first layer of paint to dry before applying a second, or he can make a duplicate stamp.

Let the finished design air-dry before setting the color (see the paint manufacturer's directions) and washing and drying the shirt.

102

Designer T-shirts

FamilyFun crafter Maryellen Sullivan has shirt decorating down to a T. Here are a few of her favorite ideas.

Materials

- Prewashed T-shirt
- Nontoxic fabric paints and paint-brushes, fabric dye, or fabric pens
- Disposable paint containers
- Pom-poms
- Fabric glue

Monster Mania: Paint on a brilliant purple monster with pom-poms glued to the tops of his spiraling antennae.

Identi-Ts: Fill the center of the shirt with your child's first initial and have him paint all of his favorite things around the letter — tiny cars, music notes, pets, sports equipment, or even his favorite foods.

Hanging Out: Paint a zigzagging clothesline across a T-shirt and hang a miniature wardrobe out to dry.

Works of Art: Have your child thumb through colorful art books to find a picture he likes, then help him decorate a T-shirt with his own rendition of the artwork.

Two Tones: Create the sea and sky by dyeing the bottom half of a T-shirt blue and painting in an underwater world. On the top half of the shirt, paint sunshine, seagulls, ships, and leaping fish. For a farm scene, dye a shirt bottom green and paint a field of farm animals. Add a barn, a butterfly, and even a rainbow above the horizon.

Novel-Ts: Children can translate their favorite songs, stories, or poems onto a T-shirt by printing the words with colorful fabric pens and illustrating the piece in fabric paint.

Monster Mania

Hanging Out

Works of Art

Two Tones

Novel-T

SPLATTER SHIRTS

This free-form splatter technique is especially suited for young T-shirt designers. All it takes is fabric paint and a flick of the wrist to create a wearable masterpiece.

First, hang one or more prewashed white T-shirts outside on a clothesline (be sure the clothesline is far away from unintended targets). If the day is windy, it's a good idea to slip a rectangular piece of cardboard inside each shirt to keep it rigid.

Next, pour nontoxic fabric paints into disposable containers, such as aluminum pie plates, plastic lids, or muffin pan liners, and let your children (dressed in smocks or old bathing suits) dip paintbrushes into the paint and flick it onto the shirts. Don't worry about giving much artistic direction for this part. The flicking will come easily to children and will no doubt be accompanied by dribbling, splattering, smearing, or long-distance slings, so just stay clear.

Leave the shirts on the clothesline to dry thoroughly. If you don't want the paint to run even more, take them down and allow them to dry flat.

Refer to the fabric paint package for specific directions on setting the color and washing the shirt.

Ready to Wear

Socks & Shoes

Slipper Socks

Your kids will get a kick out of this zany slipper craft — it lets them apply puffy designs to their socks. The three-dimensional fabric paint, which is sold at most craft or fabric stores, comes in a variety of colors and costs about $3 for a 1-ounce bottle. It provides plenty of traction on slippery floors.

Materials

- Cotton socks
- Cardboard
- Pencil
- Nontoxic three-dimensional fabric paints

First, prewash and dry the socks, but do not use fabric softener. Next, set a pair of your child's shoes on top of a piece of cardboard and trace around them with a pencil. Cut out the two shoe shapes with scissors. Then, fit the cardboard feet into the socks so that they are pressed flat against the soles of the socks (this will keep the socks flat while decorating).

Now, your child can paint stars, fish, letters, or any other designs he likes on the sock bottoms. Most 3-D paints can be applied straight from the bottle — just press the nozzle gently against the sock to make sure the paint sticks.

Let the paint set overnight before removing the cardboard and wearing the slippers. You'll also want to wait about three days to machine-wash and dry them (refer to the bottle for the proper heat setting).

Fancy Flip-flops

Footwear trends may come and go, but flip-flops have long reigned as the unofficial shoe of summer. Here's how your kids can make their flips truly hip:

- ✂ **Attach small plastic toys, such as plastic goldfish, with a hot glue gun.**
- ✂ **Wrap the straps with colorful embroidery thread.**
- ✂ **Tie on beads or jingle bells.**
- ✂ **Make a smiley face by gluing on a pair of googly eyes and painting your toenails red.**

Slipper Socks

Tie-dyed Socks

Although there are dozens of methods for tying socks to achieve bright, bold designs, the circle pattern design is ideal for beginners — it's easy to master and looks great with a single color of dye. You might want to reserve this project for a sunny day and work outside.

Materials

- Plastic bowl or pan
- Nontoxic fabric dye
- White socks
- Rubber bands
- Pennies or buttons
- Plastic spoon

Begin by covering your work area with layers of newspaper or garbage bags. In a plastic bowl or pan, dissolve a packet of nontoxic fabric dye, such as Rit, in hot water according to the package directions. Add more hot water until there is enough to cover a couple of pairs of socks.

Dampen the white socks with clear warm water, then bundle them up in rubber bands. To make stripes, wrap three or four thick rubber bands around the foot and/or top of the sock. To make circles (great for the heels), pinch a section of the sock and tie, about an inch down, with a rubber band. For a pattern of tiny rings, slip pennies or buttons into the socks and wrap bands around them.

When the socks are bound, submerge them in the warm dye and stir occasionally with a plastic spoon. After twenty minutes or so (remember that the color will lighten after the fabric is rinsed and dried), run them under cool water, squeezing until the water runs clear. Remove the bands, smooth out the socks, and rest them flat on layers of newspaper. Let the socks dry overnight. Wash them separately for the first few times to keep any bleeding dye from tinting other clothes.

Tie-dyed T's: Instead of socks, use a prewashed white T-shirt.

Tie-dyed Socks

Tips on Tie-Dyeing

✄ **Wear rubber gloves when handling dye. If you do get dye on your skin, scrub with soap and a nailbrush — do not use household bleach.**

✄ **To tie-dye with more than one color, use small plastic cups to slowly pour dye onto the fabric. Start with lighter colors and work directly over the central container so that the excess spills back into it. Squeeze out the fabric after each application. When the color is dark enough, rinse the section with cool water and cover it with a plastic bag secured with a rubber band, to protect it from the next color you use.**

When the whole garment is finished, squeeze out any moisture still left in each section before undoing the rubber bands to prevent colors from dripping into each other. Then, lay out the garment to dry.

✄ **When washing tie-dyed garments, always use cold water.**

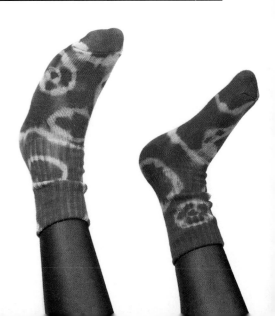

Hats & Hair Ties

Hold On to Your Hats

With this whimsical hat design, your kids might not make headline news, but they'll be wearing it. Fashioning one is simple; all you need is paper and tape.

Materials

Colored tissue paper, crepe paper, gift wrap, or newspaper

Masking tape

Unfold several double sheets of newspaper or cut colored tissue paper, crepe paper, or recycled gift wrap into pieces of comparable size. Place the paper on top of your child's head, fanning out the sheets in different directions. Then, form the crown of the hat, using your hands to gather the paper, all the way around, at eyebrow level. For a brow band, wrap the base of the crown with a long piece of masking tape. Reinforce with a second layer. For taller styles, such as a stovepipe or a Stetson, bundle up the paper so that it rises several inches above your child's forehead before you apply tape.

Once you fashion the crown, remove the hat from your child's head and use scissors to shape the brim. Round the edges to make a floppy bonnet, then decorate with a ribbon sash and silk flowers. To style a derby, trim the brim an inch or two from the brow band and adorn with a feather. For a baseball cap, cut the brim flush with the brow band along the sides and back. Then, round the front brim to create a visor. Another style is a watch cap: merely roll up the brim all the way to the band.

Hold On to Your Hats

Cover a large surface with newspaper and have your child spread out all of the items she may use. Next, cut out a piece of poster board that is slightly larger than the barrette back. Have your child sketch a pattern on the cutout and fill it in with buttons, balloons, pins, old puzzle pieces, or miniature bows. Once she's finished the design, carefully push aside the materials and cover the poster board with hot glue (a parent's job). Then, press the collage items onto the glued surface and hot glue the decorated poster board onto the barrette.

Recycled Barrettes

By the time *FamilyFun* reader Lauren MacDonald, from Orlando, Florida, was eleven years old, she had an impressive collection of barrettes. "I have three sisters," says Lauren, "so we have drawers full of barrettes with nothing on them." After gathering up their supply, Lauren and her eight-year-old sister, Kara, adorned them with bows, buttons, balloons, and ribbons.

Materials

Poster board
Ribbons, buttons, shells, and other trinkets
White glue
Plain barrettes
Hot glue gun

Ready to Wear

No-Sew Scrunchies

There's no such thing as having too many scrunchies. With this no-sew technique, your child can turn out a snappy collection in no time.

Materials

Old necktie
12-inch-long piece of sewing elastic
Masking tape and a pencil
Hot glue gun

Cut a 24-inch length from the necktie. Thread the sewing elastic through the center of the tie by taping one end of the sewing elastic to the end of the pencil and then pulling the material down over the pencil. Once the elastic is threaded through, remove the tape and tie together the elastic ends.

To complete the scrunchie, pull one end of the tie over the other end and hot glue the loop closed (a parent's job). Lastly, adjust the tie so that the gathered material is evenly distributed around the circle.

Herringbone Braid

This decorative hairstyle, also known as the fishtail, is just right for festive occasions.

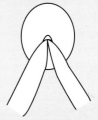

1. Pull your hair into a ponytail and tie with an elastic band. Divide the ponytail into two parts.

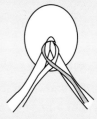

2. Pull out a narrow section of hair from under the right side, cross it over, and add it to the left side, as shown here.

3. Next, pull a small bunch of hair from under the left side of the ponytail and add it to the right side. Repeat steps 2 and 3 until the braid is the desired length.

Jewelry

First, your child will need to draw a pair of either matching or complementary images, such as salt and pepper shakers or a snowman and a snowwoman. Remind her that the images should be small (for a guide, she can mark two 1½-inch squares on the paper and then sketch within the lines). Another option is to cut designs from a magazine or gift wrap.

Next, she should cut around the finished drawings and stick them face-up onto a square of Con-Tact paper. Press another piece of Con-Tact paper tacky-side down on top of the drawings to seal them. Then, trim away the excess Con-Tact paper. For pierced earrings, poke small holes in the tops and attach the hangers; for clip-ons, glue the fasteners to the backs.

Artful Earrings

Snowman Pin
This little snowman looks frosty, but pinned on a child's jacket he's sure to prompt a warm smile. To make one, lay two buttons facedown one above the other. Position the head so that the button-holes resemble eyes; the holes in the body should look like vest buttons. Glue a pin back to the rear of the buttons. Then, glue on a small felt top hat and tie on a ribbon scarf.

Artful Earrings

The secret to designing these handmade earrings lies at the tip of a pen. With a couple of drawings, your child can make a pair to accessorize a favorite outfit or give as a gift to a friend.

Materials
- Heavyweight paper
- Fine-tipped colored markers
- Clear Con-Tact paper
- Earring hangers or fasteners (available at bead and craft stores)

Jewelry Frames

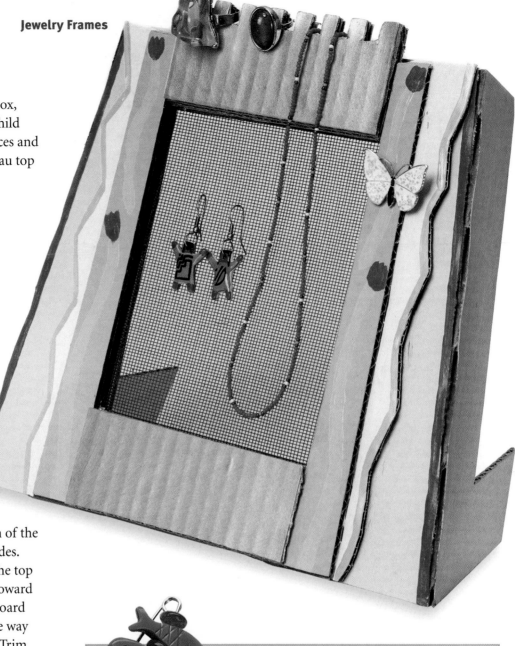

Instead of stashing jewelry in a box, this decorative screen lets your child hang up her earrings and necklaces and dress up a bedroom wall or bureau top at the same time.

Materials

- Corrugated cardboard
- Craft knife
- Wire cutters
- Metal screening (available by the foot at hardware stores)
- White glue
- Craft paints

For a freestanding earring frame, use a 9- by 18-inch piece of cardboard. Set it on a hard surface with the long edges at the top and bottom and use a craft knife (adults only) to cut a 5- by 6-inch opening in the center.

Measure and mark the bottom of the frame 3½ inches in from both sides. Draw a line from each mark to the top of the frame, slightly angling it toward the center. Then, score the cardboard along the lines (do not cut all the way through) to form foldable flaps. Trim the flaps into L shapes, angling the bottoms a small amount so the frame tilts back when standing.

Next, place a 6- by 7-inch piece of metal screening on top of the opening and glue the edges to the cardboard. Cover the screen edges by gluing on layered cardboard strips. Cut notches in the top of the frame to hold rings or necklaces and decorate the front with paint.

Pin-on Charms

Here's a jewelry-making method that's a snap for kids. First, open up a safety pin, slip a few beads over the point, and close the clasp. Then, use one or more of these charms to make a necklace or bracelet — cut a piece of leather cord to the desired length and tie half of a barrel clasp (available at bead stores) to one of the ends. Next, string on charms by threading the cord through the loop joints of the beaded safety pins. (For a jazzier effect, encourage your child to experiment a bit by tying overhand knots or stringing beads between the charms.) Finally, tie the other half of the clasp to the loose end of the cord. To redesign a necklace or bracelet, simply open the safety pins and slip on a new set of beads.

Ready to Wear

Chapter Eight

Gifts Kids Can Make

EVERY YEAR, *FamilyFun* contributing editor Lynne Bertrand makes a gift for each of her two children. One of six-year-old son Nick's first presents was a stuffed monkey; for her daughter Georgia, age three, Lynne knit a tiny Christmas sweater.

The bulk of Lynne's gift-making is done right by her children's bedside. "While the kids are falling asleep, they want me nearby," she says. "That's when I work on their presents. It means so much more to them when they see me at it, night after night. 'That's going to be for me, right?' they always ask."

As Nick and Georgia are lucky to be learning, handmade gifts are a two-for-one deal. You get the gift itself, of course. But you also get the delicious knowledge that somebody thought about you the whole time he or she was making it. While children may not grasp this concept consciously, they are easily inspired by it. They won't wrestle with dropped stitches until midnight, but they will get excited to make a jaunty button boy key chain (page 117) for a teacher, a hedgehog pincushion (page 125) for a fun-loving aunt, or a picture frame (page 124) for a friend. And just like adults, kids anticipate the gleeful reaction to the gifts they've made.

In honor of that excitement, this chapter is brimming with gifts kids can make. Some take time; others lend themselves to last-minute efforts or mass production. But every single one is a keeper. So let your kids flip through these pages — and make sure they don't skip the last few, which offer up homemade wrapping paper and gift tags for packaging that extra-special present.

Glitter Paper, page 126

Gift Basket, page 127

Kits for Crafty Kids

Craft kits are thoughtful gifts for a brother, sister, or schoolmate. First, help your child choose a craft the recipient will enjoy making. Then, gather the supplies needed. Pack everything into a box, photocopy the craft directions, and tie with a bow. Many of the crafts in this book lend themselves to a gift kit. Here are a few that beg to be wrapped up:

T-shirt kit: Along with a new T-shirt, wrap up a pile of decorating supplies. See page 100 for ideas.

Doll-making kit: For a doll-lover, give the materials for making the worry dolls (page 86) or all the accessories for finger puppets (page 87).

Sewing kit: This is a great excuse to introduce a child to sewing. For a complete kit, see page 125.

Jewelry box: Into an inexpensive jewelry box, pack the supplies for earrings (page 108), or pins (page 109).

Choose the right gift for the right person: You can enrich the gift-making experience for your child by helping him match his handiwork with the right recipients. First, choose someone who really will cherish something homemade. Next, spend some time talking with your child about what kinds of things that person likes.

Think function. People always appreciate a gift that really works for them. A child's drawing is wonderful, but it's even better (and easier to display) if you turn it into a bookmark or a picture frame with the child's photograph in it.

Over the holidays, take time to craft gifts. Instead of rushing to buy presents for everyone on your holiday list, set aside an afternoon for crafting a few. Not only are homemade gifts more personal, but making them will also give your family the chance to slow down during the busy holiday season — and to get into the spirit of giving.

Mass-produce if necessary. Around the holidays, you may need a lot of little gifts for the people in your daily life. This chapter offers a few ideas for things you can make in large quantities, such as the cutout coasters (page 121), the light switch plates (page 120), and even the birthday calendar (page 117), which

you can duplicate on a copy machine. For more specific holiday ideas, look through the Homemade for the Holidays chapter, which begins on page 129.

Let your child make one for himself, too. Kids are wonderful givers, but let's face it: they're even better receivers. If the gift you're making is something your child might enjoy, by all means encourage him to make two. Plus, your child may get a kick out of having an apron that matches Grandma's or a hand-decorated bedroom clock like the one in Mom's study.

Handprint Apron, page 118

Portable Playhouse

Just for Kids

Lightweight and cheery, this free-standing Styrofoam cottage makes a nice birthday or Christmas gift for a little sister or brother. It's roomy enough for a tea party but also can be folded together for easy storage in a closet or under a bed.

Materials

- 4 3¼- by 4-foot sheets of Fome-Cor (available at hardware stores)
- Utility knife
- Tempera paints
- Paint roller or paintbrushes
- String or thin rope

First, use the utility knife (adults only) to cut out windowpanes and a door from the four pieces of Fome-Cor to create the playhouse walls. Then, cover both sides of the walls with a base coat of paint. Paint on trim and wall decorations.

Now it's time to raise the walls. First, cut holes in each corner and centered on both sides, 1 inch in from the edge. Then, thread string or rope through the holes and tie the walls together at the corners.

To hang curtains, cut holes through the walls above each window, thread pieces of string through, and tie the rods in place. Use the same method to attach a shoe box for a window planter or a cardboard canister for a mailbox.

Portable Playhouse

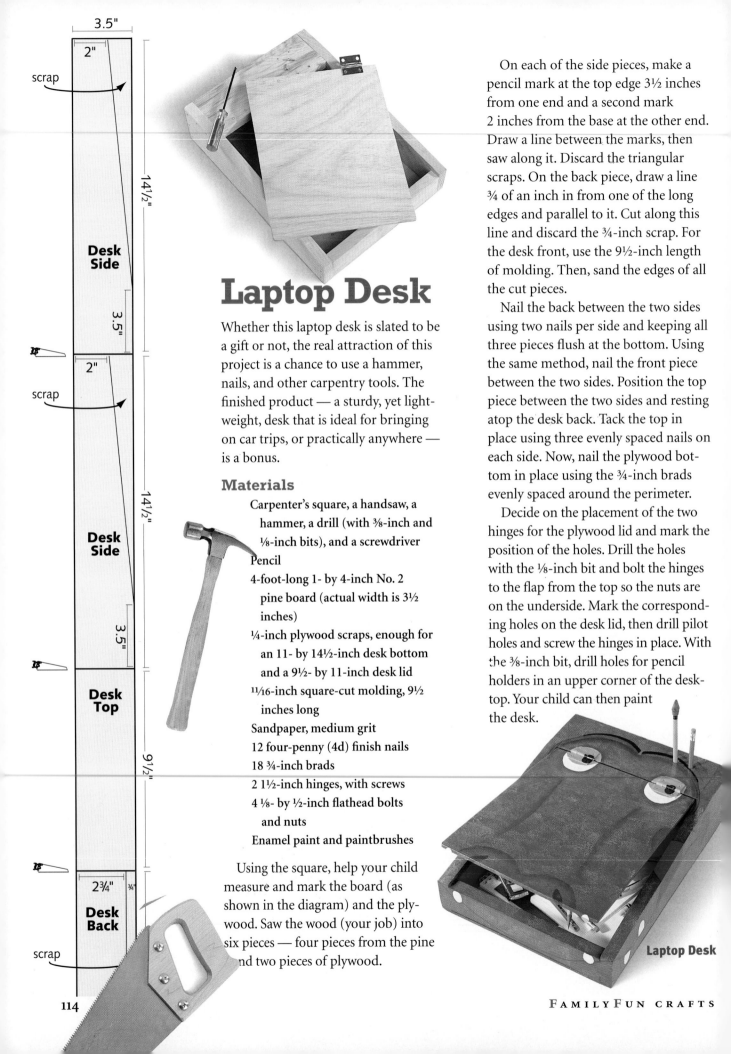

Diagram labels (left side)

3.5"

2"

scrap

14½"

Desk Side

3.5"

1½

2"

scrap

14½"

Desk Side

3.5"

1½

Desk Top

9½"

Desk Back

2¾"   ¾"

scrap

Laptop Desk

Whether this laptop desk is slated to be a gift or not, the real attraction of this project is a chance to use a hammer, nails, and other carpentry tools. The finished product — a sturdy, yet light-weight, desk that is ideal for bringing on car trips, or practically anywhere — is a bonus.

Materials

Carpenter's square, a handsaw, a hammer, a drill (with ⅜-inch and ⅛-inch bits), and a screwdriver

Pencil

4-foot-long 1- by 4-inch No. 2 pine board (actual width is 3½ inches)

¼-inch plywood scraps, enough for an 11- by 14½-inch desk bottom and a 9½- by 11-inch desk lid

11/16-inch square-cut molding, 9½ inches long

Sandpaper, medium grit

12 four-penny (4d) finish nails

18 ¾-inch brads

2 1½-inch hinges, with screws

4 ⅛- by ½-inch flathead bolts and nuts

Enamel paint and paintbrushes

Using the square, help your child measure and mark the board (as shown in the diagram) and the plywood. Saw the wood (your job) into six pieces — four pieces from the pine and two pieces of plywood.

On each of the side pieces, make a pencil mark at the top edge 3½ inches from one end and a second mark 2 inches from the base at the other end. Draw a line between the marks, then saw along it. Discard the triangular scraps. On the back piece, draw a line ¾ of an inch in from one of the long edges and parallel to it. Cut along this line and discard the ¾-inch scrap. For the desk front, use the 9½-inch length of molding. Then, sand the edges of all the cut pieces.

Nail the back between the two sides using two nails per side and keeping all three pieces flush at the bottom. Using the same method, nail the front piece between the two sides. Position the top piece between the two sides and resting atop the desk back. Tack the top in place using three evenly spaced nails on each side. Now, nail the plywood bottom in place using the ¾-inch brads evenly spaced around the perimeter.

Decide on the placement of the two hinges for the plywood lid and mark the position of the holes. Drill the holes with the ⅛-inch bit and bolt the hinges to the flap from the top so the nuts are on the underside. Mark the corresponding holes on the desk lid, then drill pilot holes and screw the hinges in place. With the ⅜-inch bit, drill holes for pencil holders in an upper corner of the desk-top. Your child can then paint the desk.

Laptop Desk

114

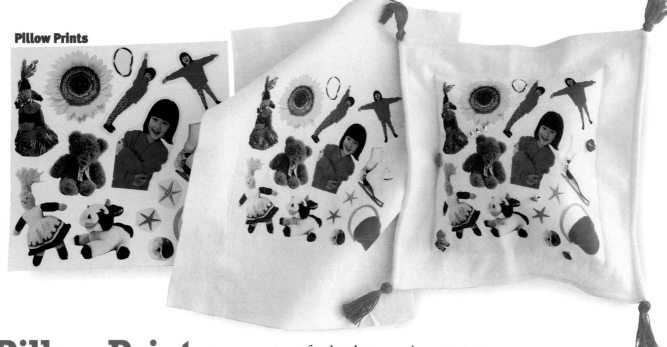

Pillow Prints

Pillow Prints

Instead of keeping all of his favorite pictures in an album, your child can display them collage style on a personalized pillow for Grandma or a best friend. Of course, he'll probably want to make an extra one — it can also come in handy for a sleepover. The project involves two steps — first, making a collage, and second, taking it to a photocopy shop to have the image transferred onto a pillowcase (the average cost is about $12).

Materials

    Photographs
    Sheet of plain paper
    Glue
    Pillowcase
    Trinkets or beads

Once your child has picked the photos he wants to use, ask him to cut out the images with a pair of scissors and arrange them on the white paper. When he is happy with his design, have him glue the cutouts in place, and the collage will be ready to take to the photocopier's.

There, ask the clerk to make a slightly reduced color photocopy of the collage to sharpen the images and then to transfer the photocopy image onto a pillowcase (you'll need to supply your own) or a piece of washable fabric you can sew into a cover. At home, your child can finish off his printed pillowcase by sewing on trinkets or beads.

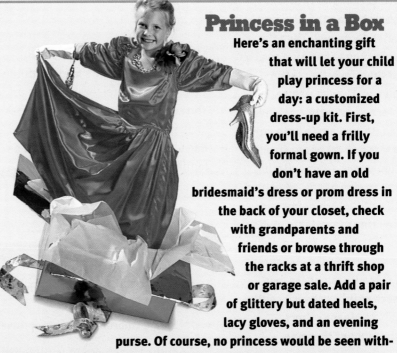

Princess in a Box

Here's an enchanting gift that will let your child play princess for a day: a customized dress-up kit. First, you'll need a frilly formal gown. If you don't have an old bridesmaid's dress or prom dress in the back of your closet, check with grandparents and friends or browse through the racks at a thrift shop or garage sale. Add a pair of glittery but dated heels, lacy gloves, and an evening purse. Of course, no princess would be seen without jewels — the incentive you need to untangle the costume jewelry cluttering the top of your dresser — and a corsage (see page 57 for instructions on making colorful paper flowers). Layer the gown and accessories in a large gift box. Then, decorate the box with shiny paper and glitter glue.

Gifts Kids Can Make

For Family & Friends

A Family Flag

GIFT CALENDAR

FamilyFun reader Susan M. Paprocki of Northbrook, Illinois, recycles her kids' most creative artwork into gift calendars. First, she photocopies the new year's calendar pages. Then the kids choose and sign twelve of their favorite master-pieces. They match each piece of art with a calendar month and paste both onto a large sheet of construc-tion paper. After collating the twelve pages, they bind them together using two key rings (available at dis-count stores). The calendars make wonderful treasures for family members, and each child's artwork contin-ues to please others throughout the year.

A Family Flag

Making a felt banner covered with symbols of everyone's favorite things is a terrific way to celebrate family pride. You can make one for a keepsake to hang in your own home or customize a flag to give as a gift to relatives at a family reunion.

Materials

2 yards of 72-inch-wide felt
Assorted 9- by 12-inch felt rectangles
3½ yards of decorative cording
Glue
Liquid embroidery paint (optional)

Trim the large piece of felt into pen-nants, one for each family member. Make an extra one for the center of the banner and glue on felt letters cut from a contrasting color to spell your family name. Individuals can decorate their own pennants by gluing on a variety of felt shapes. A dancer, for example, might choose pink ballet slippers. A sports fan could add a basketball. The family gardener could fashion a bold sunflower. And don't forget to include a likeness of the family pet. You may want to consider using liquid embroi-dery paint to inscribe a motto on the flag, such as United we stand or Do your best (great for teens to read on their way out of the house each day).

To assemble the banner, place the completed pennants on a flat surface, spacing them about 3 inches apart. Run a bead of glue along the upper edge of each one. Lay the cording on top of the glue and press down gently to make it stick. Once the glue is thoroughly dry, you're ready to raise the flag.

FunFact

According to *The Guinness Book of Records*, the largest American flag in the world spans 505 by 255 feet and was unfurled over Hoover Dam on May 1st, 1996.

Button Boy Key Chain

Is your button box bursting at the seams? With this craft project, your child can turn that surplus into a gift for a parent or friend — a colorful doll to use for a key chain or wear as a pendant.

Materials

    Heavy-duty elastic thread
        (available at fabric stores and
        most department stores)
    Measuring tape
    Buttons

1. Cut two 20-inch lengths of elastic thread. Holding the two pieces together, fold them in half and tie an overhand knot in the folded end to create a 1-inch loop. (When the doll is finished, you can use the loop to attach a key chain or necklace.)

Choose three buttons for the doll's hat. String the hat buttons onto the elastic by dividing the four strands into pairs and thread-ing each of the pairs through a separate buttonhole. Add the widest of the buttons last to create a hat brim. Next, add three medium-size buttons for the doll's head, followed by a couple of slightly wider ones for a shirt collar.

2. For each arm, cut a 6-inch piece of elastic. Thread the ends of the elastic through two different holes of a single button. Slide the button to the center of the strand. String on ten more buttons to form a stack. Knot the elastic just above the top button. To attach both arms to the body, tie the thread ends around the four elastic strands below the doll's collar. Then, add nine new buttons below the collar to create the doll's torso.

For legs, knot the elastic below the torso and, again, divide the strands into two sets. String a dozen or so buttons onto each set of threads, using slightly larger ones at the bottom for the doll's foot. Finally, knot the elastic ends below the feet and trim off any excess.

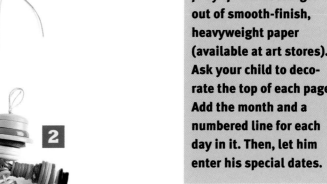

Button Boy Key Chain

Leg Threads

Birthday Calendar

Unlike a conventional calendar, a perpetual calendar has no weekday labels, so it can be used year after year. Because it's written in list form, it's a great place for your child to keep track of friends' birthdays and annual events.

For each month, cut a 7- by 17-inch rectangle out of smooth-finish, heavyweight paper (available at art stores). Ask your child to decorate the top of each page. Add the month and a numbered line for each day in it. Then, let him enter his special dates.

Handprint Apron

When her daughter Heather, now eight years old, was in preschool, *FamilyFun* reader Nancy Ojeda of Houston helped the class make a handprint apron for their teacher. The four-year-olds lined up, dipped their hands in saucers of paint, and pressed them on the apron. "It went like clockwork," she says. When they were done, the apron was covered with six-teen little handprints. Nancy appreci-ated how easy it was to make the gift. What did the kids like? "Oh, the mess!"

Materials

 Solid-colored apron
 Fabric paints
 Paper plates
 Fabric pen

Cover your work area with news-paper and lay the apron right-side up. Pour a little paint into a paper plate. Your kids can press their hands into the paint, move them around until the palm sides are covered, then place their handprints on the apron. Continue until the apron is covered with prints. Write each child's name with a fabric pen under his handprint. Let dry for at least 1 day before wearing.

Tinted Glass

Looking for a memorable end-of-the-year gift for your child's favorite teacher? Try recycling a jar into a hand-painted vase or pencil pot that will add some color to her desk.

Materials

 Acrylic or liquid tempera paints
 White glue
 Clean, clear glass jar
 Paintbrushes or Q-Tips
 Clear liquid glaze (available at
  art supply stores)

To make the paints stick to the glass, first mix the colors with some glue. Keep the paint thick so it won't run. Then your child can use brushes or Q-Tips to paint a design on the jar. To erase a mistake, she can use a paper towel to wipe off the paint before it hardens. Once it's dry, she should seal her finished design by brushing on a coat of clear liquid glaze.

Handprint Apron

For the Home

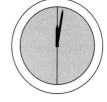

Customized Clock

With a little innovation, your child can turn a plain clock into a masterpiece, just right for hanging in Mom's or Dad's office, or his own bedroom. Dismantling and reassembling the clock may be a project best suited for kids over ten, but even the younger set will find decorating the clock face a breeze.

Materials

- Basic plastic clock (about $7 to $10 at discount or department stores)
- Sheet of sturdy paper
- Pencil and ruler
- Pin or thumbtack
- Assorted craft materials, such as paint, markers, and crayons
- Glue or double-sided tape

First, help your child detach the clear plastic shield that covers the face of his clock. It typically is held in place with plastic tabs or small screws. Trace around the shield onto the paper and cut out the circle, which will serve as the background for the clock face design. Mark the center of the clock face by gently laying the paper circle on top of the uncovered clock and using a pin or thumbtack to make a small hole in the middle.

Next, using a ruler, your child should draw two perpendicular lines through the center of the circle, creating four equal pie slices. The points where these lines touch the circle's edge are where the hours of 12, 3, 6, and 9 will be on his clock. Mark off two equidistant points between each of these four points for the remaining clock hours.

Now, your child can use paint, markers, crayons, or collage materials to customize the clock face. If his mom is a dog-lover, for example, she might like photos of the family pet; a friend who is a stargazer might enjoy a collage of planets and glow-in-the-dark stickers. He also can use cutouts or stickers instead of numerals to mark the hours.

When the design is complete, draw a straight line connecting 6 and 12 o'clock and cut the circle in half along this line. Then, use the knob on the back of the clock to rotate the arms clockwise until they align at 12 o'clock. Following the diagram at right, slip the decorated face into the clock, one half at a time (you may have to cut a small notch in each half to fit around the clock arms). If the clock face fits loosely, secure it with glue or double-sided tape. Finally, replace the plastic shield and reset the clock.

Customized Clock

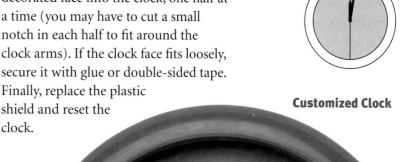

Gifts Kids Can Make

Jazzy Light-switch Plates

One way to brighten up a child's bedroom or a family room is with a gift pack of hand-decorated light-switch plates.

Materials

- Magazine photos, candy wrappers, postage stamps, or other printed paper
- Light-switch plate
- White glue
- Warm water
- Soft paintbrush

While your child cuts out images she'd like to use from the printed paper, mix together three parts glue and one part warm water. Then, your child can use the paintbrush to coat the back of each cutout before mounting it on the plate (the glue mixture will look white when applied, but it dries clear). Remind her to leave the openings for the screws and switch uncovered.

Fold paper pieces that extend over the edge under the plate to prevent them from curling up. If curling persists when the glue is dry, apply another coat of glue or use strips of clear tape folded over the edges of the plate.

Wallpapered Light-switch Plate:

Place a light-switch plate facedown on a piece of wallpaper. Trace the switch openings with a pencil and draw a ¾-inch border around the plate. Cut around the border and then clip a ¾-inch square from each corner of the cutout. To remove the paper where the switch slot goes, cut an *X* from corner to corner with scissors or a craft knife. The two screw openings can be poked with a sharp pencil. Attach the paper to the front of the plate with an even coat of white glue mix. Fold back the borders and the switch slot flaps to the underside of the plate.

Clay-covered Light-switch Plate:

To create a clay-covered plate, roll out a ⅛-inch-thick slab of Fimo or Sculpey III on a flat working surface. Using a toothpick or plastic knife, carve shapes out of the clay. Bake the shapes on a cookie sheet (be sure they are lying flat while they heat) according to package directions. When cool, the clay can be painted and then attached to a switch plate with a generous coat of white glue mix.

Jazzy Light-switch Plates

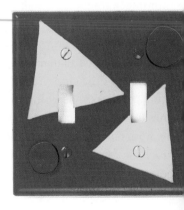

rates the top third from the bottom.

Now, pour some orange and yellow paint onto a paper plate. Press each potato stencil into the paint and then onto the fabric. Continue until you've finished your pattern. Air-dry overnight, then put in a hot dryer for about 30 minutes (this sets the paint so that it's machine-washable).

Cup Coasters

Here's a gift that your child can try his hand at making: a stack of handprint drink coasters.

Materials

    Tempera paints and
        paintbrushes
    Construction paper
    Clear Con-Tact paper

Stamp handprints (or another design that will fit under a cup) on construction paper and cover the prints on both sides with clear Con-Tact paper. Then, cut them out with enough of a plastic margin to keep fluids off the table.

PLACE MATS

You can turn your child's artwork into a gift set of place mats by preserving it in plastic. Take a set of 11- by 17-inch drawings or paintings to your local photocopy shop and ask the clerk to run it through the laminator (the

fee is generally about $3 each). Or, for a less glossy finish, cover them yourself with clear Con-Tact paper.

Cup Coasters

Table Linens

Stamped with potato-print acorns and leaves, these hand-decorated napkins and table runner lend a child's imprint to a grandparent's dinner table.

Materials

    Potatoes
    Craft knife
    Yellow and orange acrylic paints
    Paper plate
    Cloth napkins and table runner

To make a leaf stamp, cut a potato in half lengthwise (a parent's job). Using a craft knife, cut three wedges out of each side of the potato's cut surface. Carve a stem at the bottom and veins out of the leaf's center.

For an acorn stamp, cut a 1-inch square from a potato. Round the edges, leaving a stem, and cut a line that sepa-

Gifts Kids Can Make

For the Hobbyist

Gardener's Flowerpot

Using this quick-printing method, your child can create the ideal gift for an indoor gardener — a handsome and colorful planter. Terra-cotta pots look especially nice when printed this way, but plastic ones work well, too. Remember that new pots may be printed on immediately, but used ones should be thoroughly cleaned and dried before applying paint.

Materials

> Small leaves from trees and houseplants
> Acrylic paints and small paintbrushes
> Scrap paper
> Terra-cotta or plastic flowerpot

Your child can begin by choosing a couple of well-formed leaves from one or more types of trees or, with your permission, houseplants. He won't need many, because a single leaf can be used to make lots of prints.

Have him practice printing on a piece of scrap paper before working directly on the flowerpot. After he brushes a thin layer of paint onto the back of a leaf (the side that has prominent veins), he should place it paint-side down on the scrap paper. Have him put a sheet of clean paper over the leaf, then gently press down with his fingers, making sure that the leaf comes into contact with the printing surface. Remove the sheet of paper and carefully peel back the leaf to reveal the print. If your child is pleased with the print's color and shape, he can repaint the leaf to use on the pot.

It is easiest to print when the flowerpot is on its side and steady, so help hold it in place or have your child wedge it between two heavier objects. Be sure he lets the paint dry on one side of the pot before rotating it to continue printing. Encourage him to experiment with overlapping prints and different patterns and colors (wash off the leaf with a wet paintbrush before switching to a new color).

If your child likes, he can also embellish the flowerpot with stripes, splatter prints, dots, geometric designs, fingerprints, and even his own name. When the printing process is finished, let the paint dry completely, then add the crowning touch — a pretty houseplant.

Gardener's Flowerpot

Tin Can Chimes

Tin Can Chimes

Sometimes scarecrows are just too soft-spoken to intimidate the birds. Your child can solve the dilemma for his favorite gardener with this gift — a clanging noisemaker.

Materials

- Hammer
- Nail
- 2 jar lids
- Empty can
- Twine

Use the hammer and nail (adults only) to poke a hole through the center of the jar lids and the bottom of the empty can. Knot one end of a piece of twine and string on the lids, knotting the twine between them. Tie another knot 1 inch above the upper lid. Next, thread the twine through the hole in the can so that one lid serves as a clapper and the other catches the wind. Tie a loop in the end of the twine, and the can is ready to hang in a garden.

Gardener's Gloves and Apron

Cultivating a green thumb takes practice, patience, and a few handy accessories, like this personalized apron a gardener can use to keep all her tools within reach.

Materials

Painter's or carpenter's canvas apron and cotton gardening gloves (available at hardware stores)
Fabric paints and paintbrushes

Help your child design a garden pattern for the apron and gloves, such as a row of bright yellow sunflowers or a bunch of carrots. Then, she can decorate the set using fabric paints. When dry, heat set the paint according to the package directions. Then, fill the apron pockets with seed packets, a garden trowel, and a plastic misting bottle.

Gardener's Gloves and Apron

GARDEN SIGNS

A gardener can stake out the rows of his garden in style with these hand-crafted signs. First, cut out the pictures and names of specific vegetables and flowers from a garden catalog or seed packets. Next, cut 2- by 4-inch rectangles out of corrugated cardboard and fit an end of a small stick into each one (between the grooves, centered along the lower edge). Then, glue on the pictures and names and let dry thoroughly. Waterproof the signs with clear, sturdy tape or Con-Tact paper. Then tie the set together with a green gift ribbon.

A Shutterbug's Frame

Made from three layers of cardboard, this frame is sturdy enough for any decorating method your child can dream up. When he's done, he can slip in a photo of himself, and he's got the perfect gift for Grandma and Grandpa. The frames shown here fit a horizontal 4- by 6-inch photo, but you can adjust the dimensions to suit any shot.

Materials

- 12-inch-square piece of corrugated cardboard
- Pencil and ruler
- Craft knife
- Glue or rubber cement
- Small piece of ribbon
- Decorating supplies, such as paints, colored markers, puzzle pieces, buttons, or other trinkets

On the piece of cardboard, measure and mark off two 6- by 8-inch pieces, three 1- by 6-inch pieces, and one 2- by 5-inch piece. Cut out the shapes. In the center of one of the 6- by 8-inch pieces, mark off a 3¾- by 5¾-inch opening for your photo and cut it out with a craft knife (adults only).

Lay the frame facedown and collect the three cardboard strips (these will form a pocket that holds the photo). Center, then glue one of the 1- by 6-inch strips about ⅛ of an inch away from the bottom of the frame opening (as shown at left). Glue each of the other two 6-inch strips about ⅛ of an inch away from the sides of the frame opening.

To make the frame's stand, your child should evenly bend the 2- by 5-inch piece of cardboard about 1 inch in from one end. Using glue or rubber cement, attach the folded section against the the second 6- by 8-inch cardboard rectangle (the frame back), 1 inch below the top. To prevent the stand from weakening, glue a short length of ribbon between the back panel and the bottom end of the stand.

Now, your child can embellish the frame front. A map or a collage of stamps makes a nice border for a travel photo or a coat of bright paint enhances a portrait of a good pal. For a three-dimensional look, he can glue on layers of puzzle pieces, buttons, pennies, or seashells. When he's done decorating, your child can glue the frame's back to the pocket strips. The last step is to slip the photo into the frame pocket.

A Shutterbug's Frame

Hedgehog Pincushion

A seamstress needs to keep track of pins and needles, and this little felt hedgehog is up for the job.

Materials

Fabric pen
Felt
Embroidery floss
Large-eye needle
Straight pins
Batting
Googly eyes and a black button

Use a fabric pen to trace a 6-inch circle on a felt square. Cut out the circle and then cut it in half. Thread six strands of embroidery floss through a large-eyed needle and knot the ends.

To form the hedgehog's back, pin together the curved edges of the felt pieces and sew them up using a blanket stitch

Next, stuff the body loosely with batting and place it on top of a second felt square. Pin the straight edges to the square and trace around them. Draw a tail at one end of the body, then cut the felt on the traced line.

Stitch the back to the bottom, leaving a 2-inch opening. Fully stuff the hedgehog and stitch up the opening. Glue on googly eyes, sew on a black button nose, and fill with pins.

Gifts Kids Can Make

Sewing Basket

Not only will this gift delight a young seamstress, but it also makes great use of last year's lunch box.

Materials

Plastic lunch box
Fabric scraps or felt
Glue
Plastic or cloth tape measure
Cardboard egg carton

First, decorate the outside of the lunch box by cutting out shapes or letters from the fabric scraps or felt and gluing them on. Cut the tape measure to fit around the box top and then glue it in place. You can even wind and glue a colorful ribbon around the lunch box handle.

Next, furnish the inside of the box with a thread spool holder — trim one end off an empty egg carton so that it will fit inside the box and then place a spool of thread in each cup.

Starting a Sewing Kit

Every starter sewing kit should include pins, a thimble, a pincushion, scissors, a variety of sewing needles, and an assortment of thread (both dark and light colors). Shears for cutting fabric, tailor's chalk for marking fabric, and a tape measure also come in handy, as do buttons, zippers, and fabric scraps.

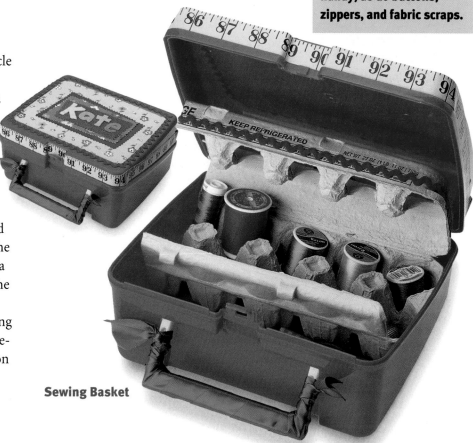

Sewing Basket

Wrap It Up

Yarn Paper

Plaid Paper

Paper Bag Cutting 101

To turn a grocery bag into wrapping paper, cut along one side seam. Next, cut along all four sides of the bottom of the bag and remove the cut panel. Open the bag up, and it's ready for decorating and wrapping.

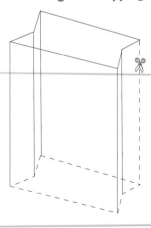

Plaid Paper

One way to dress up a package is in stripes or plaids. Here's how you and your kids can turn an ordinary brown paper bag into colorful gift wrap.

Materials
    Paper bag
    Acrylic paints
    Paper plate
    2- to 4-inch-wide paint roller

Cut open the paper bag, then spread it out on a flat working surface. Squeeze a dab of paint onto the paper plate. Have your child run the paint roller through the paint to coat it, then roll stripes onto the paper. Let each color dry before adding contrasting colors. (To clean the roller, simply rinse it with water.) Once your artist has mastered stripes, it's time to try plaids.

Yarn Paper

With this design, you can wrap and decorate all at once.

Materials
    Paper bag
    White glue
    Scraps of yarn

Help your child wrap a gift in a cut-open paper bag. Then, glue the scraps of yarn onto the package. The best method for younger children is to dribble a thin line of glue randomly on the paper and lay yarn along the line. Older kids can try tying the yarn into bows, weaving it into patterns, or making pom-poms. The decorations can then be glued onto the package. Allow the glue to dry thoroughly before presenting the gift.

Glitter Paper: For a dazzling effect, have your child drizzle a pattern of glue onto a flat sheet of brown paper. She can make stars, squiggly lines, and other abstract shapes. Then, sprinkle glitter onto the glue. When the glue is dry, carefully shake the excess glitter back into the jar. Then, use gold or silver markers to outline the designs. Allow the paper to dry thoroughly before wrapping the package.

ow to Make a Pretty Bow

s basic bow is easy to
and it will lie flat on
kages.

ter wrapping a length of
on around your gift and
tting it, grasp both rib-
ends and bend them into
ple loops.

2. Cross the right loop over the left loop

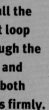

ll the
t loop
ugh the
and
both
s firmly.

raighten both loops and
and, if you like, notch
nds of the tails or cut
at an angle.

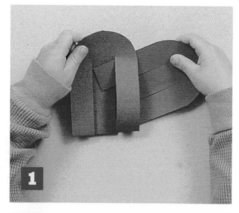

1

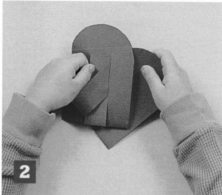

2

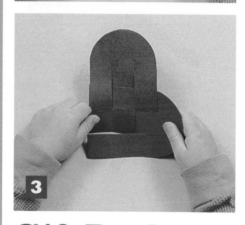

3

Gift Basket

This woven paper heart is handy for kids who want to surprise a friend with fresh flowers or candy. Just fill it up with goodies and anonymously hang it from a doorknob.

Materials

- 2 3- by 9-inch pieces of construction paper
- 1- by 9-inch strip of construction paper
- Ruler
- Pencil
- Glue

First, fold the 3- by 9-inch paper rectangles in half lengthwise (this forms the two halves of the heart). Place them on a table so that the creases are at the bottom. Then, measure 3 inches up from each crease and use a pencil to lightly draw a straight line across the paper. With scissors, round off the top of each half, above the line.

On each half, mark 1-inch increments along the crease. Make a straight cut up from each mark to the pencil line to form three flaps for weaving the two halves together.

1. Now, hold one half of the heart in each hand, as shown.

2. Weave the upper flap of the right half through the flaps of the left half by slipping it through the center of the first one, around the middle one, and through the third one.

3. Next, weave in the middle flap of the right half, this time slipping it around the first flap, through the second flap, and around the third flap.

Finally, weave in the last flap following the same sequence you used with the upper flap. If done correctly, the woven heart will open into a basket.

For a handle, just glue the ends of the construction paper strip to the inside of the heart, and the basket is ready to fill.

Gift Basket

127

Chapter Nine

Homemade for the Holidays

ASK ANY CHILD to describe his favorite holiday memory, and he probably will use the word *always*. We always carve jack-o'-lanterns on Halloween; we always decorate eggs at Easter; we always make ornaments at Christmas. The holiday isn't just one day — it is a tradition, built year upon year, affecting all the senses.

It is in this spirit that we've put together the crafts in this chapter — activities that your family will want to turn to every holiday. This year, you may try crafting the homemade valentines on page 133 with your kids — and sharing holiday hopes and memories while you work with your hands. Next year, that same session at the table will seem familiar — the doilies will come out for the first time since last Valentine's Day. Five years later, you won't be able to imagine the holiday without this ritual.

Crafts add richness and importance to any and all of the calendar's holidays. Taking time to make a mask for Halloween, a card for Mother's Day, an ornament for Christmas, or a noisemaker for New Year's extends the holiday — and ensures that those days will *always*

Fingerprint Hearts, page 135

Holiday Crafts for Kids

Paper chains: For any holiday, you can create paper chains out of construction paper in seasonal colors — pink and red for Valentine's Day, green and red for Christmas, orange and black for Halloween, blue and white for Hanukkah, and so on.

Quick cards: Cut hearts, Easter eggs, pumpkins, Christmas bells, and other holiday symbols out of construction paper and let your kids decorate them with markers or glitter.

Easy table decorations: Stamp a paper tablecloth with holiday symbols and let it dry before draping over your table. For quick napkin rings, cut cardboard tubes into 2-inch-wide sections, then paint or cover with strips of ribbon, paper, or a collage of magazine clippings.

Decorate your door: Welcome your guests with a holiday greeting — a giant paper jack-o'-lantern with a crooked grin, a paper Santa with a cotton ball beard, or a valentine with a sweet message written in colored glue.

stand out in your family's history.

Look ahead. Pick a craft that you think you and your family will like to do, year after year, such as making an ornament for the Christmas tree or decorating Easter eggs. It won't be quite the same each year; people and crafts both evolve over time. Still, the core activity may become a tradition.

Think back. In this chapter, you'll find many new crafts to add to your holiday repertoire, but be sure to try crafts you did as a child — or ones that are traditional from your ethnic or religious heritage. These activities teach kids about family history and are a special way to connect one generation to the next.

Don't try to do too much. One or two crafts at Christmas are enough, especially if you're also making gifts, baking, or entertaining. If you try to do more, you'll only add to your holiday

stress. You don't need to spend a lot of time on the craft — a holiday decoration you've made in minutes could last for years.

Create a box for each holiday. Store holiday craft supplies and homemade decorations in one box so that the following Halloween, Easter, or Christmas, you'll know just where to find them.

Buy supplies for next year. At the end of every holiday season, stock up on craft supplies, such as holiday-themed stickers, wrapping papers and ribbons, at a discount rate.

Get in the spirit. Play Christmas carols while you make wrapping paper or spooky music while carving jack-o'-lanterns. Munch on jelly beans as you dye eggs at Easter or put on a Pilgrim's hat for crafting Thanksgiving decorations.

Holiday Crafts for Kids

New Year's

Party Hats

For *FamilyFun* reader Gayle Selsback of Minneapolis, New Year's Eve is an occasion for homemade haberdashery. Her family celebrates the last evening of the year with an early supper and a hat-designing extravaganza. The Selsbacks create fancy party hats from colored paper, paper cups and plates, old Christmas ribbons, and whatever else they can find. Then, they don their creations, count down the New Year, and parade through the house banging pot lids together and yelling, "Happy New Year!"

Materials

Construction paper
Hole punch
Elastic cord
Glue, stickers, or tape
Colored paper, foil, stickers, feathers, pipe cleaners, and other decorations

1. Fold a large rectangular piece of construction paper in half by bringing together the shorter sides.

2. Turn down the corners along the crease so that they line up (as in paper airplanes), then individually fold up each open edge to create the brim.

3. Make a chin string by punching holes on each side or each end of the hat and threading a piece of elastic cord through the holes.

Now, offer your kids supplies for decorating their hats. Roll up thin strips of paper to make curlicues or cut fringes out of colored foil paper, then attach them with glue, stickers, or tape. As a finishing touch, add feathers, pipe cleaners, or any other odds and ends — the wilder the hats, the better.

Homemade for the Holidays

Party Hats

Cone Hat: Roll a large square or rectangular piece of paper into a cone, staple down the sides, and trim the edges for an even brim. To make a shorter cone, cut a semicircle with a diameter of about 1 foot out of a piece of construction paper. Holding the paper at the midpoint of the straight edge, fold the semicircle into a cone. Staple down the ends and trim around the brim. For both sizes, punch two holes on opposite sides of the hat, and thread a piece of elastic cord through the holes for a chin string (you may want to secure the holes with paper reinforcements).

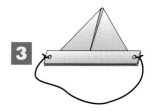

To make the wand, roll the acetate into a tube about 1½ inches in diameter. Close up one end of the tube by cutting slits in the sides, folding the strips over, and taping them down.

Using a small funnel made from paper, slowly pour the homemade confetti into the wand. Cork the open ends with wads of tissue paper; remove at midnight and wave the wands through the air.

Confetti Balloons: When it comes to making a big bang, popping balloons is unparalleled — and even more thrilling if streams of confetti come pouring out. Prepare your New Year's balloons by setting the kids to work making confetti. Stuff as many confetti pieces as you can into each deflated balloon using a funnel (you can improvise one by cutting a plastic soda bottle in half). You may also want to write fortunes on small pieces of paper and slip them into the mix. Blow up the balloons and hang them high, but still within your children's reach. A few moments before the appointed hour, hand out the pins. When the time is right, let that confetti fly.

QUICK CONFETTI

Making confetti is a great way for little hands to join in on the decorating, as well as a quick and inexpensive way to create party magic. When the party's over, these tiny decorations can be vacuumed up.

Grab a hole punch and a collection of colored paper, old gift wrap, mail-order catalogs, and aluminum foil (if you don't have a hole punch, you can simply rip paper into confetti-size pieces). Fill a medium-size mixing bowl about half full with confetti and stir to distribute the color. If you wish, add in a few tablespoons of glitter.

Confetti Wands

These sparkling wands are a blast to wave through the air — the only downfall is the cheerful mess they tend to make on the floor.

Materials

6-inch by 1½-foot piece of medium-thickness acetate (available at art supply stores)

Tape

Homemade confetti (see Quick Confetti, at right)

Tissue paper

FunFact

As much as 3,000 pounds of confetti are thrown in Times Square every New Year's Eve.

Valentine's Day

Bag of Hearts

Sweet Temptations

Scores of *FamilyFun* readers said their kids couldn't resist these Valentine's Day suitors, who came bearing sweet treats. The idea was inspired by the creative children's craft book *The Best Holiday Crafts Ever!* (Millbrook Press).

Materials

- Playing card (hearts, of course)
- Thumbtack or straight pin
- Ruler
- 2 8-inch pipe cleaners
- Construction paper
- Googly eyes
- Glue
- Markers
- Lollipop

First, use the thumbtack to poke arm- and leg-holes 1 inch from the top and ½ inch from the bottom of the card. For arms, fit the ends of one pipe cleaner through the upper holes from the back of the card. Fit the other pipe cleaner through the lower holes for legs. Bend the ends to shape feet.

For a head, cut a heart out of construction paper. Glue on googly eyes and draw on a nose and mouth. Then, glue the head to the card. Finally, wrap one arm around the lollipop. Write a message on a mini card and slip it in the card's free hand.

Bag of Hearts

Need a tote for carrying your cards? This one can be assembled in a flash.

Materials

- Colored paper
- Brown bag (lunch size works well)
- Ribbon
- Markers (optional)

Glue a few colored paper hearts onto a medium-size bag. For handles, use two pieces of ribbon. Cut holes in the bag; thread the ribbon through and knot the ends.

Dress in Red

Scarlet, after all, is the order of the day. Help your kids dig up an all-red ensemble from their closets and use ribbons or rickrack for belts, shoelaces, and hair ties. Paint nails with hearts in all the shades of red polish you've collected. You even can tattoo your arms with beet juice, cutting a fresh beet into heart-shaped stamps.

Sweet Temptations

Homemade for the Holidays

My Punny Valentine

Lovebug Brooch

FamilyFun contributor Shannon Summers made one of these ladybugs in first grade for her mother, who decades later, still pins it on. Young kids can make this project nearly independently — and the finished brooch looks more sophisticated than the usual macaroni jewelry many moms get on Valentine's Day.

Materials

Plaster of Paris
Plastic spoon
Safety pin
Red and black
 acrylic paints
Small paintbrush
Clear varnish (optional)

Help your child mix up the plaster, then fill and level off the spoon. Press the safety pin into the wet plaster so that it opens out. Allow the plaster to harden for an hour. Your child can pop out the brooch and paint it red. Using the black paint and small brush, she can draw eyes, wings, and a head on the lovebug, then cover the wings with hearts, as shown above. If your child makes other brooches, she can decorate them with any simple design, as in the one below. To seal in the colors, a parent can apply a protective coating of clear varnish.

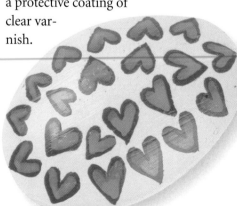

Lovebug Brooch

Paint a Romantic Rock

This activity, which brings the family outside for fresh air on Valentine's Day, can become downright obsessive. Search for heart-shaped stones in the rockiest places near you: a stream bank, a driveway, the parking lot. They don't have to be perfect, as long as they have the two telltale lobes of a heart and some sort of point at the bottom. Then, set everyone to work painting the rocks.

My Punny Valentine

Why are valentines always filled with puns? We don't know, but we love it.

Materials

Old magazines and catalogs
Construction paper
Glue

Cut out letters and pictures of animals from the magazines and arrange them into punny cards, using a bit of glue to hold them onto the paper. A cat remarking, "I have felines for you," a horse noting, "Bubba, you're my mane man," or a dog sending this sweet nothing to Mama, "I'll hound you till you're mine," are all gems.

Button Hearts

For an easy, handsome addition to any Valentine's Day outfit, dress up your shirt buttons by cutting heart shapes out of a piece of felt.

Materials
- Felt
- Googly eyes
- Glue

Cut romantic shapes out of a piece of felt (they should be about 1 to 2 inches tall and wide). We chose hearts, but you could try flowers, stars, or whatever you like. Cut slits that are the size of your buttonhole in the center of the shapes, then slip them in place. For a goofy-face button slip, glue on googly eyes above the slits.

Fingerprint Hearts

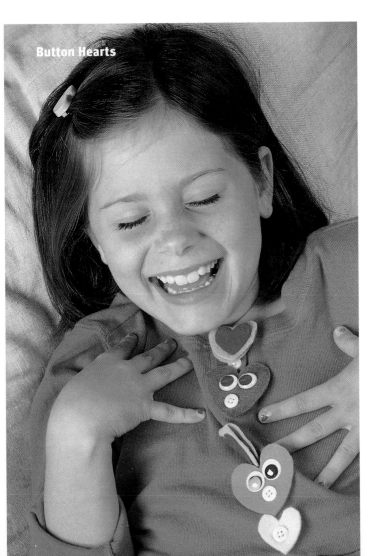

Button Hearts

QUICK VALENTINE CARDS

Lots of kids love glamorous, store-bought Valentine's Day cards. But homemade valentines are the most fun to give, even when you have to mass-produce them. We suggest starting a card-making workshop a few days before the big day. Or, to save time, you can make one card, then color-copy it.

Fingerprint hearts: This is the perfect little-kid card. You'll need a nontoxic stamp pad, scrap paper, and notepaper or postcards. Have your child stamp a V-shaped heart by joining two index-finger prints at the bottoms. Once your kids master the technique on scrap paper, let them add hearts to folded notepaper or postcards or to each frame of a paper accordion card (see below).

Accordion hearts: Cut a long narrow rectangle from a piece of paper, then fold it in four, accordion style. Next, make a heart stencil out of scrap paper. Use the stencil to cut out heart shapes from magazines, wrapping paper, doilies, or old photographs. Children can then glue down a heart cutout on each square.

Chinese New Year

Dragon Mask

Dragon Mask

In Chinese folklore, dragons guard the earth's jewels, govern the weather, and watch over the rivers. It's no surprise, then, that this mythical creature is also charged with leading the Lantern Festival street processions that cap off the Chinese New Year. With this costume version of the legendary beast, your kids can take turns heading up the traditional Chinese game described below.

Materials

6- by 30-inch piece of yellow poster board
Stapler
Ruler
Colored construction paper
White glue

Wrap the poster board around your child's head with the ends meeting in front of his face; staple them together an inch or two from his forehead. Remove the poster board and make the dragon's face by gluing together the poster board flaps that project from the brow band (the brow band will serve as its neck).

Cut out the dragon's mouth and contour the top of its face. Glue construction paper scales to its neck, face, and chin. Add paper eyes, flaring nostrils, teeth, and horns. Finally, glue the base of a red paper flame to its lower jaw.

Chase the Dragon's Tail

This time-honored Chinese game can be played with ten kids or more. One child is the head of the dragon and wears the mask. The other players line up behind him with their hands on the shoulders of the person in front of him. The head has one minute to tag the last kid in line without causing the line to break apart. If he succeeds, he wins; if not, he becomes the tail, and the child behind him wears the mask.

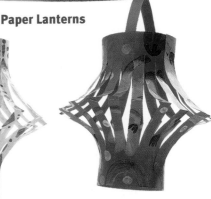

Paper Lanterns

Paper Lanterns

During the Lantern Festival, children carry candlelit lanterns in the street. This construction paper version is wonderfully decorative and doesn't need to be lit — but if you want to, you can rig up a mini flashlight inside.

Materials

> 8½- by 11-inch piece and a ½- by 6-inch strip of lightweight paper, such as gift wrap or decorated newsprint
>
> Ruler

Fold the larger piece of paper in half lengthwise and cut eighteen slits 3½ inches long, into the fold and parallel to the short edges (begin cutting an inch from each edge and leave a half inch between each slit). Unfold the paper and staple or glue the short edges together, then glue the small strip to the sides at the top for a handle.

Stamp Your Name

When a Chinese artist signs his paintings, he uses a carved stone block — called a chop — to print his symbol on the canvas. To personalize her art or stationery, your child can make her own signature stamp out of Styrofoam and cardboard.

Materials

> Pen
> Tracing paper
> Clean Styrofoam meat tray
> Glue
> Cardboard
> Cardboard tube
> Ink pad

1. First, have your child write her initials on tracing paper, making the letters as ornate as she likes or incorporating them into a unique design. Next, place the paper printed-side down on a clean Styrofoam meat tray. Trace over the design with a pen, bearing down to leave an impression in the Styrofoam.

2. Cut out the design, leaving a narrow border all around, and glue it onto a piece of cardboard trimmed to the same size. For a handle, glue a cardboard tube to the back. Then, press the stamp onto an ink pad and stamp it on stationery.

Chinese Calendar

The Chinese calendar dedicates each year to one of twelve animals. Have your kids find the animal that matches their birth years and draw a picture of it.

Rat: 1972, 1984, 1996
Ox: 1973, 1985, 1997
Tiger: 1974, 1986, 1998
Hare: 1975, 1987, 1999
Dragon: 1976, 1988, 2000
Snake: 1977, 1989, 2001
Horse: 1978, 1990, 2002
Sheep: 1979, 1991, 2003
Monkey: 1980, 1992, 2004
Rooster: 1981, 1993, 2005
Dog: 1982, 1994, 2006
Pig: 1983, 1995, 2007

1

2

Stamp Your Name

Homemade for the Holidays

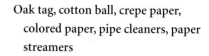

Easter

Easter Bonnets

On Easter morning, your kids can parade around the yard in these fanciful Easter bonnets, made of paper bowls and plates.

Materials

- Paper bowl
- 10-inch paper plate
- Glue
- Tape
- Craft knife
- Tempera paints and paintbrushes

Oak tag, cotton ball, crepe paper, colored paper, pipe cleaners, paper streamers

To make either bonnet, set the inverted bowl on your child's head to see if it fits. To make it smaller, cut the bowl into quarters, refit the pieces so the edges overlap (use tape to get it right), then glue the seams.

Rabbit Cap: To make the visor, cut a 7- by 5-inch rectangle from the flat portion of a paper plate. Trace the rim of the bowl along one long edge of the rectangle. Using this line as a guide, cut out a 3-inch-wide crescent shape (see top left). Glue the bowl rim to the inner edge of the visor. Paint the cap and let it dry. Next, cut foot-long ears out of oak tag paper, leaving a ½-inch tab at the bottom of each. Paint the ear backs and front edges to match the cap. Once dry, shade the centers with a lighter hue. Use a craft knife (parents only) to make two ½-inch slits in the top of the hat. Push the ear tabs through and glue them to the inside of the hat. Finally, glue a cotton ball tail to the cap back.

Flower Bonnet: To make the brim, center the fitted bowl rim-side down on top of an upside-down paper plate and trace around it. Cut a circle from the middle of the plate, staying ½ inch in from the line. Glue the rim of the bowl to the inner edge of the paper ring. Paint and dry thoroughly. For a hatband, glue a strip of crepe paper around the hat, above the brim. Next, cut flowers out of colored paper and tape pipe cleaner stems to the backs. To attach, push the stem end through a hole in the hat and secure with tape. For chin sashes, tape an 18-inch paper streamer to the inner brim on both sides of the hat.

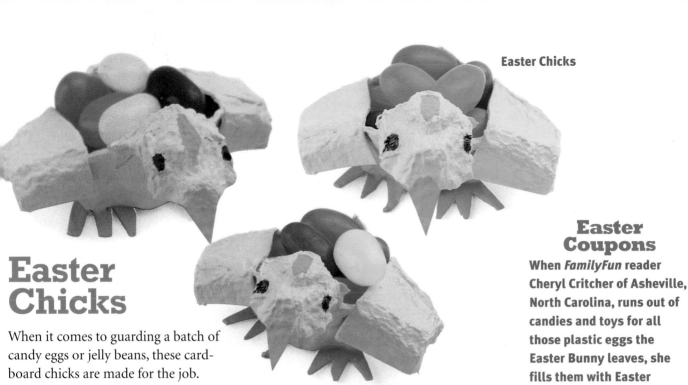

Easter Chicks

Easter Chicks

When it comes to guarding a batch of candy eggs or jelly beans, these cardboard chicks are made for the job.

Materials

- Cardboard egg carton
- Colored markers
- Glue
- Watercolor brush
- Yellow tempera paint

1. To make each chick, cut a single egg cup from the egg carton for a body. Trim along the top edge, keeping the sides of the cup as tall as possible.

2. Then, with a colored marker, outline a chick's head and neck on the underside of the carton top. (Use the molded portion of cardboard that separates the eggs, as shown.) Cut out the head and glue the base of the neck to the inside of the body.

3. For the chick's wings, cut a second egg cup from the carton, this time trimming the sides about ½ inch from the bottom. Then, cut the cup into halves. Holding the half cups with the bottoms up, fit them onto the sides of the chick's body and glue them into position.

Once the glue dries, brush on a coat of yellow tempera paint. Allow the paint to dry thoroughly. Next, use colored markers to tint the beak orange and draw on eyes.

Finally, cut a pair of feet from carton scraps and color them orange. Glue the feet onto the bottom of the body, and the chick is ready to fill with Easter candy.

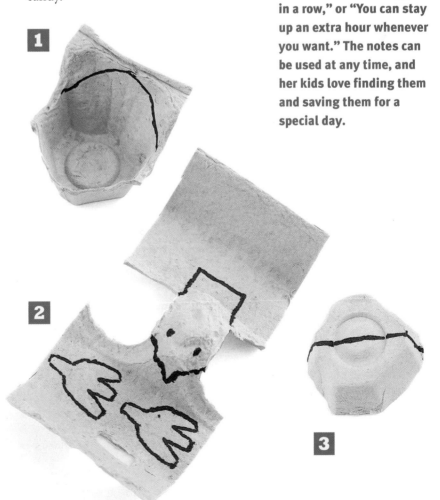

Easter Coupons

When *FamilyFun* reader Cheryl Critcher of Asheville, North Carolina, runs out of candies and toys for all those plastic eggs the Easter Bunny leaves, she fills them with Easter "coupons." These slips of paper say things like, "You can go to lunch at the place of your choice," "You can skip your chores three days in a row," or "You can stay up an extra hour whenever you want." The notes can be used at any time, and her kids love finding them and saving them for a special day.

Homemade for the Holidays

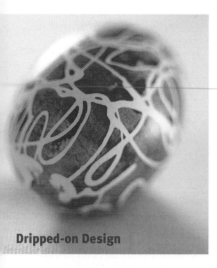

Dripped-on Design

Dripped-on Designs

Kids will get a kick out of letting rubber cement gloop and dribble all over (the egg, that is).

Materials

Hard-boiled eggs

Egg dye

Rubber cement with applicator brush

To start, rest the egg in an empty egg carton lid or on a section of paper towel tube set upright. Next, using the applicator brush, dribble rubber cement over the egg. When the cement has dried, dip the egg into a bowl of dye. When the color is bright, remove the egg and let it dry. Peel off the glue and repeat to add additional colors, if desired.

Sticker Stencils

These eggs are especially fun for little kids to work on — all they need is a few stickers or paper reinforcers.

Materials

Hard-boiled eggs

Egg dye

Stickers (paper reinforcements, store-bought stickers, or designs cut from self-adhesive shelf paper or mailing labels)

Begin with a cooled egg and cooled dye; otherwise, the adhesive gets sticky and difficult to remove. Cover the egg with stickers, then dip the egg until the color is bright enough. Let the egg dry and remove the stickers. If you wish, you can remove only some of the stickers and dip the egg in a second color.

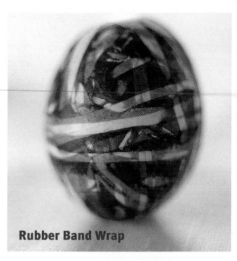

Rubber Band Wrap

Rubber Band Wrap

Twisting rubber bands around an egg can challenge small hands, but the result is a snazzy, colorful creation.

Materials

Hard-boiled eggs

Egg dye

Rubber bands, various sizes

Wrap rubber bands around the egg, covering it completely. When you dip the covered egg, the dye will seep under the bands in some areas and be blocked out in other areas. Remove from the dye when the color is bright enough. Blot dry with paper towels and remove the rubber bands. If you wish, repeat with a new color.

Sticker Stencils

Sponge-print Eggs

Sponge stamps are easy to use and leave a clean, sharp design. Create your own patterns or just stampede (as it were) at random.

Materials

    Hard-boiled eggs
    Kitchen sponges
    Tempera paints

Cut out shapes, about ½ inch wide, from a sponge (we used a thin rectangle to make our zigzag pattern). Dip the sponge into the paint, dab off the excess, and make a pattern of stamps on the egg. To keep colors fresh, make a sponge stamp for each color.

Sponge-print Egg

Painted Chick

In this particular case, the age-old question is settled: the egg definitely came first.

Materials

    Air-drying clay
    Cardboard or cutting board
    Plastic knife
    White glue
    Blown eggs (see tips on page 140)
    Tempera paints and paintbrushes
    Rolling pin

Homemade for the Holidays

Painted Chick

Roll out the clay on cardboard. Using the plastic knife, shape the clay into a beak, comb, and feet. Rub a dab of glue onto the clay parts and press into place on the egg. Hold for 1 minute until the glue starts to dry, then set the egg aside to dry completely. Paint on eyes, wings, and feathers. Finally, paint the clay features.

THE EGGHEADS

Have you ever looked at your Easter eggs and wondered what's missing? This year, give the bald ones a head of hair. Use a small nail to make a hole about the size of a quarter in one end of an egg, then drain the egg and rinse out the shell. Draw or paint funny faces on the shells and put them in the egg carton. It's a good idea to use permanent markers so the colors won't bleed when you water the hair. Use a spoon to fill the shells with soil, then plant with grass seeds (follow package directions).

Moisten the soil, cover with plastic wrap, and place the shells in a sunny window until the seeds sprout — it generally takes less than a week. When the eggheads have a thick, green mane, remove the covering and place them on a stand (try using empty film canisters). Style the hair into pigtails, buzz cuts, or Mohawks and water it every day.

Fourth of July

Firecracker Hats

Kindergarten teacher Jean Alston of Roanoke Rapids, North Carolina, sent *FamilyFun* snapshots (and one newspaper clipping) of six kindergarten classes all sporting these fluttery hats at the same time — apparently, the kids were

such an astonishing sight that they made the front page of the local paper.

Materials

- 2 full sheets of newspaper
- Ruler and pencil
- Blue, red, and white tempera paints
- Wide paintbrush
- White construction paper
- Tape and glue

First, unfold the two newspaper sheets one atop the other as if you were reading them. Thereafter, treat them as a single two-ply sheet — this will strengthen the hat and provide a double layer of fringe.

To make the brow band, mark a line 3½ inches from the bottom edge of the sheet and fold up along that line. Roll the band up once more and flatten the fold. Paint the brow band blue. When dry, paint broad red and white stripes on the flip side of the newspaper (this will be the inside of the hat). While waiting for the paint to dry, cut star shapes from the construction paper.

Fit the hat by wrapping the brow band around a child's head and taping the overlap securely. At this point, the hat should resemble a tall cylinder.

Glue the stars to the brow band. Finally, fringe the top of the hat, making cuts an inch or so apart that extend most of the way down the cylinder.

Firecracker Hats

Statue of Liberty Crown

Statue of Liberty Crown

If your bored masses are yearning for a Fourth of July costume, try making this Statue of Liberty headband and Miss Liberty's torch.

Materials

    2 sturdy paper plates
    Green construction paper
    Stapler
    Glue
    Green paint
    Glitter

First, cut 2½ inches from each of the bottom rims of two sturdy paper plates, then cut out their centers, leaving a 2-inch-wide headband (this fits most children's heads snugly, but if it's too tight, carefully trim more away from the edge).

Next, cut six triangles from green construction paper. Each one should measure 4 inches across and 9 inches high. Space these evenly across the front of one headband with the points radiating outward and staple into place. Glue the other headband across the first to conceal the staples. Paint it green, then "oxidize" with glitter.

Miss Liberty's Torch:

Fashion a torch out of a cardboard tube, poster board, and yellow tissue paper. Touch up both to look like Miss Liberty's crown with green paint and glitter.

Homemade for the Holidays

Patriotic Bike Parade

Let kids celebrate America's birthday by dressing up their two-wheelers in red, white, and blue and riding in a Fourth of July parade.

➤ Weave colorful crepe paper through the wheel spokes.

➤ Tape lengths of ribbon to the handgrips and string the ends with beads or mini bells.

➤ Make a flag out of construction paper. Instead of drawing fifty stars on each side, apply silver star stickers. Trail glue along the left edge of the finished flag, roll about 1½ inches of the paper around a thin dowel or branch, and hoist it up.

➤ As a treat, provide each child with a helium balloon on a short string for each child to fly from his handlebars.

Star-printed T-shirt

Star-printed T-shirt

These star-spangled T-shirts are easy to make — whether you use a star fruit (also called a carambola) as a stamp or make your own out of a potato or a gum eraser (see page 121 for directions).

Materials

- Newspaper or piece of cardboard
- Cotton T-shirt
- Fabric paint
- Pie tin
- Knife
- Star fruit (or potato star stamp)
- Paper towel

Insert several sheets of newspaper or a piece of cardboard inside the cotton T-shirt. Then, pour some fabric paint into a pie tin. Slice the star fruit in half and dry both the cut surfaces with a paper towel. Dip the fruit into the paint and use it to press stars onto the shirt. Once the prints dry, follow the fabric paint instructions to heat-set the design.

Margarine Tub Drum

No Fourth of July parade is complete without a noisemaker (or ten). This one won't quite drown out the firecrackers, but it comes pretty close.

Materials

- Small margarine tub and lid
- Colored duct tape
- Craft knife
- ⅜-inch dowel cut to an 8-inch length
- 2 6-inch pieces string
- 2 wooden beads

First, decorate the tub and lid with shapes cut out of the tape. Use a craft knife (parents only) to cut a ⅜-inch hole through one side of the tub and slide the end of the dowel through it. Poke a small hole in each side of the tub 90 degrees from the dowel. Thread a piece of string through each hole and knot the ends inside the tub. Tie a bead onto the free end of each piece of string. By rolling the dowel back and forth in his hands, your child can make his own one-drum salute.

Uncle Sam Hat

To make the Uncle Sam hat the cyclist is wearing on page 143, start with a 12- by 14-inch piece of poster board. Mark each side with a dot at the halfway points of 6 and 7 inches, respectively. Measure 2½ inches in from each dot and mark an additional dot. Connect the outer dots with a curved line to form an oval; repeat with the inner dots. Cut away the corners of the outer oval, then cut the inner oval sides and rear, leaving the front intact. Raise the inner flap and fold it forward. Trim the top and sides of the flap to square it off and decorate the hat.

Margarine Tub Drum

Halloween

Stack-o'-Lantern

When trick-or-treaters come knocking on your door this Halloween, greet them with our three-story jack-o'-lantern. It's no more difficult to fashion than three conventional ones — in fact, that's really all it is. And its triple glowing power can help keep all those creepy Halloween shadows at bay.

Materials

- 3 pumpkins (a big one on the bottom with progressively smaller ones above; the top pumpkin should be no less than 9 inches deep)
- Paring knife or craft knife
- Large spoon or ice-cream scoop

First, cut the tops off all three pumpkins (adults only). Don't make the openings too wide just yet (leave some room for error) and cut in at a generous slant to provide support for the pumpkins above. Ask your kids to gut the insides with the spoon or ice-cream scoop. The more they scrape, the brighter the pumpkin will glow — but go gently on the bottom.

Test-fit your pumpkins as you go; you may need to trim so upper ones sit firmly in lower pumpkins (see illustration). Once your stack fits together properly, unstack them and carve faces. Light a candle in each pumpkin and carefully restack them.

Say Boo!

Say Boo!

What can you do with four odd-size pumpkins? This solution — making each one a letter of a word — is so clever it's scary.

Materials

- 4 small pumpkins
- Pen
- Paring knife, craft knife, or pumpkin carving tool
- Large spoon

First, draw the letters and exclamation point in pen on the pumpkins. Cut the tops off with a sharp knife (a parent's job); for best results, carve at an inward angle. Cut a small hole in each cap to allow heat from the candle to escape. Remove the seeds with the spoon and scrape the walls until they are about 1 inch thick. Cut out the drawn letters with the knife or carving tool.

Choosing a Pumpkin

Look for large, heavy, evenly shaped pumpkins. Those that will be lit by candles should be at least 9 inches high. A curly stem can add personality, but it may be delicate and should not be overhandled (remind kids never to pick up a pumpkin by its stem).

Homemade for the Holidays

Pumpkin Painting

Kids who are too young to carve their own jack-o'-lanterns can paint dastardly faces on this seasonal squash.

- Pumpkin
- Tempera paints and paintbrushes
- Plastic yogurt containers filled with water for rinsing brushes

On a covered surface, set out the paints, brushes, and plastic yogurt containers filled with water. Then let the kids paint goofy, surprised, or creepy faces on the pumpkins.

CARVING TIPS

✂ **For stability, work from the center out (nose before eyes, eyes before eyebrows, mouth last).**

✂ **While huge, gaping features look really cool, they also get mushy quickly. For fine details, use a craft knife or saw through the pumpkin with a piece of thin wire.**

✂ **For creepy facial highlights, cut trenches just far enough into the pumpkin's skin that the candlelight glows eerily through (in other words, don't cut all the way through the pumpkin).**

Pumpkin Painting

If your belfry is looking a bit bare this year, scare up a swarm of these clip-on bats.

For each bat, cut an extended-wings shape from black construction paper. Next, cut out an oblong body with pointed ears and feet and glue it onto the wings. Add round, beady eyes cut from yellow or red paper. Glue a clothespin to the back of the bat, and it's ready to hang onto a curtain.

Black Cats

There's no need to worry about these black cats crossing your path. Bright-eyed and bushy-tailed, they're meant to stand on a table or a doorstep as a surprise greeting for Halloween callers.

Materials

Black poster board
Pinking shears
Yellow construction paper
Glue

1. First, cut an 11- by 6-inch rectangle out of the poster board. Fold it in half so that the shorter edges meet and make a crease. Using the crease for the cat's backbone, cut out a four-legged body. Trim the bottom of each foot with pinking shears to create toes.

Still using the pinking shears, cut out a bushy, upright tail. With regular scissors, make a small vertical snip in the backbone above the hind legs and fit the base of the tail into it.

For the cat's head, use a 6- by 3½-inch rectangle. Match up the short ends

and make a sharp crease in the center. Unfold the rectangle and lay it flat so that the short ends are at the top and bottom. Then, form ear tabs. With a pencil, mark both sides of the rectangle 2½ inches up from the bottom. Make a diagonal cut from each mark up to the crease (see above).

2. Refold the rectangle and push up the triangular tabs to create the cat's ears. With the scissors, shape the cat's chin and neck. Then, glue on a black poster board nose and whiskers. Add yellow construction paper eyes. To attach the cat's head to the body, make another cut in the top of the back (this time above the front legs) and fit the lower edge of the neck into it.

Black Cats

Gauze Ghosts

It takes practically nothing to make this family of mischievous sprites.

Materials

Assortment of different-size
    plastic milk jugs or juice
    bottles
Aluminum foil
White gauze or cheesecloth
Liquid laundry starch

Top each milk jug or bottle with a ball of crumpled aluminum foil. Next, cut the gauze or cheesecloth into 18-inch squares, one for each ghost. Dip the gauze squares into a bowl filled with laundry starch. Pull them out one at a time and squeeze out the excess moisture. Drape a square over each bottle.

To shape the ghosts' shoulders and arms, loosely pile crumpled aluminum foil around the bottle and drape the gauze over it. Flare out the lower edges of the gauze and let dry overnight. (To make the dog, simply drape a small square of gauze over shaped foil.) Once they've dried, carefully lift the ghosts from their bottles. They should stand freely on a flat surface.

Egg Carton Pumpkins

Greet your trick or treaters with a row of mini pumpkins perched along your windowsill.

Materials

Cardboard egg carton
Glue
Orange acrylic paint and
    paintbrush
Paper clip
Green pipe cleaners or crepe paper
Black marker

Homemade for the Holidays

Gauze Ghosts

Cut two cups from the egg carton. Run a bead of glue along the top edge of one cup. Invert the second cup and position it atop the first, making sure the cut edges align.

Once the glue dries, coat the shell with orange acrylic paint. When the paint is dry, use the end of the paper clip to poke a hole in the top of the pumpkin. Make a stem and curly vines out of the green pipe cleaners or twisted green crepe paper and push the ends through the hole. Use the black marker to draw on a spooky jack-o'-lantern face.

Egg Carton Pumpkins

Ghost Prints

This is an easy party activity for little ghouls. Have kids fold a piece of black construction paper in half, then dribble white paint into the crease. When they briefly press the paper back together, then open it, a ghost will appear.

Mr. Bottle Bones

Start saving your empty plastic gallon jugs — with a snip here and a hole there, you can resurrect a life-size skeleton. Punching holes and tying on bones is a job for little kids; cutting out and gluing together the pieces is a job for older children and parents. If you like, you can paint Mr. Bones a neon color to make him glow.

Materials

- 8 or 9 clean, plastic gallon jugs
- String
- Craft knife or heavy-duty scissors, such as kitchen shears
- Hot glue gun
- Hole punch

Head: Choose a jug with a pair of circular indentations opposite the handle and turn it upside down. In the corner, opposite the handle, use the craft knife or scissors (parents only) to cut out a large, smiling mouth, centered under the indented "eyes." Make two small slits in the top of the head and tie a loop of string through them for hanging the finished skeleton.

Chest: Cut a vertical slit down the center of a right-side-up jug, directly opposite the handle. Cut and trim away plastic to make the rib cage. Glue the head and chest together at the "neck" by connecting the spouts of the two jugs with a thick band of hot glue (adults only). Hold the jugs together for a few minutes until the glue cools.

Shoulders: Cut off two jug handles (leaving a small collar on the ends) and attach them to the chest section with hot glue. Punch a hole at one end of each shoulder.

Hips: Cut all the way around a jug, about 4½ inches up from the bottom. Take the bottom piece and trim away a small smile shape from each side to make a four-cornered piece. Punch holes in two opposite corners.

Mr. Bottle Bones

Waist: Cut out two spouts, leaving a ½-inch collar on each. Glue the spouts together and let dry. Then, hot-glue the waist to the bottom of the chest and the top of the hip section.

Arms and legs: Cut eight long bone shapes from the corner sections of three jugs (cut into the curved shape of the jug to make the bones even more realistic). From four of these bones, cut out the center to make lower limbs (forearms and shins). Punch a hole through the ends of all eight bones. Tie two arm sections to each shoulder, and two leg sections to each hip, with string.

Hands and feet: Let the kids trace their hands and feet onto the side of a jug, then cut out the shapes. Punch holes in the hands and feet and tie them onto the arms and legs.

Monster Jugheads

Ever notice that an empty milk jug looks a little like Frankenstein? We did — and we convinced *FamilyFun* reader Rachel Schwartz of Scarsdale, New York, too. She made these monster heads with her whole family — including a three-year-old, a preteen (who thought the project was weird enough to warrant a try), and her husband, whose skills were employed to insert the bolts into Frankie's neck.

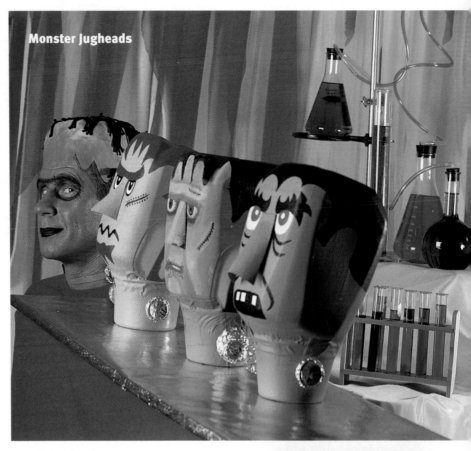

Monster Jugheads

Materials

- Clean, plastic gallon jug
- Plastic deli container
- Duct tape
- Tempera paints and paintbrushes
- Milk caps
- Aluminum foil
- Pushpins
- Thin piece of cardboard

Turn over a clean, gallon jug and rest it inside a plastic deli container (the deli container helps the monster head stand upright and also makes Frankie's thick neck). Attach the jug to the container with duct tape, then coat both with tempera paint. When the paint is dry, paint on bloodshot eyes, wicked scars, and a head of greasy black hair. To create bolts in the sides of the monster's neck, cover milk caps with foil and attach them with pushpins. Cut a nose from a thin piece of cardboard, then slip it through a slit cut in the monster's face.

Monster Mouth Game

To make this game of skill, cut monster teeth out of the edge of a shoe or cereal box and invert it so the teeth touch the table. Decorate to look like a monster with paint or construction paper, googly eyes, and goofy ears. Place the box on the ground and mark off a masking tape starting line. Offer the kids marbles to flick into the monster's mouth. If you're playing with big kids, give each tooth a score (the smaller the hole, the higher the score). The highest scorer wins.

Spooky Spiders

Here's a bunch of itsy-bitsy spiders that won't take long to hatch.

Materials

Cardboard egg carton
Black acrylic paint and paintbrush
Paper clips or pushpin
12 black pipe cleaners
Glue stick
12 pairs of googly eyes

Cut the cups off an empty egg carton and place them on newspaper. Have your kids cover the cups, inside and out, with a coat of black acrylic paint. Use the end of a paper clip or a pushpin to poke four holes along the bottom edge on one side of the cup. Poke matching holes on the opposite side of the cup.

To make fuzzy legs, cut four black pipe cleaners into 7-inch lengths. Thread a pipe cleaner through one of the holes, into the cup, and out the corresponding hole on the other side. Make sure the ends protrude an equal length from both sides of the cup and bend them upward at the base of the spider's body. Fold in the opposite direction midway down the legs to create knees and bend the tips to make feet. Finally, glue on googly eyes.

Dinner Ghosts

Butternut squash, rather than pumpkin, is the Halloween centerpiece at the Hardy-Johns household in Tampa. *FamilyFun* reader Kimberly Hardy-Johns reported that her oldest daughter, Rachael, came up with the idea. She started by covering three butternut squashes in white paint. To complete her ghosts, she added a mouth and eyes of black construction paper, using straight pins to attach them. (Permanent black marker would work just as well for facial features.) As you can see, each squash took on quite an individual personality.

Turnip Top Flashlights

Carving jack-o'-lanterns is a tradition that got its start in ancient Ireland, where kids used hollowed-out turnips filled with embers to light the way on Halloween night. With these directions, you can make a nonflammable (but still spooky) trick-or-treat lantern.

Materials

Medium-size, purple-top turnip
Paring knife and spoon
Flashlight

Slice off the very top of the turnip and hollow out the inside using a sharp paring knife (parents only) and a spoon. Then, carefully carve facial features in one side, as you would for a pumpkin. Cut a circle in the bottom of the turnip to fit over the end of the flashlight. Finally, turn on the flashlight to give Jack a glow.

Turnip Top Flashlights

Thanksgiving

Village People

Setting the Thanksgiving table became an art rather than a chore for *FamilyFun* reader Shelby Powell of Ava, Illinois, and her two children, Neil, age six, and Adi, age four. They had fun creating and naming one placeholder for each of the twenty-six guests at their Thanksgiving table.

Materials

- Cardboard tissue tube
- 4- by 6-inch rectangle of colored paper
- Glue
- Fine-tipped markers
- 2- by 3-inch piece of paper
- Colored paper scraps

For each figure, wrap a cardboard tissue tube with a 4- by 6-inch rectangle of colored paper and glue the paper in place. Draw the facial features on the 2- by 3-inch piece of paper with fine-tipped markers. Glue the face onto the tube. For the hair, cut fringe along one side of a small paper rectangle. Roll the hair around a pen to make curls, trim it, and glue it in place.

Native Americans: Cut and decorate headbands and feathers for the Native Americans and draw a string of beads with a fine-tipped marker.

Pilgrims: Cut and decorate collars for the Pilgrims. To make the Pilgrim girl's bonnet, wrap a 2- by 5-inch paper rectangle around the top of the tube with the ends overlapped and glued at the back. For the Pilgrim boy's hat, cut out a black circle 2½ inches in diameter. Roll and glue a black 2- by 5-

inch paper rectangle into a tube shape. Cut slits along one end, fold in the tabs, and glue them to the center of the paper circle. Add a ½-inch band and square buckle and glue the hat to the boy's head.

Native American

TABLE FOR FOUR

When *FamilyFun* reader Eileen Allen of Draper, Utah, hosted Thanksgiving dinner for the first time, her kids were thrilled — until they realized that having all those guests meant they would have to sit with their cousins at a card table. To make this fate more appealing, Eileen suggested they decorate the table. So, Brent and Adam wrapped the table legs with colored crepe paper, made canvas place mats, and even made Pilgrim and Native American headbands. Eileen picked up Silly Straws, candy kisses, and napkin holders in the shape of turkeys. Sure enough, the cousins thought the table was "rad," and nobody complained about not sitting with the adults.

Homemade for the Holidays

Tiny Toms

back of the pinecone, starting from the underside and twisting them together a few times on the top of the pinecone to secure them. Then loop both ends of each pipe cleaner to shape tail feathers.

Gobbler Gloves

Here's a project kids will be happy to lend a hand with — a turkey puppet that doubles as a Thanksgiving centerpiece.

Materials

> Gardening glove
> Felt
> Glue
> Liquid embroidery paint
> Googly eyes

Use the gardening glove for the bird's body. Cut feathers out of felt (make them a bit wider than the glove fingers), fringe the edges, and glue one to each glove finger. Cut a wing shape out of felt and glue it to the palm. Use paint to enhance the plumage.

For a beak, cut a pair of small felt triangles and glue them to opposite sides of the thumb tip. For the wattle, cut a 2-inch-long hourglass shape out of red felt. Drape the wattle over the base of the beak and glue it in place. Glue on googly eyes. To use the turkey puppet as a table decoration, stuff newspaper into the glove and roll up the cuff.

Tiny Toms

This is one turkey that won't get eaten this Thanksgiving. Your kids can make a flock to decorate the dinner table.

Materials

> Yellow and red felt
> Tacky glue
> Googly eyes
> Brown pom-poms
> Pinecones
> Pipe cleaners

For each turkey, cut out a yellow beak and a red wattle from felt. Then glue the beak, wattle, and a pair of googly eyes onto a pom-pom to create the turkey's head.

Glue the pom-pom head to the tip of a pinecone. Allow the glue to dry.

Wrap a pipe cleaner around the middle of the turkey's cone body, starting from the top and twisting it together a few times on the underside. Separate the ends of the pipe cleaner (below the twists) and bend each tip into a 3-toed foot.

For the turkey's tail, individually wrap 3 or 4 pipe cleaners around the

Gobbler Gloves

Terra-cotta Turkey Planter

A more charismatic flowerpot we never did see — and he doubles as a handsome Thanksgiving centerpiece.

Materials

- Self-drying modeling clay (brown)
- Butter knife
- 7½-inch-tall terra-cotta pot
- 2 white pebbles (painted, if necessary)
- Black permanent marker
- 1 walnut in the shell
- 1 red pipe cleaner, 9 inches long
- 6 corn kernels
- Hot glue
- Corn husks (available at grocery stores)
- Potted mums (in a pot at least 1 inch smaller than the terra-cotta pot)

The head: From some of the modeling clay, shape two balls, each 3 inches in diameter, and a third ball that is half the size of the other two. Sandwich the balls so that the smallest ball is in the middle and press together. Smooth the balls together to form a head, neck, and chest. Tip: To smooth cracks or rough edges, wet your finger to smooth the clay.

With a butter knife, cut a vertical slit halfway up the center of the bottom ball. Slide it over the rim of the terra-cotta pot. Press the two sides of the clay ball together to secure the turkey's head to the pot. Lightly flatten the clay on the inside of the pot.

The face: For eyes, use the marker to draw black circles in the centers of the white pebbles. To make the turkey's face, firmly press the eyes and walnut (for a beak) into the clay head. For the wattle, fold the pipe cleaner in half and twist the ends together. Press 1 inch of the pipe cleaner into the clay just above the beak and bend down the protruding end.

The feet: From the clay, make two 3-toed turkey feet. Press a kernel of corn onto each toe. Next, press the feet onto the front of the pot.

The wings and feathers: Once the clay is dry, secure any loose pieces with hot glue. Next, hot-glue dried corn husks onto the sides and the back of the pot (on the inside) to make the wings and feathers. Once everything has dried, insert the potted mums into the turkey planter.

Puffed Corn

This year, add a festive touch to your holiday table by filling a vase with colorful paper cornstalks. To make each stalk, cut three 18-inch lengths of natural-colored paper twist (sometimes called raffia paper).

Untwist them, then trim the edges to resemble corn husks. Fan out the husks so that they overlap, as shown, and use a few drops of glue to hold them together. From yellow poster board, cut out an ear of corn (about 10 inches long and 3 inches wide) and glue it atop the husks.

Now crumple a bunch of 3-inch colored tissue paper squares to create rounded kernels and glue them to the ear. Lastly, gather the husk bottoms and tie them together with a strip of raffia.

Homemade for the Holidays

Stained-glass Hanukkah Windows

Hanukkah

Stained-glass Hanukkah Windows

Brighten the eight nights of Hanukkah and enjoy each other's company by crafting these "stained-glass" candles. Each night, hang another one in your window or door until you have all eight.

Materials

- Black construction paper
- Craft knife
- Colored cellophane or tissue paper
- Tape
- Cheese grater
- Old crayons
- Waxed paper
- Iron
- Glue
- String or yarn

Use the craft knife (parents only) to cut out a candle shape from two black construction paper pieces placed back to back (cut the candle stem and flame separately). Next, pick a color of cellophane or tissue paper and cut a rectangle slightly larger than the candle stem shape. Tape the colored paper to one piece of black paper so it covers the cutout shape.

To make the flame, grate shavings from yellow, orange, and red crayons. Then, cut two squares of waxed paper at least 4 inches square. Spread the crayon shavings across one square, then place the other square on top. Cover both sides of the crayon sandwich with newspaper and press lightly with a dry iron. Let the creation cool, then cut out a piece slightly larger than the candle flame shape and tape it to the black paper. Glue the second sheet of black paper to the back of the first. Punch a hole in the top, thread with string, and hang.

Star of David

Representing David, the Jews' greatest hero-king, the six-pointed star graces the Israeli flag and is Judaism's most recognized symbol worldwide. With some kitchen science, kids can turn pipe cleaners into a crystal Star of David.

Materials

- Widemouthed jar
- Borax (available at grocery stores)
- Food coloring
- Pipe cleaners
- String
- Pencil

Fill the jar with boiling water (adults only). Mix borax into the heated water, a tablespoon at a time, until you notice powder settling on the bottom of the jar. Stir in food coloring to add a tint.

Next, bend a pipe cleaner into a six-pointed star. Tie one end of the string to the star and the other end around the pencil. Rest the pencil on the jar lid so that your pipe cleaner is suspended in the solution. Set aside overnight.

As the water cools and evaporates, borax molecules will stack together. By morning, the star will be covered with crystals. Remove it from the jar, let it dry, and hang. To make a three-dimensional star like the one at right, make two six-pointed stars and nest one inside the other before dipping into the borax. (This may look like rock candy, but remind your kids that these are toxic and nonedible.)

Star of David

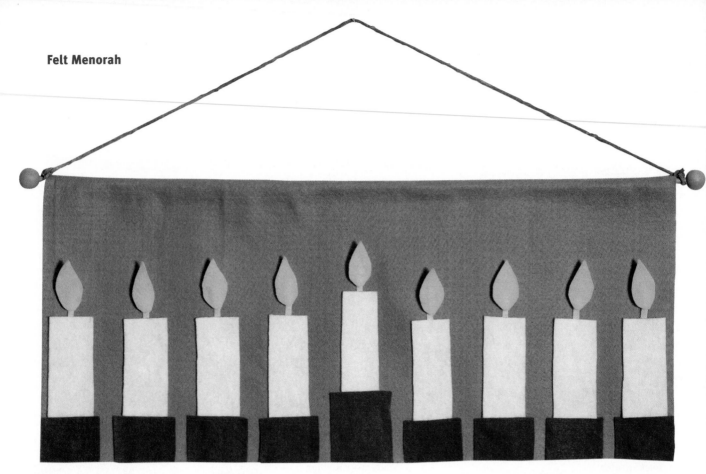

SIMPLE MENORAHS

Natural menorah: Find a steady branch, about 10 inches long, then glue or nail metal bottle caps onto it to hold the special menorah candles (melt the bottom of candles to affix them to the bottle caps).

Thread spool menorah: Nail painted wooden thread spools to a board. Widen the holes with a drill (parents only) and be sure to take care as the menorah candles burn down.

Clay menorah: Shape candleholders with clay, poke holes with a menorah candle, then paint when dry.

Felt Menorah

One of the high points of Hanukkah is getting to light the family menorah. This holiday wall hanging features felt candles and stick-on flames, which makes it easy, and safe, for even very young kids to participate in the ritual.

Materials

> White and blue felt (the colors of the flag of Israel)
> Yellow felt
> 2- by 1-foot piece of felt (of any contrasting color)
> Glue
> Velcro
> Wooden dowel
> 2½-foot piece of cord

Cut nine 3½- by 1½-inch candles from the white felt and nine flames from the yellow felt. From the blue felt, cut eight 2-inch squares and one 3- by 2-inch rectangle for candleholders.

Place the felt banner on a flat surface and glue the candleholders along its lower edge. Space them equally apart and put the larger holder in the center for the shammes candle, which is used to light all the other candles. Glue a candle above each holder. For wicks, glue one side of a ¾-inch Velcro strip above each candle. Glue a matching strip to the back of each flame.

Fold over the top of the banner 1½ inches from the edge. Glue the edge to the back of the banner and insert the dowel. Tie the cord to the ends of the dowel, and the menorah is ready to hang.

On the first night of Hanukkah, remind your child to "light" the shammes first and then the candle to the far right. Each night thereafter, he can add a new flame, always starting with the candle to the left of the one he lit last.

Kwanzaa

Kwanzaa Mobile

From December 26th to January 1st, African American families can pay tribute to their heritage by celebrating Kwanzaa. This simple holiday decoration will help teach your kids the seven principles of Kwanzaa — Unity, Self-Determination, Collective Work and Responsibility, Cooperative Economics, Purpose, Creativity, and Faith.

Materials

Red, black, and green felt (the three colors of Kwanzaa)
Glue
3 wooden paint stirrers
Tempera paints and paintbrushes
Pushpin
Fishing line

With your kids, brainstorm symbols that represent the seven principles of Kwanzaa (a drum for Creativity, say, or a star for Purpose). Cut the shapes out of felt and glue on the first letter of the principle each stands for.

To form the hanger, paint the paint stirrers red, black, and green. Stack them so their tips fan out like the spokes of a wheel and glue in position. Once dry, use a pushpin to poke a hole 1 inch in from each of the ends. Make a seventh hole through the hub. Thread a 1-foot piece of fishing line through each hole and tie a knot at the top. Poke small holes through the tops of the felt shapes and tie them to the fishing lines.

To suspend the mobile, thread three 2-foot pieces of fishing line under the crossed stirrers. Gather the six ends above the stirrers, secure with a knot, and hang.

Homemade for the Holidays

Felt Kufi

Get into the Kwanzaa spirit by crafting this classic Kufi hat, adapted from *The Kids' Multicultural Art Book* (Williamson Publishing).

Materials

Red, black, and green felt
Stapler
Masking tape or duct tape

Cut and staple a 2-inch-wide brow band of red felt. Next, cut a pair of 1- by 12-inch strips out of red, black, and green felt. With each pair, form an X and staple together in the center. Pile the X's on top of one another so the felt strips extend out like the spokes of a wheel. Attach to the band by folding up the ends and stapling in place. Finally, cover the staple prongs by lining the inside of the brow band with masking or duct tape.

Cowrie Beads

With pasta shells, kids can make beads that resemble cowrie shells, symbols of good fortune in Africa. Hold a shell with the inside facing you with the curled flap at the top. Apply glue to the inner edge of the lower flap. Hold a second shell as if it were a bowl and slide its open flap behind the curled flap of the first shell. Once set, paint with black, red, and green acrylics and let dry. String the beads in alternating colors on cord.

Felt Kufi

Christmas

Paper Tree

Decking your halls, doors, mantels, and tabletops with homemade decorations will put your family in the holiday spirit, especially if the crafts are quick, like this miniature Christmas tree.

Paper Tree

Materials

Green poster board
Stapler
Acrylic paints and paintbrushes
Cardboard tissue tubes
Large Styrofoam cup
Styrofoam block
18-inch wooden dowel
Glue
Construction paper
White puffy paint

1. Using a dinner plate as a guide, draw a circle on the poster board and cut it out. Cut out five more circles, each an inch or so smaller than the previous one. Make a cut from the edge into the middle of each circle and cut a hole in the center.

2. Tuck one cut edge under the other so that the circle becomes slightly cone-shaped.

3. Staple together the edges. Cut out small triangles around the edges of the circles.

Paint the outside of the cardboard tissue tubes green and cut them into 1½-inch sections. Turn the Styrofoam cup upside down and push the dowel into it, using a Styrofoam block in the cup to hold it secure. Start with one tube ring for the trunk, then stack the green circles on the dowel, separating each one with another ring. Put glue on the top and bottom rims of each ring to secure it. Paint the base and glue a construction paper star on the treetop. Use puffy paint to tip the branches, glue on paper ornaments, and if you like, twine around a store-bought gold garland.

Pasta Angel

We've all heard of angel-hair pasta, but a pasta-haired angel? This one has a mess of jaunty curls and will brighten up any Christmas tree.

Materials

Dried lima bean
Glue
Markers
Assorted dried
    pasta (tiny soup
    pastas, rigatoni,
    noodle, wagon wheel, elbow
    macaroni, bow-tie pasta wings)
Thread

To create a pasta angel, start with a dried lima bean for the head. For curls, let your child brush glue on one side of the bean and press it into a pile of tiny soup pastas. Then, she can use markers to draw on a face. Use a rigatoni noodle for the body. Glue on a wagon-wheel pasta collar, elbow macaroni arms, and bow-tie pasta wings. Glue the head onto the body. For a hanger, tie on a loop of thread below the bean.

Pasta Angel

Air Santa

Air Santa

A high-flying Kriss Kringle, complete with billowing white silk scarf, pilots this old-fashioned biplane. Children who love miniatures and model-making enjoy inventing cool trimmings for this clothespin flying machine.

Materials

Old-fashioned clothespin
2 Popsicle sticks
Wooden coffee stirrer
Fine-point marker, paint, and small
    paintbrushes
Small wooden bead
Glue
White yarn and ribbon
Gold-colored thread

Before your child glues his plane together, he should paint its body (the clothespin), its wings (the Popsicle sticks), and its propeller (the stirrer). With a paintbrush or marker, he can decorate the wooden bead with a Santa face and hat. Next, glue one wing on top of the clothespin and one wing to the bottom of it. Glue the pilot's head in place just in front of the wings. Snap the stirrer in two and affix one half onto the plane for a propeller.

Decorate the biplane with stripes, numbers and letters, polka dots, or holiday designs. Poke a piece of white yarn into the top of the bead to make the pom-pom on Santa's hat and tie a short length of ribbon around Santa's neck for his aviator's scarf.

SHOOTING STAR

Brighten up your Christmas tree with this two-tone star. Draw a five-point star (about 3 inches across) and a slightly smaller star on thin cardboard and cut the shapes out. Trace the larger shape onto purple felt and the smaller shape onto red felt; cut out both stars. Next, cut three 8-inch strands of one color ribbon and three 8-inch strands of another. Gather the ribbons, making sure the ends are even, then staple them together across one end. Lay down the purple star, place the stapled end of the ribbons in the center, squirt with glue, and center the red star on top of the purple one. Once dried, poke a hole in the top and thread a ribbon through it to hang.

Growing Tree

This felt Christmas tree is a true evergreen that can serve as a visual record of your family's growth from year to year. After measuring it, your kids can print their heights on felt ornaments and add them to the tree.

Materials

- 2 yards each of red and green felt
- Fabric glue
- Two plastic 6-foot tape measures
- Felt scraps, assorted colors
- Wooden dowel
- 20-inch piece of yarn
- Fabric paint

Cut a 6- by 2-foot piece of red felt and lay it on a flat surface. Apply glue to one long side. Press a tape measure onto the glued edge, with the 1-inch mark at the bottom of the banner. Glue the second tape measure to the opposite side.

Cut out a 7- by 5-inch tree trunk from the felt scraps. Center it on the banner 2 inches from the bottom and glue it in place. From the green felt, cut five triangles that measure 20 inches tall and 17 inches across the base. Glue a triangle onto the banner, overlapping the top of the trunk by an inch or so. Glue on a second triangle over the top half of the first one. Add the other triangles in the same manner. Top the tree with a felt star.

Fold over the top of the banner and glue the edge to the back. Insert the dowel, then tie the ends of the yarn to the ends of the dowel.

Finally, cut out a bunch of colorful 3½-inch circles on which your kids can note their heights and the year with fabric paint. When gluing the ornaments onto the tree, line up the tops of the circles with the appropriate marks on the tape measures.

Growing Tree

Poinsettia Napkin Rings

Because there's no sewing involved, this craft lets young kids make something elegant with little fuss. It will seem magical to them that three pieces of felt, folded properly, can become a napkin ring so pretty it wins a place at the table.

Materials

- Poster board
- Red and green felt

Measure and cut out poster board templates for the shapes pictured above: a four-pointed leaf (about 5 inches across), four rounded petals (about 3½ inches across), and a dog

Poinsettia Napkin Rings

bone shape (about 9 inches long and 4 inches high). Trace around the leaf template on the green felt and around the petals and dog bone on the red felt.

Cut out the shapes and then cut 1-inch slits in the center of the petals and leaf. Lay the red petals over the green leaf, fold the dog bone shape in half, pull the ends up through the slits, and open the felt into a flower.

Gingerbread Garlands

String these cheery garlands along your mantel, on the front door, or across a special present. Made from old grocery bags, this project is an easy one to whip together at a moment's notice.

Materials

- Brown paper bags
- Construction paper
- Glue
- White puffy paint (for the gingerbread "icing")

Cut a 5- by 16½-inch strip from a brown paper bag. Fold up the rectangle, accordion style, five times. On the top layer, draw a gingerbread person, either by hand or by tracing around a cookie cutter. Make sure the hands and feet extend out to the folded edges.

Now cut through all the layers of paper *except* where the hands and feet touch the fold, as shown below. (If you have young kids, you may want to do this and leave the decorating to them.) Cut scarves, hats, boots, mittens, and skirts out of construction paper and glue them in place. To put the "icing" on the "cookies," use puffy paint. Squirt on buttons, hair, smiles, and eyes. To make a long garland for hanging on the tree, tape together a few chains.

Homemade for the Holidays

**Pipe-Cleanosaurus,
page 188**

FamilyFun
Boredom Busters

Edited by Deanna F. Cook
and the experts at FamilyFun magazine

EDITIONS

NEW YORK

Contents

Pipe Cleaner People,
page 188

Doggy Digs,
page 217

Bottle Beings,
page 280

Horse around,
page 218

The Boredom Bottle,
page 170

Boredom Bottle

CHAPTER ONE

Ready, Set, Play!

What do you do when there's nothing to do? Try a healthy dose
of family fun and games.

IT'S NINE A.M. on a Saturday — the kind of day that is fairly bursting with possibility. Still, the house needs cleaning, the lawn has to be mowed, and that laundry is piled high. So what are you going to do? Squander the day on chores while the kids sit around bored and complain that there's nothing to do? Or find some time to make the day special and have fun together as a family?

At *FamilyFun* magazine, we know this dilemma all too well. Our readers, our contributors, and the parents on our staff all understand that family life is a real juggling act between what we have to do and what we want to do — kick back and have fun with our kids. We may not be able to give you any extra hours to get your chores done, but we can share with you our secrets for making the most of the time you do have.

In this book, we have gathered hundreds of our favorite activities from *FamilyFun*. Each project is family tested and proven to keep boredom at bay.

Some of the ideas are as simple as playing a calculator game when you're waiting in the doctor's office (see page 183) or blowing a double bubble with soap in the backyard (page 192). Others are more involved — crafting a hiking stick for a nature walk (page 258), learning and playing a new game with the kids in the neighborhood (Chapter Three), or cooking up a real mud pie in the kitchen (page 241).

The next time boredom strikes in your household, have your kids flip through these pages and flag a few activities to try. Once you settle on one, you will have the perfect excuse for throwing your responsibilities to the wind. What's more, the project will not require much money or planning — only a firm resolve to seize the day.

So put the rake back in the garage. Childhood doesn't last forever, and your garden, rest assured, will get by just fine until tomorrow. And remember, sometimes a single special afternoon is all you need to make the memory of a lifetime.

Jump-starting Activities

Classic Boredom Busters

+ Make a paper bag puppet
+ Paint a face on a rock
+ Construct a cootie catcher
+ Design a paper airplane
+ Juggle sock balls
+ Build a couch-cushion fort
+ Blow bubbles
+ Play slapjack
+ Fly a kite
+ Sing along with your favorite tunes
+ Read a story together
+ Start a collection (rocks, buttons, bottle caps — whatever's easy to find around the house or yard)
+ Make a paper-clip chain
+ Draw your favorite person (or place, cartoon character, sport, et cetera)
+ Bowl with a tennis ball and a few empty plastic soda bottles
+ Cut up a catalog and make a collage
+ Dab watercolor designs onto paper coffee filters
+ Do a jigsaw puzzle

IF YOU'VE EVER TRIED to pull your child away from an elaborate game of make-believe or a half-done drawing of outer space, then you know the problem is not *keeping* kids interested in an activity — it's getting them started. This book is both a planning tool and an emergency resource: the more involved activities can be planned for and set up in advance, while the hundreds of quick, simple activities can serve as instant antidotes to the inevitable lulls in your kids' imaginations. Here are a few basic tips for inspiring activity:

Post a list of your favorite boredom busters. Your kids can consult it when boredom strikes and add to it as they find new projects they love. Keep a pad of sticky notes handy for marking activities in this book.

Create fun zones. Set up places in the house for your kids to go to when they need something to do. Designate a project table where your kids can work on activities (puzzles, models, crafts) without having to clean up every time.

Nestle books in a comfy reading corner.

Be spontaneous. You'll see that the surprise factor goes a long way toward keeping your kids entertained. Choose an activity that is out of the ordinary, like making aliens out of bottles (see page 280), building a geodesic dome out of newspaper (page 274), or mixing up a batch of washable window paints (see page 276).

Have a few tricks up your sleeve. For that endless snowstorm or week home sick, you'll want to have a handful of extraspecial activities planned. Set aside a giant box of new crayons or put together a box of supplies for a project in this book.

The Boredom Bottle

Here's the next best thing to a genie in a bottle — a handy stash of activities your kids can conjure up with a shake of the wrist.

1. Have your kids label a plastic bottle and decorate it with stickers.

2. Together with your kids, make a list of easy activities or challenges requiring little or no explanation and write the name of each activity on a small paper square (see the list at left for ideas). When your kids aren't looking, you might also want to slip in a few unexpected treats, such as "Bake a batch of chocolate chip cookies."

3. Fold the paper squares in half and drop them into the bottle. When after-school boredom strikes, have your kids shake out an idea — the anticipation and surprise are sure to enhance the fun.

Gathering Objects of Fun

SOME DAYS, a small rubber ball or a handful of shells is all your child needs to keep busy for hours. Other times, all the board games in the world won't fill the deep pit of boredom. Our solution? Keep on hand a good supply of versatile toys and materials — many of the supplies called for in this book will inspire imaginative play. In addition to inviting creativity, a well-stocked craft closet, pantry, and tool kit save you needless trips to the store when your child has the urge to tackle a project. Here are some basics:

Craft supplies. For instant craft projects, stock up on paper (white, construction, and a large roll of newsprint), paints (tempera, watercolor, and acrylic craft), paintbrushes, scissors, glue (glue sticks, white glue, and a low-temperature glue gun), markers, crayons, colored pencils and a sharpener, tape, and clay. Keep your craft supplies stocked, well organized, and accessible in a canvas shoe bag like the one at right.

Game basics. Stock your garage with balls, sports equipment (baseball gloves and bats, soccer balls, bikes and helmets), marbles, and colored chalk. Inside, stack a low shelf with board games, puzzles, and playing cards.

Toys and activity kits. Assemble playthings in well-labeled boxes and store them in key places around your house.

Gather some office supplies, such as paper clips and memo pads, in a Junior Executive Kit (see page 183) and leave them by your desk. Keep a musical instrument box by the stereo for impromptu jams. Stock a magnifying glass, bug jar, and butterfly net in a nature kit in the garage.

Eco-friendly materials. Don't toss handy recyclables, such as egg cartons, toilet paper tubes, bottles, and cardboard boxes — save them for craft projects and make-believe props. Collect nature finds, such as acorns, shells, and shiny rocks for game pieces and quick crafts.

Tools. Providing a selection of kid-size tools is an inviting way to say, "Wanna help?" Have on hand a junior set of cooking utensils (cookie cutters, rolling pins, and more) and kid-size carpentry or gardening tools.

Extras. As you select projects from this book, examine the materials list closely to see what you and your child need to complete the project. Sometimes little things — like googly eyes, pipe cleaners, or craft foam — can make all the difference.

Encouraging Independent Play

Surprise Bags

Fill paper bags with a few ingredients for fast fun and set them aside for emergencies (sick days, snow days, terrible moods, after-school blues). Here are some suggestions:

✦ A bunch of googly eyes, pom-poms, and glue for making creatures

✦ A recipe for play clay (see page 174) with all the ingredients to make it, plus a few sculpting tools

✦ A set of paper dolls, plus scissors and gift wrap for making a wardrobe

✦ A yo-yo and a book of yo-yo tricks

✦ A pair of plain sneakers and some fabric markers

✦ A magnifying glass, a "spy notebook," and a secret code to break

IN AN IDEAL WORLD, our kids would get home from school and we would give them our full attention — the phone would never ring, bills would never need to be paid, and the house would look after itself. But in our actual lives, there are times when our kids need to fend for themselves while we work behind the scenes to make a home for them, and we don't always want to pop in a video. This book is full of projects and ideas kids of all ages can carry out successfully on their own. We've gathered a few tips to encourage further independence:

Encourage pretend play. Left to their own devices, children are inclined to see the world as a place of endless opportunity for fantasy-filled fun. The smallest catalyst from you can inspire wonderful reactions. Gather a pile of old clothes and accessories (see page 222) and see what kinds of costumes they inspire. Or pull a bunch of chairs into a line, and before you know it, your kids will be on an imaginary train headed for the North Pole.

Create play scenarios. Challenge your kids to build a palace for their dolls or to set up a grooming station for their animals. How about a Grand Prix for toy cars? Multiuse toys like blocks, dolls, and adventure sets really foster imaginative play.

Rotate their toys. When kids' toys are out of sight (a few favorites excepted), they are also out of mind. By keeping a box of these playthings hidden away, you will always have an ace in the hole when boredom creeps up. An unexpected reunion with a forgotten Barbie, set of figurines, or board game can really spark up a dull afternoon. Plus, storing some toys in a cupboard means your kids will have less stuff out to keep tidy.

Make cleanup part of the project. Not only will your kids learn responsible habits, but that final five minutes of cleanup may just give you the extra time you need to finish your own project.

Playing With a Purpose

WHEN YOUR KIDS have already put together their puzzles and built an entire city in their sandbox, the best boredom buster might be a real job. If they are young enough, they probably still think housecleaning is some kind of game, and cooking is a science experiment. By helping out, your kids will become contributing members of your household, and they'll have a whole lot of fun doing it. Just be sure to thank them enthusiastically when they finish.

Enlist their help. Fill a bucket with soapy water and let your kids scrub the car or shampoo the dog. Turn on the music and see if they can pick up all their toys by the end of the song. The more fun you make the chore, the more likely it is your kids will chip in.

Do a good deed. Ask for kids' advice about random acts of kindness: they might craft a get-well card for a friend with the flu, bake cookies for an elderly neighbor, or even clean their old toys and donate them to a child in need.

Give kids real responsibility. Kids love to be praised, and they love to feel important. Take advantage of this by giving them challenging and rewarding tasks: watering plants, caring for pets, or cooking a pancake breakfast for the whole family.

The Cleanup Game

"To make housecleaning fun, I made up an activity called the Cleanup Game. Everyone in the family takes paper and a pencil and walks from room to room looking for messes. Each of us records instructions on the paper, such as 'Pick up and fold hand towels' or 'Put away Monopoly game.' These commands are put in a bag, and everyone takes turns picking them and doing the jobs. It's a riot, and it teaches kids to notice messes."

— Carol Saunders, Livingston, New Jersey

Ready, Set, Play!

Cultivating Creativity

Endless Roll of Paper

What can you do with a large roll of white or butcher paper? Anything you like!

+ Make a cheering banner to decorate the front of your house ("Welcome Home" or "Happy Spring" is reason enough to have a celebration)

+ Draw an imaginary roadway and city for toy cars, or a magical landscape for figurines

+ Illustrate a running story with panels you add to daily

F NECESSITY IS the mother of invention, then boredom must be the father of creativity. We've found that sparking bored kids' imaginations requires three things: having art supplies on hand, encouraging pretend play, and creating an environment in which imaginations flourish.

Emphasize the process. When beginning a craft or cooking project, it's fine to have an end result in mind — older kids, particularly, are proud of finished projects. But try not to be so determined to follow directions that your child can't add his own flair. The end result, after all, is no more important than the steps that lead up to it.

Model enthusiasm. Your willingness to plunk a brush into a jar of paint will inspire your kids to do the same. Similarly, if you're game to join their imaginary games, your kids may feel even more excited about playing them.

Allow plenty of free time. Imagination thrives in an unhurried environment. As often as your schedules allow, let your children just hang out, with no planned activities. You may be amazed by the games and activities that evolve spontaneously in this free — and *freeing* — time.

Best-ever Play-clay Recipe

When it comes to busting boredom, a batch of this sculptable stuff is like money in the bank. Store it in airtight containers for weeks of hands-on fun.

INGREDIENTS

1 cup all-purpose flour	1 cup water
1/2 cup salt	1 teaspoon vegetable oil
1/2 teaspoon cream of tartar	Food coloring

Mix the flour, salt, cream of tartar, water, and oil in a saucepan. Cook over medium heat until it holds together (keep mixing or it will stick to the bottom of the pan). When the clay is cool enough to touch, knead it on a floured surface, divide it into smaller balls, and add a different shade of food coloring to each ball.

Making Time for Family

W E LIVE IN an overscheduled age, and there are lots of duties we parents cannot avoid. But there may be some we can postpone for the sake of creating time to spend with our families doing something fun, or doing nothing at all.

Let the chores pile up. Decide where your schedule can give a little — and let it. This may mean a shaggier lawn, it's true, but you can promise yourself to turn into the perfect homemaker after the kids leave for college. Do a project or take a field trip with them instead.

Play with your kids. Your kneeling down on the floor to *vroom* trains around with your children will give them — and you — tremendous pleasure. Throw a football around the yard. Spend the afternoon hunched over the Monopoly board. You'll feel like a kid again, and you'll get to know your own kids better.

Have a do-nothing day. Commit a full day to relaxing play with your family. This means no big outings, no big projects, and no serious entertaining. Play the games your kids are always begging you to join in on, or sit on the floor with coloring books. Read a story together, even if your kids can read on their own. Prepare leisurely meals together.

Watch TV deliberately. Is there a show your whole family loves? By all means watch it together. There is a wealth of wonderful educational programming that can make for a fun evening tube-side. But you may want to let the television stay quiet sometimes. Keep an eye on channel surfing as an antidote to boredom.

Make Fridays Family Night. Make a weekly date to play a family game. Rent a video, pop popcorn, and snuggle under a big blanket for movie night. Eat dinner in your pajamas or all dressed up. Have a monthly planned outing to a restaurant or show, or set up a tent and have an indoor camp-in.

However you do it, making regular time for your family to spend together will guarantee a great time — and a treasure trove of wonderful memories

Family Traditions

Set up a monthly date with each child. Whether you go out to lunch or see a movie, both you and your child will look forward to this one-on-one time.

Keep a family journal in a prominent place in your house and encourage everybody to contribute at least one entry a week.

Talk about your day. At dinnertime, go around the table and have everyone share the Best Thing/Worst Thing that happened that day.

Have a TV-free week. Pull the plug on the TV for one week and fill your time with family activities: biking, walking, swimming.

Backpack Danglers,
page 190

CHAPTER TWO

Instant Fun

In a pinch? Kids getting bored? Thirty minutes to dinner? Try our quick games, easy crafts, and other ideas to fill 15 minutes of free time.

WHEN OUR KIDS step off the school bus after a long day of dueling fractions, they are ready to devote themselves wholeheartedly to the pursuit of fun. But by the time they unwind, eat a snack, and unload their backpacks, there's sometimes as little as a half hour of free time left before dinner.

The truth is, much of family life takes place in brief intervals: the 15 minutes you have before soccer practice; the 30 minutes until your child gets picked up for a play date; the 20 minutes riding in the car. These slices of time are usually unplanned — and unwanted. But they don't have to be. Instead of approaching them as time to kill, we advocate appreciating such snatches as time to fill.

With that carpe diem attitude in mind, we offer you a chapter full of our favorite 15-minute-and-under activities: games, crafts, and tricks to harness the bits of spare time that life offers you.

When you have a few minutes of free time, let your children pick an idea from the following pages to suit their mood and companions (or lack thereof). The projects in this chapter require only readily available supplies and very little, if any, parental assistance. Some, like Crocodile Crawl on page 195, are rowdy energy burners; others, like the quick and easy Foil Family on page 184, can happily occupy a lone child when zip is in short supply. These are just a few ideas for living fully in the moments you find. To make the most of your family time, keep these fast-fun principles in mind:

Find fun where (and when) you can. Whether you're at a restaurant, in the car, or just plain waiting, you may discover that you have much more family time than you ever thought possible. Instead of making grocery shopping a chore, for instance, turn it into a field trip and send your kids on a hunt for the cheapest cornflakes or the products that match the coupons. Stuck in traffic?

Pipe Cleaner People, page 188

Peanut Pal, page 187

See who can find the most animals in passing billboards, or who can come up with the catchiest blues riff in the backseat.

Prepare an Emergency Fun Kit. Fill a bag with props and keep it on hand to chase away any sudden bouts of boredom. Consider including such versatile items as tooth-picks, a rubber ball, buttons, a full deck of cards, dice, pipe cleaners, rubber bands, aluminum foil, and marbles.

Stock up on supplies. Having basic art supplies accessible can do wonders to keep your kids busy and independent. A pad of paper and a pencil, crayons and coloring books, scissors, stickers, construction paper, glue stick, and play clay — with minimal setup, these basics can spearhead a 10-minute doodle or quick paper craft.

Use your imagination. Once you get going, your kids will come up with their own quick games. When it comes to instant fun, silli-ness and spontaneity are true virtues.

5-minute Fun

Need some ideas for licket split fun? Sometimes simp is better:

* Thumb wrestle
* Hold a jacks tournamer
* Stage a silly-song session with a tape recorder
* Turn a paper tablecloth into a giant crayon canv
* Play crazy eights
* Build structures with toothpicks and mini marshmallows
* Spin a yo-yo
* Ref an impromptu contest with an egg tim

Tabletop Games

QUICK GAME

Tabletop Hockey

2 If you want to score some instant fun on a rainy day, cut a plastic berry box in half. Invert one half and set it at one end of a table. Now your kids can line up at the opposite end and try to score by flicking button pucks into the net.

EASY CRAFT

Play With Buttons

1 What do you do on those days when your kids' favorite toys suddenly lose their entertainment value? Empty out your button box on the kitchen table and try the following quick activities.

MATERIALS

   Assorted buttons

   Glue, fabric, yarn, poster board

   Pie plate

   Elastic thread

   Dabble in button art: Glue buttons and bits of fabric or yarn onto poster board to create a textured portrait or landscape.

   Pan for buttons: Place a pie plate on the floor near a wall, line up 10 to 12 feet away, and see who can pitch the most buttons off the wall and into the pan.

   Make button jewelry: String elastic thread through the holes of assorted flat buttons, then tie it into a loop for a wrist or ankle bracelet.

   Build a button tower: See who can stack the most buttons without toppling the tower.

INSTANT TOY

Funny Faces

3 This felt man is a master of disguise — just give him a shake and he'll put on a new face. With a marker, draw a profile of a person, leaving out the front of his face, on a felt-covered piece of cardboard. Use a nail to poke a hole in the forehead and the neck, then loosely thread through a length of ball chain, taping the ends to the back of the cardboard. Now hold the drawing flat and jiggle it — the chain will form a nose and chin.

Pinch Your Pennies

5 With this coin-gobbling bank, saving your pennies can become downright habit-forming.

MATERIALS

- **Poster board or card stock**
- **Mason jar with a metal rim (you won't need its flat inner lid)**
- **Glue**
- **2 googly eyes**
- **3 pom-poms**
- **3 pipe cleaners**

For the bug's face, cut out a poster board circle to fit inside the metal rim of the mason jar. Use scissors to cut out a rectangular mouth large enough for a quarter to drop through.

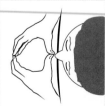

Glue on googly eyes and a pom-pom nose. Set the finished face on top of the jar opening, then screw on the rim. To add antennae, wrap a pipe cleaner around the metal rim, twisting the ends together once to secure. Then bend the ends slightly to form a V and glue pom-poms onto the tips. Use the same method to attach a pair of pincher arms to the jar just below the metal rim, this time twisting together the pipe cleaner ends to within a half inch of the tips.

A Penny Pool

4 For some quick fun on a rainy day, ask your child to guess how many drops of water he can fit on a penny. Then hand him a drinking straw for a dropper and see how close he comes to his estimate. Because water droplets cling together, he may fit as many as 24 drops if he's careful!

FUN FACT

Here's a penny for your thoughts: the coin-y motto "E pluribus unum" means "One from many" and describes the United States (although we think it's a pretty good slogan for a family too!).

Penny Basketball

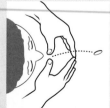

6 Wanna shoot some hoops? Find a penny, a partner, and a tabletop and follow these NPBA (National Penny Basketball Association) instructions:

1. Put the penny into play by spinning it on edge.

2. Trap the coin between your thumbs, one on each side of the coin.

3. With the sides of your pinkies on the table and your fingertips together (see drawing), flick the penny up with your thumbs so that it swooshes through the basket that your opponent, across from you, is making with her fingers. Take turns shooting. You score two points per basket. The first player to score 10 points wins — and keeps the penny.

House of Cards

7 Requiring little more than a deck of cards and a box of toothpicks, this no-frills game is a testament to the adage that less is more.

MATERIALS

Paper and pencil

Deck of cards (including 2 jokers)

Box of toothpicks

The object of the game is to build a house (strictly two-dimensional) out of toothpicks. Whoever finishes construction first is the winner. For each player, draw a simple model house like the one below on a sheet of paper. Make sure you indicate the number of toothpicks needed (you can do this by using broken lines, one for each toothpick).

Shuffle the cards and place the entire deck facedown on the table. Players alternate picking a card from the top of the deck. Moves depend on which card you pick (see "What the Cards Mean," at right).

Once your child has chosen a card and followed the directions, she should place it facedown next to the original deck. If players run out of cards before the game ends (and it's likely that they will), reuse the discards, shuffling them first. **Tip:** Each player might vary the game by drawing a different house — a tent, say, or a treehouse.

What the Cards Mean

Any face card (king, queen, or jack): Take one toothpick and use it to build your house.

Any ace: Take two toothpicks and use them to build your house.

Joker: Put back one toothpick. (If you don't have one yet, do nothing.)

Any eight: Use one of your toothpicks to help build the house of the opponent on your right. (As with the joker, if you don't have any toothpicks yet, you don't have to do anything.)

Two of spades: Players who draw this unlucky card must put back all their toothpicks and start over.

All other cards: No value.

BRAIN BOOSTER

A Straw Stumper

8 Arrange 12 drinking straws, as shown. Can you remove two so that you're left with just two complete squares? (Answer below.)

Answer: Remove any two adjacent straws of the four inside the large square. You'll be left with a small square inside a large square.

FUN FACT

Question:

Which straw broke the camel's back?

Answer:

At .025 ounce each, that would be roughly the 786,000th!

INSTANT TREAT

Citrus Sipper

9 You don't need a pitcher to make this lemonade — in fact, you don't even need to stir. Simply break a peppermint stick in two and insert one half directly into an uncut lemon. Suck on the peppermint stick as you normally would, and after a few minutes (surprise!), you'll taste lemon juice! Here's how it works: as you suck on the candy, tiny holes are created, turning the stick into a straw. The sour juice of the lemon combines with the sweet and minty taste of the peppermint stick for an instant treat.

TRY THIS NOW

Turn Straw Into Gold

10 Just because restaurants give them out by the handful doesn't mean straws aren't a valuable raw material for the creative crafter. Consider these two nifty projects:

MATERIALS

Drinking straws
Ping-Pong ball
Tape
Magazine cover

Balancing Ball Blower

This probably demonstrates some key principle of aerodynamics, but all we know is it's cool. Carefully slice a flexible straw's end and bend out the arms. Place a Ping-Pong ball in the cradle and blow hard and steady. The ball will hover. Sheer magic!

Double-O Glider

Believe us, this thing really flies. Cut two strips, 6 inches and 9 inches long and at least an inch wide, from the magazine cover. Tape into O's and slide them into slits cut in the straw's ends. Hold the straw with the small O facing forward and throw.

Home Office Kit

11 When you are busy paying bills or working at home, hand your kids this Junior Executive Kit so they can play independently. With the right supplies, business will boom.

MATERIALS

- **Inexpensive briefcase or plastic case**
- **Calculator**
- **Notebook**
- **Pens, paper clips, and other office supplies**

Assemble a home office kit in an old briefcase or plastic container, using assorted office supplies from your own stash. Include Post-its, a roll of tape, a stapler, paper clips, and other supplies for your pint-size CEO. For fun, include a set of business cards (printed up at a copy shop or on your home computer).

TRY THIS NOW

Word Processing

12 This game is great for entertaining your kids during those endless doctor's office waits. Just turn on a pocket calculator and challenge them to see how many number combinations they can come up with that spell words when the calculator is turned upside down. Here are a few numbers to get you started (for answers, see page 313).

a. 663   d. 77345   g. 7714   j. 637
b. 604   e. 5508   h. 618   k. 35007
c. 771   f. 733   i. 3045   l. 7738

TRY THIS NOW

Clipboards, Inc.

13 Hand your kids clipboards (to set an industrious mood) and give them each an assignment. For example, they might need to draw a treasure map, invent a better flyswatter, create a secret code, or write a mock newspaper article about what's happening outside the window.

FAMILYFUN READER IDEA

Bored Book

One mom's list of things to do when there's nothing to do

"When my daughter, Jade, couldn't find anything to do, I came up with the perfect solution. I made a list of all the activities we have around the house, including toys, sports equipment, puzzles, and board, electronic, and computer games. I compiled the list, added pictures to make it look like a fun vacation brochure, and placed it in a three-ring binder. Because many of the toys and games were tucked away, we had forgotten what we had. Now whenever Jade and her younger sister, Jazlyn, are looking for something to do, I refer them to our book."

— *Cindy McNeely, Tallahassee, Florida*

Quick Crafts

Pet Rocks

14 Part of the fun with this 1970s-inspired craft is hunting for the perfect rocks to decorate. This makes it a fitting project to do after a nature hike. Encourage your kids to look for natural features in the rocks that resemble noses, chins, ears, and so on. Help little kids stick pebbles, googly eyes, and pom-poms in place with double-sided tape or glue. Kids can use fun fur for hair, mustaches, and beards or apply additional features with acrylic paint.

Party of One

"To help my five-year-old, Amy, learn to entertain herself, we invented the 15-minute game. I fill paper bags with materials for a short project, seal them, and keep them for special times. For example, in one bag, I placed the makings for a bird's nest, including yarn, twigs, clay, and even candy eggs. I have also filled bags with postcards, pens, and stamps for writing to Grammy, or simply enclosed a long-forgotten toy. The game has been a hit — I get 15 minutes when I need it, and she gets a new activity to enjoy."

— Jennifer Caputo,
Lawrenceville, Georgia

The Foil Family

15 Unlike your average tin men, these foil characters have plenty of heart. All it takes is a pinch here and there to make them strike any pose your child likes.

MATERIALS

Rectangular sheet of aluminum foil (about 10 by 15 inches)
Scissors

Make two cuts down from the top of the sheet and one cut up from the bottom, as shown below (for a pet, make two cuts up from the bottom). Now scrunch together the center of the sheet to form a torso and pinch and mold the upper corners into arms and the lower corners into legs and feet. Finally, shape the upper midsection into a head and neck (the lower midsection makes the pet's tail).

Release a Paper Dove

16 Here's one critter that you won't mind invading your next picnic: a high-flying dove made from paper plates and plastic spoons.

MATERIALS

Paper plate
Pebble
2 plastic spoons
Rubber band
Tape
Markers

Cut the plate in half, then cut one half into three equal wedges and tape one wedge to the bottom of the intact half, as shown.

Now sandwich the pebble between the spoon bowls and bind the spoons with the rubber band.

Finally, tape the spoons to the bottom of the paper plate half and draw a face on the top spoon.

To make the dove fly, throw it like a paper airplane. Adjust the pebble size to improve flight.

185

Paint to Music

17 **For a quick and soulful project, let your kids put on some tunes, grab a paintbrush, and paint what they hear. Does the mood of the music suggest a color? How about painting the shape of a slow melody or moving the brush along with the energy of the rhythm? Try Vivaldi's** Four Seasons, **the Beatles, melodic pop songs with varied textures, Prokofiev's** Peter and the Wolf, **Saint-Saëns's** Carnival of the Animals, **or almost anything by Mozart.**

Sponge Away Boredom

18 Transform a sponge into a squeaky-clean superhero. With suction cups for feet, he's well equipped to cling to a window and ward off a case of the rainy-day blues.

MATERIALS

Glue

2 large googly eyes

Small pom-pom

Small sponge

Permanent marker

2 rubber suction cups

3 pipe cleaners

Craft foam

Ribbon

Glue the googly eyes and a pom-pom nose onto the upper front of the sponge (the type that stays soft when it dries). Use a permanent marker to draw on the mouth.

For legs, remove the metal hooks from the suction cups. Tightly wrap the middle of a pipe cleaner around the knob atop each cup, then twist together the ends of the pipe cleaner, as shown above. Insert the tops of the legs into the bottom of the sponge, using a little glue to secure them.

To make each arm, insert an end of a 4-inch pipe cleaner length into the side of the sponge and use glue to hold it. Next, cut two small ovals out of craft foam and glue them sandwich style onto the end of the arm to create a hand.

Now cut out a craft foam cape. Glue the midsection of a length of ribbon to the upper back edge of the cape. Once the cape is thoroughly dry, tie it onto the sponge just above the arms.

Instant Stickers

19 Kids can never have too many stickers, and here's a fun way to keep your family well supplied. Cut a bunch of pictures from old magazines, comic books, or gift wrap. Then dissolve 2 tea-spoons of flavored gelatin in 5 teaspoons of boiling water (adults only). With a small paint-brush, coat the backs of the cutouts with a thin layer of gelatin solution. Let them dry, and the stickers are ready to lick and stick.

Bean Scene

20 Want to see bean soup moonlight glamorously as a mosaic? Have your child arrange a bunch of colorful dried peas and beans into a festive legume collage. To begin, sketch a design on a piece of corrugated cardboard. Next, use a paintbrush to cover a small portion of the design with a thick coat of white glue. Now arrange beans on top of the glued area, following the drawn figures and shapes. Continue gluing beans until the entire design is filled in.

Peanut Pals

21 If you're looking for a quick and easy project to keep your peanut gallery amused, we recommend rounding up a few peanut buddies.

MATERIALS

Brown lunch bag
Newspaper or packing peanuts
Tape
Colored markers
Brown paper
Glue

Stuff the lunch bag with newspaper or, better yet, packing peanuts. Seal the top of the bag with tape, then scrunch the middle so that it resembles the shape of a real peanut. Draw on a face with colored markers. For stalklike arms and legs, accordion-fold brown paper strips and glue them to the body. Lastly, glue peanut-shaped paper feet to the ends of the legs.

FUN FACT The average American eats about 11 pounds of peanuts per year, and most kids will have consumed some 1,500 PB & J's by the time they've graduated from high school.

Bean Soup Relay

22 Ending up with the biggest hill of beans is the goal in this 3-minute relay. For each team, place a bowl filled with dried beans at the starting line, then set a grocery bag 20 feet from each bowl. When the race begins, the first person on each team uses a wooden spoon to scoop up beans from his team's bowl, then races off to dump them in the team bag. He hands off the spoon to the next person, who follows suit, and so on, until the time is up. The team with the most beans in its bag wins.

Pipe-Cleanosaurus

23 This lumbering giant roamed the earth during the Craft-aceous Period, which followed the snack and rest periods.

MATERIALS

- 8 green pipe cleaners
- Glue
- Googly eyes

STEP 1: Connect three green pipe cleaners end to end.

STEP 2: Wrap them around a thick marker for the body.

STEP 3: Connect two green pipe cleaners end to end.

STEP 4: Wrap half around a pencil for the head, then coil some for the neck. Leave a 1-inch stem.

STEP 5: Attach the head and neck by inserting the stem into the body. Glue.

STEP 6: For the tail, coil one green pipe cleaner around a pencil, leaving a 1-inch stem.

STEP 7: Insert the attaching stem into the body.

STEP 8: Make legs by bending two green pipe cleaners into V's, then coiling each end around a pencil.

STEP 9: Insert the legs into the body, between the coils. Glue. Glue on googly eyes.

Pipe Cleaner People

24 Don't be put off by their twisted appearance: making pipe cleaner humans is a snap. Fortunately for the pipe cleaner sculptor, pipe cleaners come in all colors — just like people.

MATERIALS

- Pipe cleaners
- Fingernail clippers
- Glue
- Googly eyes
- Markers

STEP 1: Make a V with a pipe cleaner and twist a small loop at the top.

STEP 2: Twist together the two ends a few times to make the torso.

STEP 3: Coil another pipe cleaner around a pencil.

STEP 4: Slide the coil onto the torso.

STEP 5: Clip a pipe cleaner in half with fingernail clippers and slide one half through the loop.

STEP 6: Wrap a pipe cleaner around a pencil and stick it on the loop to make a head.

STEP 7: Make loops at the ends of the arms and legs for hands and feet.

STEP 8: Glue on googly eyes and pipe cleaner accessories: hair (a C-shaped snippet of brown), a necktie (looped from red), and a briefcase (a length of black bent back and forth).

Thread Heads

HOMEMADE TOY

Hunt for Buried Treasure

25

At first glance, this homemade toy may look like nothing more than a bottle of rice, but roll it once or twice and a host of hidden objects will appear before your eyes.

MATERIALS

Clean, clear plastic soda bottle

Assorted trinkets (beads, buttons, charms, plastic insects, dime-store jewelry)

Uncooked rice

Remove the label from the bottle. Gather up the trinkets and put them in the bottle. Add rice to fill the bottle two thirds of the way, then tightly screw on the cap. Shake well to conceal the objects. Now your child can twist and turn the toy to see how many treasures can be spotted inside. **Note:** Heavy objects such as coins and pebbles tend to gravitate into the middle, while lightweight plastic beads, buttons, and trinkets are easier to spot.

26

Grab your sewing basket and round up a few of these amusing kooky characters.

To make one, peel away the labels from the top and bottom of a plastic thread spool. Then cut yarn into two dozen 6-inch lengths and divide them into four groups of six. Sandwich each group in a pipe cleaner bent in half. Then fit each set of the pipe cleaner ends into a separate hole in the center of the spool, pulling the ends through just far enough to secure the yarn in place.

When all of the yarn hair is attached, trim four of the pipe cleaner ends protruding from the bottom of the spool so that they are flush with the plastic (a parent's job). Pose the remaining four ends to resemble arms and legs. Finally, glue button eyes and a nose to the thread-covered spool for a face.

TRY THIS NOW

No-peeking Sketches

27

With its potential for silliness, this fun drawing game is a great thing to try with your kids. To begin, write the names of a dozen simple items, such as house, dog, plane, and so on, on strips of paper, place the strips in a hat, and have each person take one. Without showing their word to anyone else, players take turns sketching the object with their eyes closed, while the others attempt to guess what is being drawn.

Backpack Danglers

28 As any kid will tell you, there's no greater fashion faux pas than a naked backpack. So we devised these jazzy danglers to dress up even the drabbest canvas. You'll need to lay in some inexpensive supplies ahead of time, but once they're handy, your kids can whip up new danglers to suit their daily whims. We've described three methods below, but your kids will undoubtedly dream up their own.

MATERIALS

Narrow ribbon

Buttons with a large threading loop on the back

Large safety pins and diaper pins

Elastic cord

Beads

A

Button Dangler: Fold 8 inches of ribbon in half and thread the loop through the opening of a button. Tie the loose ends in a knot beneath the button to hold it in place. Thread the loop through the closed safety pin, then the button through the loop, as shown above (A).

B

Diaper Pin Dangler: Fold a 10-inch length of elastic cord in half and loop onto a safety pin, as shown at left (B). Thread beads onto the cord, then knot the cord beneath the last bead. Repeat with three to five more strands.

Bead Dangler (shown at top): Tie a few short lengths of elastic cord onto the circular joint of a safety pin. Thread beads onto the cords, then knot the cords beneath the last bead on each strand.

Bounce a Band Ball

29 Instead of stuffing stray elastics into a desk drawer or (worse!) shooting them across a classroom, your kids can turn them into a bouncy ball with this simple project. To make one, pinch together the ends of a single rubber band and tie it into a loose double knot. Wrap and twist a second band around the knot repeatedly, until it is taut. Continue adding rubber bands one at a time until the ball is as large as you like, or you run out of bands. You also can speed along the process by starting out with an inner core made of wadded-up newspaper or aluminum foil and then covering it with rubber bands.

Friendship Pal

30 Here's a new twist on a summer classic: the friendship bracelet. These dolls are even quicker to make, and they use just one knot, a simple half hitch (see Figure A, below). Kids can make a bunch for their friends and themselves, then pin them to shirts, use them for zipper pulls, or dangle them from their backpacks.

MATERIALS

Embroidery floss

Safety pin

Two-hole button

Permanent marker

1. Cut eight pieces of floss, each about 12 inches long. Hold all the strands together and tie a knot roughly 5 inches from one end (the extra will become hair). Stick the safety pin through the knot and pin it onto your pants or backpack to make the knotting easier.

2. Separate out two strands on each side for arms. Divide the remaining four strands into two groups (call them pair X and pair Y), which will be knotted to each other to form the body, then knotted individually to form the legs. Begin by holding pair X straight and taut. Loop pair Y over pair X, then send it back up through the loop (as shown in A, below). Pull up the knot to the top and tighten. For the next knot, alternate the strands, holding pair Y straight and taut and sending pair X over and up through the loop. Pull the knot up snugly to the first one. Repeat, alternating sides, until the body is about an inch long.

3. To make the left leg, separate the two strands of pair X and loop one around the other. Continue, but don't alternate sides: simply knot one strand around the other until the leg is about three quarters of an inch long (B). Tie off the ends and trim. Repeat for the right leg and both arms.

4. Attach the button head by running another piece of floss through the buttonholes and knotting it in place above the body (C). Make a hairdo for your pal from the loose ends and draw a face on the button with a permanent marker.

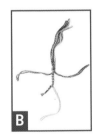

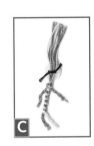

Make Your Mark

Sure, you can color and draw with markers, but what about all the other amazing superpowers they have? Here are some of our favorite marker tips and techniques.

With permanent markers, draw on a balloon, let dry, then inflate it to see the art grow.

Make a drawing with a white crayon, then color over it with a washable marker.

Photocopy a photograph, then colorize it with markers of different colors.

To create a metallic look, draw with permanent markers on a sheet of aluminum foil.

Wacky Fun

Blow Bubbles

31 Need some good, clean fun for your kids and their friends? Just mix up a batch of our tried-and-true bubble solution, twist a few pipe cleaners into homemade wands, and try your luck at a couple of bubble tricks on the next page.

INGREDIENTS

3 cups water

1 cup dishwashing liquid

¹/₃ cup light corn syrup

In a large plastic container, stir the water, dishwashing liquid, and corn syrup. (Although you can use any brand of dish detergent, we found that Joy and Dawn produce the best bubbles.) Store the homemade soap in a covered container. When your kids are ready for some bubble-making fun, make a few homemade wands, following the directions on the next page. **Tip:** The best time to blow bubbles is when the air is calm and muggy, such as after a rain shower (bubbles last longer when there's more humidity).

FUN FACT The longest bubble was 105 feet long, created with a wand and home-made soap by Alan McKay of New Zealand.

TRY THIS NOW

How to Blow a Double Bubble

32 Here's a trick from bubble-ologist Casey Carle (www.bubblemania.com). 1. Balance a bubble on your wand. 2. Wet the bottom two thirds of a straw in bubble solution. 3. Poke the straw through the side of the bubble until the straw's end is in the bubble's center (wetting the straw keeps the bubble from popping). Blow gently!

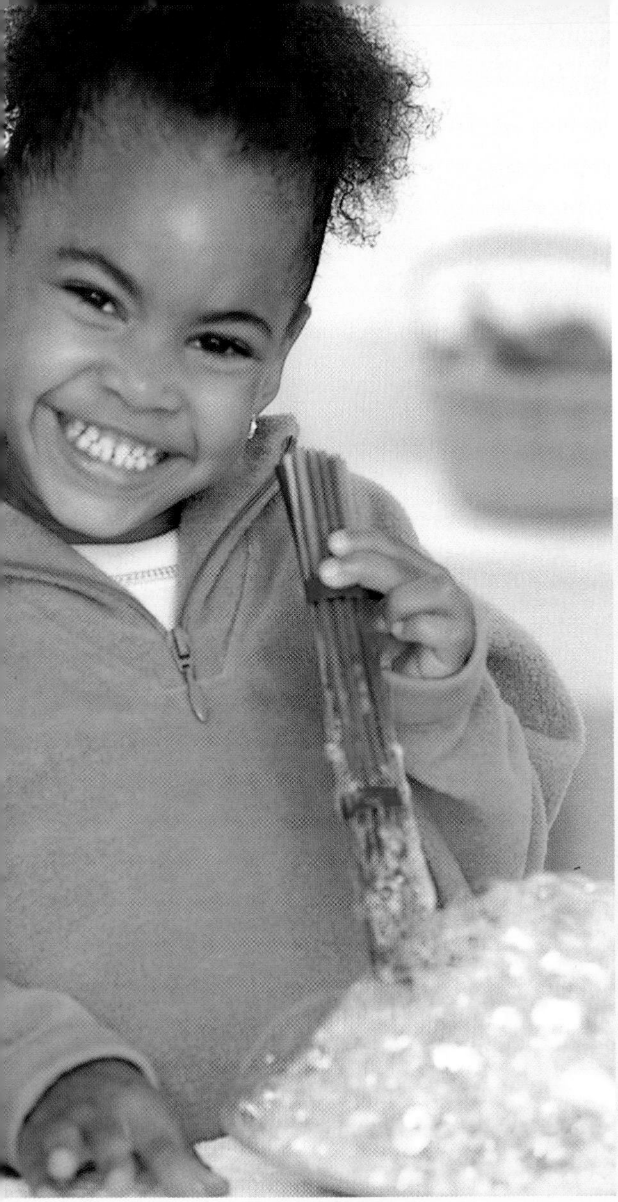

Make Tiny Bubbles

33 For a slew of miniature bubbles, tape together a bunch of plastic drinking straws, as shown in the photo at left. Dip one end in the bubble solution, hold the other about 1 inch from your mouth (do not put your lips on the straws), and blow.

Bubble Magic

34 Need an ice-breaker for a summer party? Set out a pie plate filled with home-made bubble soap (see recipe on the previous page), try these two tricks, and your guests will be bubbling over in no time.

Poke it: Blow a bubble and catch it in your hand. Stick one finger into a cup of water and then immediately through the top of the bubble. It won't pop!

Hand it over: See if you can catch one bubble in your palm. The trick is to dip your hand in the soapy solution first, since it's dryness, not sharpness, that usually bursts a bubble. Then try passing it to someone else.

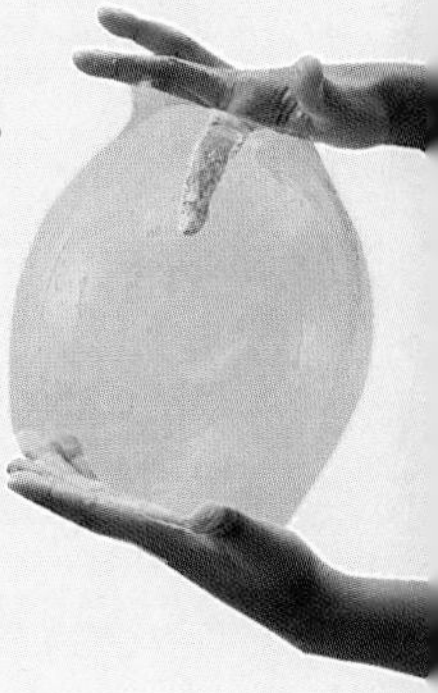

Homemade Wonder Wands

35 When you're creating something magical, the right wand is crucial (just ask Harry Potter). Here are a few good ones — from mini to monster — all made from household items.

MINIATURE PAPER CLIP WAND

How to make it: Bend a paper clip into a bubble wand shape. **Dipping container:** Cap from a small jar. **What you'll get:** A single baby bubble.

FLYSWATTER BUBBLETTE WAND

How to make it: Grab a clean fly-swatter. **Dipping container:** Flying disk turned upside down. **What you'll get:** Cumulus-cloudlike masses of mini bubbles.

CLASSIC COAT HANGER WAND

How to make it: Bend a hanger into a circle and handle. Wrap the circle with string. **Dipping container:** Upside-down trash can lid. **What you'll get:** A looong bubble.

GIANT HULA WAND

How to make it: Dig out your hula hoop. **Dipping container:** Kiddie pool (hold hoop as shown above). **What you'll get:** Say aloha to the biggest bubbles ever.

String Knot

36 Your mission? To tie a knot in a 2-foot-long string without letting go with either hand. It's a cinch if you cross your arms first and then pick up the string by both ends. Next, uncross your arms, and you'll automatically knot the string.

Doorway Liftoff

38 Here's a fun way to get a rise out of your child. Ask him to stand in a doorway with his arms at his sides. Then have him press his arms outward, so that the backs of his hands and wrists push against the door frame, for a full minute. Next, have him quickly step forward out of the doorway. What happens? His arms will seem to float up and away of their own accord!

Why? While he stood in the doorway, his arms became accustomed to pressing out against the resistance of the door frame. Once he stepped out of the doorway, his arms were still trying to press outward, and with no door frame to hold them back, away they went.

Hole-in-one Relay

37 In this game, players have to pucker up for a sticky pass-off. The object is to pass a Life Savers candy from teammate to teammate using only drinking straws held between their teeth.

MATERIALS

Plastic drinking straws

Life Savers candies

First, cut a bunch of straws into halves and give one to each player. Then ask teammates to line up side by side with everyone holding their half straws between their lips, keeping their arms behind their backs. Slip a Life Saver (alternatively, you can try using rigatoni noodles and straws, or even doughnuts and chopsticks) onto the straw belonging to the first person in each line.

When the relay starts, players try to slide their team's candy from straw to straw (remember, no hands allowed) all the way down the line and then back again. If a candy gets dropped along the way, that team must start again from the beginning of the line. The first group to complete the task wins.

MORE WACKY FUN Still looking for a silly game? Race through the Stuff-stacle Course on page 204 or splash in the Soggy Jog on page 205.

Shadow Show

39 Looking for a bit of fun before the sun goes down? Invite your kids to join in some shadow fun and games.

Dancing shadows: Pair up and, keeping the beat to a familiar tune, see if you can make your shadows clap hands without your real hands actually touching.

Hold a shadow race: Line up all the contestents with the sun at their backs so that the heads of their shadows are just behind the starting line (taller kids may need to stand a bit farther back than shorter children). The person whose shadow crosses the finish line first wins.

Martian Mallow Meltdown

40 It's an alien! It's a s'more! Actually, it's both, made with just a few scissor snips and a blast of "radiation" in the microwave.

1. Snip a marshmallow into a triangular head and another into a torso with arms. Insert mini chocolate chip eyes.

2. Assemble the Martian Mallow on a chocolate "flying saucer" wafer. Place him in your nuclear transporter (microwave).

3. Ten seconds on high, and he's s'morphed! After he cools down, let him visit Planet Mouth.

Crawl Like a Crocodile

41 When a crocodile races across land, it drops onto its belly and weaves from side to side, moving all four legs as fast as it can. Your kids can get up to croc speed in this wriggly challenge. The game starts with three or more players lying on their bellies, about 5 feet apart from one another. The object is to wiggle across the floor (tummy touching) and tag all of the other players with your hand before they tag you.

CHAPTER THREE

Backyard Games

Our favorite lawn, pool, and blacktop games are a snap to learn — and will motivate even the busiest families to come out and play

ROWING UP in a family of nine, *FamilyFun* backyard expert John Porcino always looked forward to those summer evenings when the kids could persuade Mom or Dad to play outside with them after dinner. Whether the game was kickball or kick the can, charades or flashlight tag, those lingering summer hours in the backyard remain some of his happiest memories. "These days after dinner, it's *my* shirt that gets tugged on by kids, specifically by my son and daughter and their neighborhood friends," John tells us. They know that John's collected quite a pocketful of games, having worked as a camp director, teacher, and storyteller. "Some evenings, my thoughts lean more toward a lounge chair and the newspaper," John admits, "but then I recall the delight I felt as a child and try to dig out a game or two."

The following games include some of the Porcino family's favorites — and a host of other popular games from the pages of *FamilyFun* magazine. Like the best backyard classics, they require little or no equipment, are easy to learn, and can be played by groups of all sizes. Ever adaptable, they serve equally well as a 5-minute diversion before bathtime or as an entire day's entertainment, ended only by the sounds of parents calling in their reluctant kids through the darkness.

Playing simple outdoor games with friends and family does more than just pass the time. Kids huff and puff and get into shape without realizing that's what they're doing. And, as John points out, "It lets us rediscover a bit of childhood's magic." That's something to keep in mind next time you too feel the tug.

Allow us to offer some homespun backyard coaching:

Play along with your kids. Kids and parents have been playing games together as long as there have been backyards and Saturdays. But for the

Chalk games, page 209

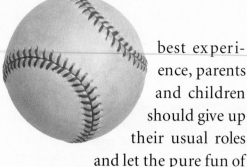

best experience, parents and children should give up their usual roles and let the pure fun of the game take over. Laugh a lot, be silly, and enjoy the fresh air.

Change the rules to suit your audience. When playing games with your kids, it's important to adapt the games to their ages and abilities. If your child is ten, for instance, tailor the rules to the skill level of a ten-year-old.

Don't be the referee. Acting as an umpire or coach will put you above the kids, not bring you closer. Even well-meaning advice can spoil the fun of playing the game. So let the kids decide the teams and the rules.

Make time for time-outs. During high-action games, designate a safe spot (you can call it the Clinic) for kids feeling a bit tired, roughed up, or out of breath. A shady patch of grass, a blanket to sit on, or the top of a cooler all work fine. Provide a large water bottle. The point is to create a refuge, especially for the little ones who want to join in the play (although we've seen plenty of teenagers head there for a cooldown as well).

Store your equipment at kid level. Set up a system for storing balls, rackets, and other backyard playthings that helps your kids find what they want, when they want it.

One family we know lines up inexpensive plastic garbage cans in the garage to hold all kinds of sports equipment. A trash can full of balls is right next to another that holds baseball bats and hockey sticks.

Teach sportsmanship. Playing games can teach kids important — perhaps even difficult — lessons about winning, losing, and trying their best. Remind your kids to praise opponents who make a good play — and to shake hands and say, "Nice game," whoever wins.

Remember that fun comes first. Kids are into games for the fun, the excitement, the participation, and to be with their friends. So when the game is over, don't ask your kids if they won; instead ask, "Did you have fun?"

Backyard Classics

Considering all the backyard games kids have played over centuries, you'd think we'd n be at a loss for something fu play. But standing in the twi with a group of kids milling about, it's all too easy to for the classics. Here's a remind

* Simon says
* Duck, duck, goose
* Red light, green light
* Mother, may I?
* Red rover
* Hopscotch
* Sardines
* Kick the can
* Dodgeball
* Pickle/running bases
* Spud (see page 202)
* Capture the flag
* Frisbee golf (below)

Ball Games

Ready, Set, Go!

With a stopwatch and a bit of imagination, your kids can clock hours of kooky contests.

+ How many baskets can you shoot in 2 minutes?
+ How long does it take to blow a perfect bubble after you put a new piece of gum in your mouth?
+ How long does it take to run around the house?
+ How many times can you snap your fingers in a minute?

TRAINING GAME

Soccer Dodgeball

42 Many classic kids' games make great training games for your young athletes. Kids can try their hands — or feet! — at this version of dodgeball. Instead of throwing the ball, you kick it.

WHAT YOU NEED

Soccer ball

4 to 6 players

Have the kids form a ring with one kid in the center. The outside players take turns shooting at the player on the inside, who's scrambling to avoid the ball. Whoever hits the target player gets to take his or her place. Watch to make sure players keep their kicks low.

FUN FACT In a typical soccer game, players run as many as 4 to 6 miles.

Backyard Games

Football Defender

43 A football and a grassy field can add up to hours of good, sweaty fun. After playing a few rounds of touch football, try this twist.

WHAT YOU NEED

Football

3 players

Defender is a pass-and-catch game, with a quarterback and receiver matching up against a defensive back. For young kids, a shorter, narrower field works best. The object is to move down the field and score a touchdown, but the offense can proceed only by completing passes; there's no running with the ball after the catch (and thus no tackling). Three completions make a first down. If the offense fails to complete the three passes in a four-down series, the players switch positions — quarterback to receiver, receiver to defender, and defender to QB — and play marches back down the field in the opposite direction. An interception automatically entitles the defender to switch places with the quarterback.

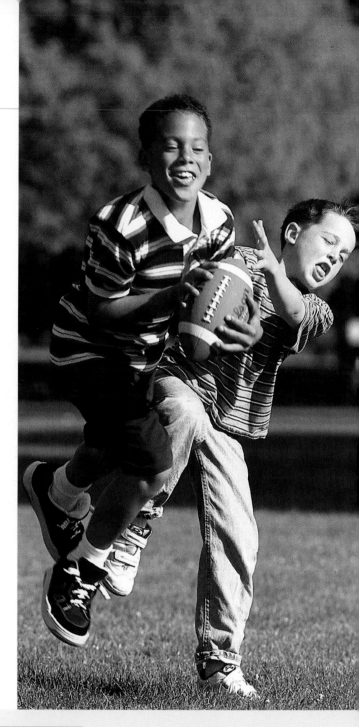

Goal Tending

"To help mark our achievements and keep the creative juices flowing, our family has come up with a special goals chart for our refrigerator. Each family member (my husband and me, Lindsey, age eight, Alex, five, and Eric, one) writes (or has someone help him or her write) a goal on a paper football — everything from 'learn to juggle' to 'learn to tie my shoes.' The footballs are dated and signed on the back, then taped to the refrigerator near a construction paper goalpost. When one of us reaches a goal, we move that football between the goalposts and celebrate with a special dinner or outing."

— Kathy Bias, Alpharetta, Georgia

Chase the Dog

44 All you need is a basketball and a bandanna tucked into each player's pocket (to resemble a tail) to get this group game started. While staying within a designated area and continually dribbling their balls, players try to grab each other's bandannas. As soon as a player loses his tail, he is out. The game continues until only one child, the top dog, is left with his tail.

King of the Dribblers

45 If your kids tire of straight-up one-on-one, let them try another driveway classic.

WHAT YOU NEED

Basketball

5 or more players

Young kids tend to look down at the ball when they dribble. Here's a game that will break them of this habit.

Designate or cone off an area (less skilled kids need a bigger area). Everyone gets a ball. Players must stay inside the area and dribble; no standing around. As they bounce the ball, they try to knock everyone else's ball away with their free hand. When a player's ball gets knocked outside the designated area, he or she is out. The last player dribbling is crowned king or queen. After right-handed dribbling, try left-handed.

Laundry Hoop

We all know the anatomy of a peeled-off outfit — that bed-side heap of dirty-kneed jeans topped by an inside-out T-shirt/ sweatshirt combo. Becky Sprague, a mother of four from Richmond, Indiana, knew it all too well. Backed by the if-you-can't-lick-'em-join-'em philosophy, she installed a basketball hoop hung with a laundry-bag net. The hoop is a yard sale find screwed to her sons' bedroom wall. The net is a mesh laundry bag with a zipper closing. She cut open the bottom and hooked the bag to the rim, zipper end down. When laundry day comes, she places her basket beneath the full bag and opens the zipper. Score!

Baseball Cupcake

46 For a grand-slam gameside treat, decorate a batch of cupcakes to look like baseballs. First, frost each cupcake with white icing. Using the stitching of a real baseball as your guide, re-create the pattern with red shoe-string licorice (or with red frosting and a writing tip). With chocolate frosting and a writing tip, have the kids sign the ball with the name of their favorite player.

Bounce a Red Ball

47 Red balls are kinder and gentler than basketballs and easier to throw than footballs — making them the perfect choice for younger children.

WHAT YOU NEED

Red playground ball

Chalk

2 players

Feat Ball: Contestants in this game take turns tossing a ball against a cement wall and catching it before it hits the ground. What's the hitch? Before making a catch, a player must complete a task posed by the challenger. For example, the first child might pitch the ball at the wall and clap his hands together before making the catch. The second player then tries to accomplish the same feat. If successful, he gets to pose the next challenge — perhaps tapping his shoulders or spinning around before catching the ball. If he fails, the first player earns 1 point and gets to pose a second challenge. The first one to score 5 points wins the game.

Bull's-eye Bounce: Draw a 5-foot-wide chalk circle on the ground about 10 feet from a cement wall. Draw a 2-foot-wide inner circle in the center. Players take turns tossing a rubber ball at the wall and letting it bounce on the ground once before catching it. If the ball lands on the center circle before a player catches it, he earns 10 points; if it bounces in the outer ring, he earns 5 points. The first child whose score totals 50 points is the winner.

Spud

48 Here's our favorite version of this time-honored recess game. Everyone counts off and stands with one foot on a designated base. The player who is "It" throws the ball high in the air and calls out one player's number. As the other players scatter, the called player tries to grab the ball. When he does, he shouts "Spud!" at which point the other players must freeze. The ball holder can take two giant steps toward any person, whom he then tries to hit with the ball. The target person can evade the throw by moving his body but not his feet. If the thrower misses or the target catches the ball, the thrower earns an S. If he hits the target, that person earns an S. Whoever earns the letter becomes It and tosses the ball to start the next round. Players are eliminated once they earn S-P-U-D. Last person still in the game wins.

Olympic Party

For her son Jackson's sixth birthday, Barbara Graydon of Columbus, Georgia, planned an Olympic party, complete with games, a medal ceremony, and for decorations, 20 international flags. This sweet Olympic finale really took the cake! "That was the best birthday party ever!" decreed the joyful Olympian.

Play Four Square

49 No keeping score, no winner, and still the best darn game at recess.

WHAT YOU NEED

Red playground ball

Chalk

4 players

Classic four square: Draw the four-square court with chalk, as shown. The player in box 1 bounces and serves the ball. The others must let it bounce in their box before hitting it into another. When a player muffs it, he moves to box 4 (or to the end of the line waiting at box 4), and the others players rotate up toward box 1.

Advanced four square: In advanced four square, you add in all sorts of variations, which are called out by the server. Each command stops the action, and players must place their feet in a specific place. The last to do so is out. Try these — **Bus stop: All must step on the outer corner of their square. Fire alarm: All must jump out of their square. Mailbox: All must step in the middle where the two lines meet. Big tomato: All must do a mailbox and then a fire alarm. Around the world colors: When players bounce the ball, they must also call out a color — or state, animal, pizza topping — whatever the category may be (no repeating). Normal: Play goes back to, you guessed it, normal.**

Tags & Relays

The Stuff-stacle Course

50 With a bit of imagination, a bunch of old toys and sporting goods can speedily transform a seemingly boring backyard into a magnificent Stuff-stacle Course.

WHAT YOU NEED

> **Stuff**
>
> **A stopwatch or a watch with a second hand**
>
> **1 to 10 players**

The idea here is to rig your stuff into an instant obstacle course. Go to your garage and dig out that old tricycle, Styrofoam swimming noodles, a pair of hula hoops, and eight winter hats you've not yet put away.

Consider it all, size up the yard, and — voilà! — the UnExtreme Games. Time the kids as they whoosh down your playground slide; wiggle through the hula hoops you've strung from a branch; sprint around an eight-hat slalom course; hurdle over the noodles, propped on overturned plastic garbage pails; crazily ride the tricycle to the garage … you get the picture. Make your own course and keep it up for a few days. Try completing it backward. Why not create a personal best chart? Then see if you can beat your top time. **Tip:** Think safety when you set up the course; there's a lot to trip over here.

Friend Tag

51 This version of tag takes the loneliness out of being "It." Two players link hands and become the taggers, chasing after the other players. When the taggers tag someone, that player becomes part of the team. Play continues until all the players are linked.

On Your Mark, Get Set, Blow!

52 Got a pack of gum chums? Try this relay at your next party. Divide into two teams and have each team form a line. The first person in line runs over to a pile of bubble gum, unwraps and chews a piece, and blows a bubble as quickly as possible. Once a judge has seen a legit bubble, the next person in line does the same. The first team to finish wins!

Easy-as-pie Tag

54 No matter how you slice it, this pie-shaped grid is all it takes to start a lively round of tag. On a level playing surface, draw (use chalk on blacktop or a stick in the dirt) a circle that is at least 15 to 20 feet wide. Then divide the circle into six equal sections by drawing three lines across its center. Now you're ready to play. The player who is chosen to be "It" stands in the center of the circle (where the slices of the pie meet). The remaining players position themselves around the outer edge. To begin, It yells "Go!" and then chases after the other players in an attempt to tag one. The runners may travel in any direction around the circle to avoid being tagged. But here's the catch: their feet must always land on a line. The first person to be tagged, or to step off a line, becomes the new It.

KITCHEN FUN

Edible Medals

53 If you want to make victory truly sweet, award these gold medals made from cookies to all of the players in your backyard games. To make one, just seal a sugar cookie in plastic wrap, then wrap it in a circle of gold wrapping paper (leave a wide border around the cookie when you cut out your circle). Wrap tightly and tape. Finally, tape a paper clip to the back for a hanging loop and thread through a yard of red, white, and blue ribbon. Knot the ends of the ribbon, and the medals will disappear in record time!

FUN FACT The first Olympians were awarded no metal medals! Instead, these ancient sports stars were crowned with wreaths crafted from the branches of an olive tree.

Soggy Jog Relay

55 Put on your swimsuits and start running in this wet and wild relay.

WHAT YOU NEED

- Soft, grassy area to run on
- Pair of loose-fitting sweatpants for each team
- Large bucket of water
- Lawn chair
- 1 to 10 players

Line up the teams side by side, set the bucket of water between them, and position the lawn chair 20 feet away. At the signal, the first child in each line dunks his team's sweatpants into the water, puts them on, and then runs around the chair and back to the starting line. There, he peels off the sweatpants (like a banana) and gives them to the next runner to dunk and don (inside out or right side out), and so on. The first team whose members have all completed the task wins.

Lawn Games

Mower Mazes

"In southern Florida, the grass grows very fast, especially in the summertime. One of our favorite things to do is make mower mazes in the backyard. As I mow in rows, I stop and restart the blades to make paths that begin and end randomly and that sometimes cross and loop around. After I head to the front lawn with the mower, my two sons, Luke, age eight, and Leigh, seven, love to run around and find their way to the designated end — usually the swings or the sandbox. The time the boys spend playing in the backyard gives me an opportunity to mow the front yard without interruption."

— Lori Waters, Homestead, Florida

WACKY FUN

Play Crazy Croquet

56 A cross between miniature golf, that gaudy vacation favorite, and croquet, its more mannerly cousin, this game is sure to keep kids giggling across the green.

WHAT YOU NEED

Mallets and balls from a croquet set

Assorted objects for obstacles

Create a crazy course with objects you have on hand. Instead of wickets (which can be difficult for kids to aim for) try setting up simple targets and obstacles. Perhaps the ball has to roll under the slide of your swing set, or between the wheels of a trike. Or it has to bump a large stuffed giraffe before tapping your pink flamingo lawn ornament. Picnic tables, sawhorses, spare tires: see how much of your stuff you can get into action to make your course as full and varied as possible. You can also cut large, arched openings into cardboard boxes, or make ball-guiding bumpers by lining up two rows of bricks.

Before you begin, agree on a clear course through the "wickets" and on any other silly rules you may want to add (a song that you have to sing before you swing, maybe, or hopping on one foot over to your ball). **Tip:** If the mallets are too hard to manage, teach kids how to safely throw the ball (underhand) at a low height.

Crab Soccer

57 Ten minutes of this game will leave kids bright-eyed and asking for more — and adults so spent they feel almost, um, soft-shelled.

WHAT YOU NEED

2 heavy-ply trash bags

Newspaper

Twist tie

Cloth tape

2 to 10 players

Make a crab soccer ball: double up the trash bags, stuff them with balled newspaper, twist-tie them closed, and tape the whole thing crosswise.

The game is played just like soccer, with the big exception that players can only run (make that scuttle) and kick in the crab position — in other words, in a sort of leaning-back, race-car-driver stance, with derriere just off the ground. Simply pick teams, set up two goals (marked by hats, old sneakers, and the like), gather for a kickoff, and you're in for major fun.

Summer Scavengers

"A few years ago, our family of five decided to spend our summer vacation at home. After enjoying day-trips to nearby cities, we came up with the idea of having our own Summer Scavenger Hunt. Every-one got to help choose the items on the list, which included a cookie from a local bakeshop, a brochure on Hawaii, fishing lures, a yard of material to make into an outfit for the baby, and the receipt for the smallest purchase. We had such a great time that we decided to make this hunt an annual event!"
— Dawn Segura, Mesquite, Texas

A Cheesy Caper

58 In this fun whodunit, one child plays the part of the mouse, and the others are cheese bandits. The mouse places a yellow object (like a bottle cap or a bandanna) on the ground, then stands in front of it with her back to the group. While she silently counts to 20, one of the bandits sneaks up, snatches the object, and then attempts to hide it up his sleeve or somewhere else on his person. The mouse turns around and has one chance to guess which bandit scoffed the cheese. If she is correct, she gets a second round at being the mouse. If not, the kid who has the cheese gets a turn.

Blacktop Games

TRAINING GAME

Blading

59 Using any sort of cone (sand-filled plastic soda bottles or milk jugs), invent courses to skate through. For an extra challenge, pretend your course is an art museum and the cones are priceless vases.

GROUP GAME

Switcheroo

60 Everybody wins in this fun group challenge that may remind you of that sixties party classic — Twister!

MATERIALS

Chalk

4 to 10 players

To play, use chalk to draw a row of connected boxes on a sidewalk. You'll need one more box than there are players. Then form two teams and have the players stand in the boxes with the empty box separating the two groups.

Explain that the object of the game is for both groups to successfully swap places while staying in the boxes. Now cue the players to start switching positions by moving into the unoccupied squares — a feat that may require stepping around one or more people. The only rule: just one person can occupy each box at any given time.

NEW CLASSIC

Bike Rodeo

61 All you're gonna need for this kind of bronco bustin' is a standard-issue kid's bike. Just remember to trade in your ten-gallon hat for a sturdy

helmet and to wait for the judge to call riders out one at a time.

Calf Roping: Each rider follows a chalked course, pausing at one point to set his or her feet on the ground, pick up a hula hoop, and toss it over a stool or other target before continuing to the finish line. Fastest time wins.

Barrel Racing: Riders maneuver bikes, in a cloverleaf pattern, around three cones. Give points for how close the riders come to the cones without knocking them over and how many loops they can make in a set amount of time.

Bronco Saddling: In a real rodeo, riders have to stay on a bronco for 8 seconds. To make this a bike event, draw a chalked circular course of tight turns and, if possible, hills and valleys. Time each contestant. The champion is the rider who follows the course and keeps his feet on the pedals the longest without touching the ground.

Sidewalk Creatures

62 Drawing these friendly monsters will bring out the Dr. Frankenstein lurking inside even the most mild-mannered child.

WHAT YOU NEED

Paper and pencil

Tape

Large bucket of sidewalk chalk (at least a dozen pieces)

Begin by cutting the paper into small strips, then label each strip with the name of a particular body part: ear, eye, nose, feet, hair, and so on — everything but the head. Don't forget to include monster essentials like horns and claws. Tape one label around each piece of chalk and put all the pieces in a bucket. A parent can start the game by drawing an oval (or the shape of your choice) for the head. Then each artist dips into the chalk bucket and adds to the creature whatever the label directs. Allow plenty of room for creativity, and don't be bound by naturalistic constraints — six eyes or three legs are perfectly acceptable.

Chalk Walk

63 Equipped with nothing more than a box of chalk, your kids can turn the walkway that leads to your front door into a trail of adventure for a parent or special visitors. (Don't forget to tip off guests before they arrive so they'll be prepared to play along.) For inspiration, you may want to suggest to the young designers a few imaginary obstacles, such as:

◆ A narrow, winding road with a dramatic hairpin curve

◆ A scary or enchanted forest with a pine tree maze

◆ A lake or raging river (include stepping-stones or a rickety bridge for crossing)

Mock Chalk

64 This tough version is ideal for sidewalk use. Mix 2 parts plaster of Paris with 1 part warm water and add powdered tempera paint to get the desired color. For each stick, line a toilet paper tube with waxed paper, seal one end with tape, and pour in the mixture. Tap the tube to release bubbles. Let harden.

CHAPTER FOUR

Rainy-day Play

Absorbing activities to keep your family's disposition sunny —

even when the weather isn't

WHEN IT COMES to kids, water seemingly has the power to both attract and repel. Give kids a snorkel mask, and they'll spend the entire day underwater. They'll dive into pools, jump through waves, race through sprinklers, and splash in the tub until their fingers look like raisins. But natural precipitation — especially the kind that lasts for days, or weeks, on end — is rarely met with such exuberance. When we wake up every morning to rain, rain, and more rain, we start to feel a simmering hostility toward the weather. And with a houseful of bored kids, a few rainy days can take on the proportions of a monsoon.

What's a sodden family to do? Plenty. As certain as the flowers grow after a shower, our kids' creativity actually blooms in a storm. Long afternoons beg to be filled with games — the old favorites and maybe some new ones. Kids and parents curl up with good books. Imaginations hum: a box

begins to look like a spaceship, or maybe even a grocery store.

On the following pages, you'll find some of our favorite indoor activities to do during downpours (or during a snowstorm or even a heat wave). We've avoided the obvious suggestions (presumably you've already thought of puzzles and Monopoly) in favor of alternatives, like the Pet Vet on page 221, that have worked for our families on the grayest of indoor days. With a minimum of preparation and the following tips, you and your kids will be happy to let it rain on your parade.

Jump-start an activity. House-bound kids may be quick to cry boredom, but they are equally quick to become engrossed. More often than not, a few minutes of planning, preparing, and playing an activity with our kids is all they require from us, and then they're off and running on their own. Teach them the rules to crazy eights, play a few hands yourself, then leave them to their own card tournament. Dig out the tape recorder

Fabulous Finger Puppets, page 214

and interview your kids; then they can spend the next hour perfecting the weather report — a bucket of fun, even if the news is bad.

Plan a surprise project. Do something that surprises your children, and they'll be talking about it for many a gray day to come. At lunchtime, try a change of scenery and set out an indoor picnic on the living room floor. Or fill the tub with bubbles and pool toys, invite your kids to an indoor pool party (dressed in their bathing suits, of course), and watch them soak the blues away.

Bring the outdoors in. Shake things up by suggesting that the kids play some classic outdoor games inside, such as marbles or blowing bubbles. If you have a playroom,

you might also let the kids set up a campsite with a blanket tent and flashlights. One *FamilyFun* contributor moved in her Little Tikes slide one long winter so her kids could get some exercise.

Sing in the rain. In the spirit of, If you can't lick 'em, join 'em, we offer this pleasurable last resort. Make sure your kids are dressed for the weather (say, rain jackets and rubber boots in the spring, or swimsuits and flip-flops in the summer) and send them out. Half the pleasure will be the breach of custom; the other half will be mud and sogginess. Let them kick around in puddles, or try our Watercolor Chalk Painting (page 233). They can even decorate an umbrella for the occasion (page 230).

Rainy-day Classics

* Bake a batch of chocolate chip cookies
* Write and read secret cod[es]
* Make a big bowl of popco[rn] and watch a favorite vide[o]
* Hide pennies throughout the house and have the ki[ds] find them
* Build a card house
* Have a round-robin thumb wrestling contest
* Make a paper doll chain
* Build a sofa-cushion fort
* Have a gin rummy tournament
* Fold paper airplanes and launch them in the living room

Puppets

Tiny Dancers

65 Your child will stay on her toes with this pirouetting troupe of finger-puppet ballerinas. Plus, she can use them to act out her favorite poem or fairy tale.

MATERIALS

- Poster board and construction paper
- Colored markers and glue
- Googly eyes (optional)
- 18- by 13-inch strip of Bubble Wrap
- 1 pipe cleaner
- Fingernail polish

To make a paper dancer, sketch a simple ballerina silhouette on the poster board. Draw the head, torso, and arms held upright (called *en couronne,* "like a crown") but do not include the legs. Cut out the sketch and draw on a hairdo, facial features, and a leotard with colored markers. Or you can glue on construction paper hair and clothes, as well as googly eyes. Near the lower edge of the torso, cut out a pair of legholes that your child can comfortably fit her fingers through.

For a frilly tutu, thread a pipe cleaner through one long edge of the Bubble Wrap, gathering it as you go. Then wrap the tutu around the ballerina's waist and twist together the pipe cleaner ends behind her back. Finally, your child can turn her fingernails into a pair of ballet slippers by brushing on a coat of satiny polish.

It's Showtime!

67 Pick up a roll of tickets at an office supply store – they cost just a few dollars – and use them to jump-start pretend play. Kids can collect the tickets from the audience (parents, siblings, and neighbors) for a puppet show, an at-home movie night, or an impromptu dance performance. To round out the show, set up chairs for the audience and serve refreshments (popcorn!) during intermission. Enjoy the show!

A Show of Hands

66 When it comes to entertaining kids, these stagehands are right for the job.

To create one, have your child hold his hand in a loose fist with the end of his thumb tucked into the center, as shown at right. Next, he should practice wiggling the lower portion of his thumb to simulate a talking mouth. Now create the puppet: using different shades of lipstick or face paints, draw on lips and eyes. Add eyelashes and other details with an eyeliner pencil. Finally, tape on a bunched yarn wig or a felt cone hat.

68 Fabulous Finger Puppets

Lights! Fingers! Action! Make our finger puppets and let the show begin.

Flutter Bye

Cut off a finger from an old glove for an easy start to our cheery butterfly. Then cut out a set of cardboard wings and affix dot stickers in a contrasting color. Hot-glue or staple pipe cleaner antennae onto the top center of the wings and glue on the glove finger body. Draw on a simple face — less is more for this kid-pleasing favorite.

The Not-so-scary Dragon

Don't be fooled by the fire breath — this guy is a softy. Start with a glove finger and glue on two small buttons for eyes. Cut a set of spiky scales from a piece of felt and glue on. Make a mouth from green cardboard lined with orange paper and staple tissue paper flames inside. Bend the mouth to shape it and glue it on.

Princess Pinky

Start with a tongue-depressor base. Wrap the stick in a bright fabric scrap, then secure it in place with glue and a band of decorative ribbon. Braid lengths of yarn at both ends, tie with glittery pipe cleaners, and glue in place. Top with a crown of cardboard and sequins. Lastly, draw on a sweet face with markers. **Variations:** Use a larger set of clothes to create a truly noble queen, or, with darker colors and fancier trim, an evil queen.

Big-mouth Bird

For our comical squawking bird, start with a brightly colored glove finger. Glue on two buttons for eyes. Add a cardboard mouth folded into shape with an open beak. Pierce three colorful feathers — they don't even need to match — through the glove-finger base. Add a dab of glue inside and out to hold them in place.

Good King Thumbkin

Wrap a tongue depressor in a royal shade of felt, leaving an inch or two exposed at the top. Over that, wrap a contrasting piece of felt for a dashing cape, and for a truly royal look, glue on trim of braid or lace. Use a bit of cotton ball for a beard (on the front) and hair (on the back). Glue on a paper crown and draw on a face, haughty or wise, depending on your political view of this particular royal family. Variation: A smaller suit of clothes, with yarn hair in a bowl cut, should produce a fairly charming prince.

Zoomy Rocket Ship

This easy rider starts with a base of cardboard on a tongue depressor, which is covered with construction paper and decorated with markers. Glue on tissue paper for rocket flames. Or make a car, with tissue paper exhaust. The car wheels can be part of a one-piece shape or cut out separately and glued onto the car. An important detail: build transportation only after you've got a few puppets ready. That way, you can make your vehicles with the finished puppets in mind — you want to be sure the windows are big enough for the puppets' heads to fit through, so it looks like they're really going for a ride.

Set the Stage

69 A sturdy box and tension curtain rods transform a doorway into a theater. When the show's over, it doubles as an under-bed storage corral for all the puppets.

MATERIALS

Sturdy cardboard box, 2 feet wide

Craft knife

Straightedge

Packing tape

3 tension curtain rods

Construction paper, crayons, and markers

Old curtain

1. With a craft knife (a parent's job), carefully trim the sides of the box to 7 or so inches high.

2. Cut a trapezoidal notch in one of the longer sides, as shown at right, top, to give the puppeteers more room to work.

3. With a straightedge, draw a rectangle in the middle of the box's bottom for the stage opening, then cut it out (you'll probably have to cut through two layers of flaps). With packing tape, secure the loose edges of the flaps and reinforce any weak seams.

4. Cut four holes for two of the tension rods. Each hole should be centered in the sidewall and as close to the seam as possible.

5. Now it's time to decorate. We covered the box with construction paper, then decorated it with crayons and markers.

6. Finally, thread the curtain on the third tension rod and hang it in the doorway just below the stage. The curtain will give your puppeteers the privacy to work their dramatic magic.

DRAMATIC PLAY

A Classic Tale

The key to a great puppet show is having just enough script to know what to do next, but not so much that there's no place for hilarious ad-libbing. The following plot should inspire your kids to develop more stories on their own.

The Dream Team

An evil king rules the land, and the puppets must band together to overthrow him. In the process, each discovers he has a special talent: the bird can fly and do reconnaissance; perhaps the dragon can become invisible (simply by ducking down out of the stage!); and so on. Work out the basic order of things ahead of time, as well as the final scene, in which the king is either tricked into leaving the castle and then surrounded, or tricked into giving up his crown, and thus the throne. Let each kid decide his characters' special powers. At the end, the evil king may be reformed or led away in shame to an ignominious fate as a castle servant.

Pretend Play

Stocking the Store

Open up shop with the following items:

- Tape empty boxes closed; try cereal (minis are fun), pasta, crackers, even tissue boxes
- Fill clean, empty plastic bottles with beans or colored water
- Duct-tape the sharp edges of clean, empty soup, veggie, fruit, or tuna cans (or donate a few full cans to the cause)
- Make fake food out of self-hardening clay
- Add price tags, stock up on paper bags, and get ready for business

FUN IN A BOX

Open a Corner Market

70 With some clever renovations, an empty refrigerator box becomes a store full of fun.

MATERIALS

- Refrigerator box, approximately 30 by 32 by 64 inches
- Packing and masking tapes
- Utility knife
- Yardstick and pencil
- Extra cardboard and boxes
- Paper towel tubes
- Paint roller (optional)
- Acrylic paints and paintbrushes
- Twine

Seal the refrigerator box top and bottom with packing tape. Using the utility knife (a parent's job), cut a window in the box's front and a door in one side.

To make the sloped roof, cut a 30- by 45-inch piece of cardboard and score it into thirds, as shown in Figure A, above. Cut four 8-inch lengths of paper towel tube for roof supports. Use masking tape to attach two supports to each side edge of the roof. Lay the cardboard over the supports, as shown, and tape in place.

Now it's time to decorate. Your kids can use a paint roller to apply large areas of paint to the box or use paintbrushes for more detailed work, such as stripes, trim, flowers, or signs.

To make the fruit bin, cut the flaps off an approximately 10- by 23- by 5-inch box. Poke two holes in the rear corners of the small box, as shown in Figure B, and two holes just under each corner of the store's front window. From inside the store, thread a short piece of twine out through the wall, through both holes in the bin, and back through the wall, then knot both ends of the twine. Repeat for the other end of the bin. Use this same technique to make bins or shelves inside the store. For a mailbox or cash drawer, tape a cereal or cracker box to the wall.

Doggy Digs

71 If your child has a stuffed animal that would love a place of its very own, here's just the thing — a cozy cardboard abode that's fun and easy to construct.

MATERIALS

- Cardboard box, about 12 inches square
- Utility knife
- Masking or packing tape
- Paint, sponges, and construction paper

Open the top flaps of the box and cut one quarter of the way down each corner, as shown in Figure A, below. Starting from the bottoms of these cuts, fold in two opposite flaps (the longer flaps, if you're using a rectangular box) and tape them together at the top to form a peak. Trim the two side flaps to match the roofline, as shown in Figure B, and tape them in place against the roof. Cut out an arched doorway, add sponge-painted roof shingles and a construction paper nameplate over the door, and your house is ready for its first tenant.

Build a Skyscraper

72 A big case of boredom sometimes requires a big cure — like this towering, build-it-yourself skyscraper. Start by collecting cardboard boxes in various sizes. Tape the boxes shut with packing tape, then stack and tape them atop each other. Using markers or crayons, your kids can decorate the boxes with windows, columns, gargoyles, and mailboxes. They might add some 3-D touches such as tissue paper flowers and bushes or paper flags. Crafter's Tip: If you don't have plain brown boxes, wrap yours with butcher paper or turn them inside out and tape them back together.

A

B

Shoe Store

73 Got time to fill? This soleful shop is a shoe-in. Have your child gather a row of shoes before asking customers to step right up – onto a ruler, so she can measure their feet. Let her fit a few pairs on game shoppers (set up a mirror on the floor for ogling them), then wrap the chosen shoes in tissue paper, put them in a box, and ring up the sale on a toy cash register.

Rainy-day Play

Indoor Explorer

"One winter day, my three-year-old daughter, Kara, wanted to go hiking — a great idea, except for subzero weather. So I found a cowboy hat, my wife's vest, a shoulder purse, a toy camera, and Kara's hiking boots, and dressed her up to look like an explorer. I made her wait in the family room while I hid her stuffed animals around the house. I told her that her job was to shoot pictures of each of the animals she found. The expedition was a hit!"

— Steve Argue, Wauwatosa, Wisconsin

Ride a Hobbyhorse

74 Fashioned from a pair of old blue jeans, this steed requires no sewing.

MATERIALS

- Pair of old blue jeans
- String, glue, and felt
- 140 eight-inch lengths of black yarn
- Polyester filling
- 3-foot-long, ¾-inch dowel

Cut off one jean leg about 2 feet up from the hem. Turn the leg inside out and tie it closed with string. Now turn the leg right side out and glue on felt eyes and nostrils. For the mane and forelock, arrange the yarn into four equal bunches. Tie each bunch in the center with another strand. Starting 2 inches above the horse's eyes in the center of the pant leg, cut eight ¾-inch vertical slits (spaced ½ inch apart). Weave one bunch of yarn though the first two slits so that the ends stick out and resemble a forelock. Weave the other bunches through the remaining slits to create the mane.

For ears, cut the back pockets from the jeans and tie the tops closed with string. Cut ear slits in the head and insert the tied ends of the pockets into them. Stuff the horse's head (up to its ears) with polyester filling. Insert one end of the dowel. Pack the neck with more filling and tightly tie the lower edge of the neck to the dowel. Finally, tie a string bridle around the horse's nose.

Box Car Derby

75 Cut from empty cereal boxes, this freeway will be open to traffic in no time. To cut sections of straight track from each box, draw a line all the way around the box ½ inch up from the bottom. Cut along the line, then snip away the walls on the ends. In the same manner, cut additional pieces from the sides of the box. Use the remaining scraps to cut out corners and guardrails (for a curve, staple two pieces of track to a flat pie-slice shape and staple on a narrow guardrail). Create an overpass by cutting an archway into a tea box, or use a few boxes to build a gas station. Finally, tape the track together any way you like.

Open a Doll Spa

77 When the weather is frightful, help your child warm up the afternoon with a play sauna for her dolls. Fill a basin, baby tub, or even your bathroom tub with warm water, cover the bathroom floor with towels (so you just won't care what happens), and let your kids bathe their dolls and all their tiny clothes. Use a mild shampoo, and set up a drying rack with clothespins. Have on hand a few beauty products for after the bath: hooded towels, combs, hair ribbons, and talcum powder. A toy car wash for miniature cars can be equally fun, especially if you have a handheld shower nozzle. Afterward, organize the sparkling fleet for a car show.

CREATIVE PLAY

Pretend Party

76 Barbie's big day? Surprise your child and her play date with a make-believe birthday party for their favorite doll. Round up a festive assortment of supplies: balloons, hats, and streamers create an instant party atmosphere. You can get a bit more elaborate with goody bags (just fill paper bags with saved favors from past parties), gala table settings, and iced muffins or cupcakes (add candles!). Or add a present for the birthday girl — maybe that rodeo outfit Barbie's been eyeing, nicely wrapped and ribboned (she might need a little help unwrapping it, of course).

TUB TIME

Bath Craft

78 This clever catamaran turns your bathtub into a glamorous port of call. To make one, remove the labels from two plastic soda bottles. Clamp the bottles together temporarily with rubber bands, then wrap them with colored tape, as shown below. Remove the rubber bands, then, with a craft knife (a parent's job), cut the oval seat openings. Sail away with a crew of fashion dolls, action figures, or waterproof plush toys.

Fort, Inc.

79 If your kids are in the business of serious play, take a memo: our easy blanket fort makes the perfect corporate hide-away for young tyke-oons.

MATERIALS

Sheet or blanket, card table, and couch pillows

Cardboard, scissors, markers, and junk mail

Briefcase, telephone, computer keyboard, and in/out boxes

Office supplies (see the Home Office Kit on page 183)

To make office space, your child can drape a sheet or blanket over the table and prop up a few pillows for a peaked roof. Now she can stock the office with various supplies — whatever she needs for pretend scenarios (these might include conference calls, meetings, memos, or briefings). Tape up a mail slot cut from cardboard and labeled with markers. Once or twice a day, a postal worker should drop through a new load of junk mail (finally, a good use for it!), and office workers can sort it into in/out boxes or file folders.

Indoor Camp-out

80 Answer the call of the wild with a retreat to the great indoors. Your child can set up a basic table-cushion-sheet tent (see the fort above), grab a canteen, and unfurl some sleeping bags. Other props can enhance the encamped effect: marshmallows are a must, as is a flashlight, and your camper will doubtless require a compass to locate provisions fridgeward. Finally, a book of scary stories might sound the right note, and a strategically placed teddy bear can growl around outside the tent (cuddling will likely tame the beast).

Chair Choo-choo

81 **All aboard! Please take your seats (or is that** chairs**?). When stir-crazy kids are crav-ing a little loco-motion, a make-believe train might be just the ticket. Simply set the dining room chairs in a straight line (or two by two), and the kids can pretend they're aboard the** Orient-Express **— or a jumbo jet, a horse-drawn carriage, even a roller coaster. Props might include conductors' hats, suitcases, and paper tickets with a hole punch. Destinations are limitless: the kids can chug toward Grandma's house or take the zoo-bound express, fly over their hometown ("Hey, is that our school down there?") or visit distant imaginary places (Narnia, Hogwarts, Neverland). If the trip turns out to be a long one, a designated attendant (hint, hint) can come around with juice and pretzels on a tray.**

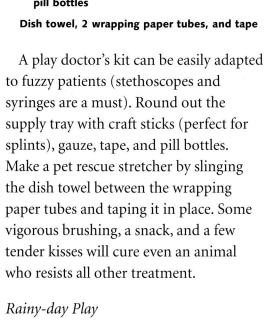

Tiny Tollbooth

83 **Rev up toy car play with an easy pasta-box tollbooth. Simply remove the transparent window from the box, then add a gate (we attached a strip of cardboard with a paper fastener) and an action-figure toll-taker. Pennies, please!**

Pet Vet

82 Got a feverish Beanie Baby? A dancing bear with a sprained ankle? Emergency Pet Vet to the rescue! Kids love to feel useful, even if it's just pretend, and the drama of nursing ill stuffies can occupy them happily for hours.

MATERIALS

   Play doctor's kit

   Tray

   Large craft sticks, gauze, tape, and empty
      pill bottles

   Dish towel, 2 wrapping paper tubes, and tape

A play doctor's kit can be easily adapted to fuzzy patients (stethoscopes and syringes are a must). Round out the supply tray with craft sticks (perfect for splints), gauze, tape, and pill bottles. Make a pet rescue stretcher by slinging the dish towel between the wrapping paper tubes and taping it in place. Some vigorous brushing, a snack, and a few tender kisses will cure even an animal who resists all other treatment.

Rainy-day Play

Dress Up

Clothes Quarters

"My daughters, Chandler and Kelsey, just love to play dress-up. The sight of their clothes all wrinkled up in a box drove me crazy, so we made each of the girls a portable closet from cardboard boxes. We cut openings for the clothes and shoes, added bars for hanging, and covered the boxes with Con-Tact paper. Now the girls each have a wardrobe fit for a princess."

— Robin Giese, Trappe, Pennsylvania

ACTIVITY KIT

Pack a Costume Suitcase

84 To encourage hours of magic, masquerade, and make-believe, pack old suitcases with dress-ups and disguises and store them under your child's bed. We recommend scouring your closets, attic, and local thrift store for the following:

- Fancy old dresses, scarves, and purses
- Hats — top, straw, witch, and cowboy hats; fedoras; Easter bonnets; baseball caps; chef's toques
- A feather boa
- A piece of sheer, velvet, or heavy fabric with a dress clip — an instant cape!
- Shoes of all kinds — cowboy boots, feathered mules, Chinese slippers, high heels
- A bathrobe or kimono
- Wigs and fake fur for beards and sideburns
- A bandanna
- Costume jewelry, including bangle bracelets and clip-on earrings
- Eyeware — think nonprescription glasses, shades, and swim goggles
- Lipstick
- A black eye pencil (and cold cream) for whiskers and mustaches
- Plastic fangs
- Wands
- A tiara
- Angel wings
- A tutu
- Masks
- Old neckties
- Silk flowers

INSTANT COSTUMES

I Want to Be a ...

Doctor: Grab a white jacket (pop some tongue depressors in the pocket), a stethoscope, a disposable dust mask (for surgical rounds), a bottle of jelly bean pills, and a pair of glasses.

Superhero: Don a cape (a towel and a safety pin will do in a pinch), an eye mask, a felt S to pin to your T-shirt, and a pair of blue tights or long underwear.

Princess: Drape yourself in everything fancy (including anything velvet or satin or rhinestone), pin on lots of ribbons and lace, thread gold cord through your hair, and don't forget a tiara!

Deep-sea Diver: Slip into your swimsuit, add fins and a snorkel mask, and hop in the tub.

Positively Presley

85 The King is reputed to have spent more than $15,000 a month on his wardrobe, but your kids can impersonate him for a song. To orchestrate your own Elvis tribute, cut out two long sideburns from fake fur (sold at fabric stores) and snip a pair of small holes near the top of each one. Thread the sideburns onto the stems of a pair of gold-trimmed Elvis-style sunglasses, and it's showtime.

Magic Wands

87 What's a wizard without his wand? No need to find out. Use a craft knife (a parent's job) to cut a foot of ¹/₂-inch clear, inflexible plastic aquarium tubing (sold in pet stores). Seal one end of the tube with a bit of modeling clay. Then your child can fill his tube with wiggle worms (metallic pipe cleaners) and dragon scales (sequins or glitter) before sealing the other end with clay.

Terrific Tiaras

86 Little princesses will love decorating their own crowns. Cut a basic tiara shape from metallic silver poster board. Trim the midsection to create a fancy edge. Your child can adorn her crown with stickers and plastic gems (sold at most craft stores) attached with double-sided tape. To fit each crown, wrap it around the princess's head and paper-clip the overlapped ends.

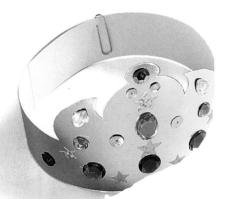

Five-minute Masks

88 Here are easy ways to go incognito using household items.

Mask 1: Tape a poster-board face with nose- and eyeholes inside the front edge of a winter hat. Add paper or yarn hair around the sides of the hat.

Mask 2: Start with a medium-size paper bag (to be worn upside down over your head). Shape it by cutting the sides and back into hair. Cut facial features into the front, and round the bottom into a chin.

Mask 3: Make an animal nose from an egg-carton cup by poking airholes in it and attaching string ties. Decorate by attaching pipe cleaner cat whiskers, a cardboard bird beak, et cetera.

Rainy-day Play

Play Cards

89 On a rainy day, let a deck of cards be your ace in the hole.

Gather some potato-chip poker chips and remind your kids of these old favorites.

Ages 4 to 6: concentration, slapjack, go fish

Ages 6 to 8: war, pig, old maid, crazy eights

Ages 8 to 10: I doubt it, spoons, casino, spit, hearts

Ages 10 and up: Michigan, rummy 500, cribbage, spite and malice

Pick a Card

90 This trick takes some practice – and a pinch of salt. Have a friend shuffle the deck and pick a card. Have another friend cut the deck into two piles. Ask the cardholder to look at his card. As he does, grab a pinch of salt (it's in your pocket). Tell him to put the card facedown on one of the piles. As you point to which pile, slyly sprinkle on a little salt. After he places his card down, put the other pile back on top. Tap the side of the deck (it should separate at the salt). Hold up the top portion: there's your friend's card.

Kentucky Card Derby

91 Here's how your family can stage some racing excitement on your own turf with a simple card game that can be just as unpredictable as the derby itself.

To get things off and running, have each player choose a suit. Take the corresponding jacks (jockeys, if you will) from the deck and place them side by side faceup on a tabletop. Shuffle the rest of the deck and set it facedown beside the jacks.

Now take turns flipping over the card at the top of the deck. If the card matches a player's suit, he gets to lay the card faceup end to end with his jack; if not, it goes into the discard pile. Continue in this manner until all of the cards have been used or discarded. The person with the longest track of cards wins.

"Do you start building from the top or the bottom?"

— The all-time favorite question asked of Bryan Berg, holder of the world record for the largest card house: a 127-story tower measuring 24 feet 4 inches, built in 1999

Game Night

"As a welcome change from TV, we invite the kids in our neighborhood over for game nights. We have a different theme each time — board games, for example — and a themed treat (such as puzzle-piece-shaped cookies on Puzzle Night). The kids learn new skills (making conversation, taking turns, and winning and losing gracefully), and they have fun!"

—Margaret Connor, Austin, Texas

Indoor Gardening

The Jug Heads

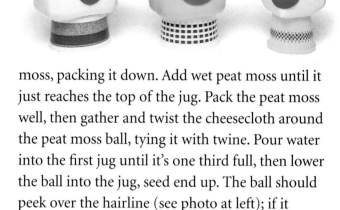

92 All it takes is water and sun to make these grassy-haired garden friends. Their jug heads make tidy, easy-to-water planters.

MATERIALS

- Pencil and permanent markers
- Two 1-gallon jugs
- Plastic milk caps and coffee-can or margarine-tub lids
- Foam mounting tape (available at craft stores)
- 1 square yard of cheesecloth
- Spray bottle and water
- Peat moss (about 3 quarts)
- Grass seed
- Twine
- Plastic margarine tub

To make a head, draw a hairline around one of the jugs, about two thirds up from the bottom. Cut away the top with scissors. Cut a nose and ears out of the excess plastic. To make the eyes, start with two milk caps. Then cut two white circles from a lid, making them just smaller than the caps. Using markers, draw an iris and pupil onto each circle, then attach the circles to the caps with foam tape. Cut a mouth from a plastic lid. Tape all the features to the jug.

To make a holder for the soil and seed bag, cut off the top of the second jug so that it's an inch taller than the first. Line the second jug with cheesecloth, letting it extend over the sides. Spray it lightly with water. Sprinkle a thin layer of peat moss over the cheesecloth, then cover the peat moss completely with grass seed.

In a mixing bowl, mix 6 cups of peat moss with 1 cup of water until the peat moss is moist. Cover the grass seed with a layer of wet peat moss, packing it down. Add wet peat moss until it just reaches the top of the jug. Pack the peat moss well, then gather and twist the cheesecloth around the peat moss ball, tying it with twine. Pour water into the first jug until it's one third full, then lower the ball into the jug, seed end up. The ball should peek over the hairline (see photo at left); if it doesn't, elevate it with a plastic shopping bag.

In a sunny spot, place the head on top of an overturned margarine tub neck. Spray with water and repeat twice a day until the grass sprouts.

93 Found Art Gardening

These whimsical planters — and even the greenery inside them — can all be scavenged from around the house.

The Pot: An outgrown rain boot

The Plant: A pineapple top

Start with a layer of pebbles, then add potting soil nearly to the top of the boot. Chop the crown off the pineapple. Remove all the fruit, cut small slices in the bottom to expose the bumpy root buds, and set the pineapple crown aside for a week to dry. Plant it firmly in the boot and water so the soil remains slightly damp but never soggy.

The Pots: Toy teacups

The Plants: Grass

Mix some sand with premixed potting soil, fill each cup nearly to the rim, and spread grass seed evenly over the top. Use a mister to keep the seed moist. When the grass is up, water it lightly but frequently using a teapot.

The Pot: Toy dump truck

The Plants:

Carrot tops

Layer the truck's bed with pebbles, cut the tops off the carrots (organic or any with greens, but snip off the greens), and gently work them into the pebbles. Cover the pebbles with water. In about a week, you'll see tiny buds, which will soon open into ferny foliage.

Tiny Terrarium

94 To grow a garden under glass, first head to your local garden center. Pick up a few plants (small ivies or palms) and small bags of stone, horticulture charcoal, and potting soil. At home, layer 1/2 inch of stone, 1/2 inch of charcoal, and 1 1/2 inches of soil in a widemouthed jar. Plant the greenery, moisten the soil, and cap the jar. Keep in a well-lit place, but not in direct sunlight. If water beads up inside, uncap the jar and let it dry out. If beading doesn't reoccur, water the plants with a mister about once every two to four weeks.

Fancy Faux Flowerpots

95 Brighten a rainy day with a pot of beaded flowers. First, thread a green bead stem onto beading wire and knot the end. Next, add color beads for the flowers and knot the end.

To create petals, bend the flower-colored beads into an oval petal shape and twist the loop closed. Repeat these steps to create three or four more petals. When the petals are complete, wrap bare wire around the center of the flower to reduce the space between petals, then snip off the excess wire.

To plant each flower, press the wire into a mini flowerpot, filled with brown nonhardening modeling clay.

Carrots: Paint Brazil nuts orange, then glue on stems of artificial foliage.

Radishes: Paint hazelnuts white and red, then glue on green pipe cleaner stems.

Tools: Cut shovel and hoe blades from a foil pie plate. Glue onto trimmed bamboo skewers.

Scarecrow: Use tacky glue to secure two sticks (one with a V for the legs) and a walnut together. Wrap the figure with fabric strips for clothes. Glue on yarn hair and a straw hat from a craft store.

GARDEN CRAFT

Tabletop Garden

96 Not only does this tabletop garden make a whimsical decoration, but it's also a great project for young gardeners who are eager for sunny weather to come.

MATERIALS

- Potting soil
- Aluminum foil tray (11 by 16 inches)
- Clear plastic bag or plastic wrap
- Shade-mix grass seed
- Craft sticks, glue, and white acrylic paint

To grow the grass for your mini yard, pour the potting soil into the foil tray and pat it down flat. Sprinkle on a layer of grass seed, then cover with a light layer of soil, pressing it down gently.

Water the soil, then loosely cover the tray (do not seal) with the clear plastic bag or plastic wrap. Check your garden regularly and remove the plastic when you see the first sprouts. Keep the soil lightly and evenly moist, and you should have a tray full of grass within three weeks. You may have to mow your grass!

To create the garden plot, use a butter knife to remove the grass from a small section of the tray and replace it with a layer of fresh potting soil. Now install a picket fence. To make each section, use scissors to trim the tops of seven craft sticks into points (a parent's job), then lay them in a row, equally spaced. Glue two uncut sticks across them. Once the glue has dried, turn over the sticks and glue two more across the back. When dry, paint the fence white. Set the fence sections in the soil and fill your garden with tiny vegetables, mini gardening tools, and a scarecrow (at right).

FamilyFun

Music Time

Thimble Fingers

98 With these clever percussion gloves on, you'll feel like you have tap shoes on your fingertips.

All you need are ten metal thimbles, an old pair of gloves that fit your child's hands snugly, white glue, and ten pens. Simply stick the pens inside the gloves (one in each finger and thumb), glue the thimbles onto the top of each glove digit, let dry, remove the pens, and you're ready. Gloves like these are sometimes used by washboard players in zydeco music (creole dance music from Louisiana) to make sounds on a ribbed metal board. Try your tappers on tabletops, bathtub tiles, and any other surfaces that sound good to your ears.

INSTANT FUN

Spin a Marker Spiral

97 Have your kids ever seen anything so archaic as a record player? While you dig out your old one, have them choose a few washable markers. Poke a hole in the center of a paper plate, set it on the phonograph as you would a record, and turn on the player. Have your kids hold the tips of one or more markers on the plate, moving them back and forth. Flip over the plate and repeat on the other side. If you like, use scissors to cut around the spiral until you reach the plate's middle, then string up one end of the strip and let it hang down in a colorful curlicue.

TAPPA TAPPA TAPPA

Rainy Days

PAINTING CRAFT

Decorate an Umbrella

99 Your child can stay dry *and* make a big splash with a hand-painted umbrella.

MATERIALS

Solid-color nylon umbrella

Pencil or soft chalk

Foam paintbrushes
1 narrow, 1 broad)

Fabric paint

Use the pencil or chalk to outline a design on the open umbrella, then use the narrow brush to paint over the outline and the broad brush to fill in larger shapes. Let the paint dry thoroughly, then head happily into the rain. Try the easy ladybug and cowgirl we show here, or one of the designs below.

Night sky: Use a stamp to decorate a navy blue or black umbrella with stars.

The solar system: Paint on a golden sun surrounded by all the planets in orbit.

Full bloom: Create a gardenful of colorful flowers or one giant sunflower.

FAMILYFUN READER IDEA

Rose-colored Windows

"On a gray day last year, to help cheer things up and satisfy our longing for flowers, we used washable paints (see page 276 for a recipe) to paint some on a window. Danielle, age six, and David, four, used paintbrushes and their fingers to make the stems, leaves, and different flower blossoms, while Jonathan, two, finger-painted the grass all along the bottom. Our row of brightly colored flowers was so beautiful that we kept it on the window even after our real flowers had blossomed outside." — Christine Nowaczyk, Midland, Michigan

Cloud Nines

101 One way to brighten a rainy day is to dish up a tropical treat: sunny pineapple slices peeking out from behind a big, billowy marshmallow-cream cloud.

INGREDIENTS

- 1/2 pint heavy cream
  A few grains of salt
- 1 teaspoon pineapple juice
- 1/4 teaspoon vanilla extract
- 2 cups mini marshmallows
  Fresh or canned pineapple slices

In a chilled stainless steel mixing bowl, combine the heavy cream, salt, pineapple juice, and vanilla extract. Whip until soft peaks form. Fold in the mini marshmallows, cover, and refrigerate for at least 1 hour. (The marshmallows will sweeten the cream as it sets.)

Just before serving, trim the outer edges of the pineapple slices to resemble sun rays. Place each pineapple slice in the center of a plate and top with a generous dollop of marshmallow cream. Serves 6 to 8.

INSTANT FUN

Splash Dance

100 Surprise your kids by encouraging their singin' and dancin' in the rain. Let them don their swimsuits, or get soaked to the skin in their clothes (they'll dry, after all!). Play some music out the window to inspire this age-old celebration of precipitation.

Lollipop Flowers

102 When it comes to brightening up a rainy day, there's nothing quite like flower power. To make a cheery bouquet of treats, cut petals and leaves from colored paper and affix them to lollipops with tape. For a blossoming centerpiece, insert the lollipop stems into a Styrofoam dome (sold at most craft stores).

MUD FUN

Make the Mud Parfait or Pie à la Mud on page 241, or play Stuck in the Mud, page 240.

Rainy-day Cake

103 Someone left the cake out in the rain — and we mean that in a good way! Our fun frosting projects brings sunshine to even the dreariest afternoon.

INGREDIENTS

1 baked 9- by 13-inch cake
White frosting
Food coloring
Pastry bag fitted with icing tips

Ice the cooled cake. Divide the remaining icing into five small bowls and mix in food coloring (we used red, orange, yellow, green, and blue). Spoon the desired color into a pastry bag (place the coupler base into the bag first, then the frosting, then roll down roll the bag down so the frosting goes into the bottom). Attach the desired tip

Tip: Twist the opening of the pastry bag shut to keep the frosting from spilling out. Squeeze the bag from the top to push the frosting out through the tip.

by screwing on the coupler ring.

To create a rainy-day scene, use a drawing tip to outline clouds, a sun, raindrops, grass, and a simple figure holding an umbrella. For the best results, wash out the tip each time you switch colors. To make flowers, use a star tip for the petals and a leaf tip for leaves. With the tip of your choice, pipe a border around the whole scene, if desired. Serves 10 to 12.

FamilyFun

A Shower of Ideas

104 One month's rain brings the next month's flowers — and plenty of chances for kids to get their feet wet with these activities.

✦ Scout out a salamander parade (see "I Spy Salamanders" on page 244 for tips).

✦ Size up raindrops — they range from smaller than a pinhead to as big as a pencil eraser. Catch some in a pan filled with 2 inches of flour, let the flour pellets dry, then compare them.

✦ Draw a tree trunk on a paper plate in crayon. With washable colored markers, top the trunk with bold squiggles. Then hold the plate in the rain and watch the "leaves" unfurl.

✦ Conduct a rain symphony by setting an array of pots, bottoms up, below a dripping roof edge.

FUN FACT A falling raindrop is not pear-shaped. Most raindrops flatten as they fall and are shaped like hamburger buns.

Watercolor Chalk Painting

105 During a gentle rainfall, hand your kids some colored chalk and let them create an impressionistic masterpiece. They can draw rainbows, family portraits, and nature scenes on the driveway, then watch the rain blur the edges (big, simple images produce the best results). To help the rain along, "paint" over the picture with a large, damp paintbrush.

Blooming Good Fun

"My four-year-old daughter's love of flowers inspired a great rainy-day activity. When she and her twin brother feel housebound, we head for our local greenhouse. The twins are free to wander through the large, open areas, protected from the weather, and enjoy the wonderful colors, scents, and textures. They also have fun seeing how the plants grow from tiny seedlings and watching the florists make beautiful arrangements. My son is especially intrigued by the hose and sprinkler system used for watering. And if you can bear to leave without making a purchase, the whole thing is free!"
— *Linda B. Jennings, Hackettstown, New Jersey*

CHAPTER FIVE

The Four Seasons

When boredom strikes, step outside and let nature work its magic

Wherever your family lives, the seasons offer a year's worth of outdoor adventures. Maybe you go apple picking every fall. Come winter, you build snowmen in the backyard and sip mugs of hot chocolate. Spring means May Day baskets to decorate the neighborhood, and summer's warmth brings long days of towering sand castles.

For many of us, these seasonal pastimes have become rituals — activities our children anticipate as the weather changes. These traditions are touch points: they help us mark the passing of time, and even slow it down just a little. They thrill us with anticipation and then comfort us with their familiarity.

And, as every parent knows, seasonal activities keep our children naturally busy. In the great outdoors, they are entertained by nature. A beach becomes a giant sandbox. An open field with wildflowers and overturned logs becomes a playground. When we attune our kids to the rhythms of nature, we offer sweet relief from the intrusions and constraints of schedules, TV, and even heaps of toys and games. Dawn and moonrise, spring and fall: natural cycles nurture a kid's creativity in fun, often unexpected ways.

On the following pages, you and your family will discover countless ways to celebrate each season. As you peruse our crafts and activities, consider the following tips:

Make the most of what the natural world has to offer. Snow, mud, sand, and leaves — these natural playthings have timeless appeal to kids. Offer your children plenty of opportunities to play with smooth sticks, skipping stones, even weathered hunks of driftwood. These humble bits of nature will capture your kids' imaginations.

Go on a seasonal scavenger hunt. Those same natural goodies that beg to be played with also beg to be collected. Give your kids a list of nature items to find and a lunch-size paper

Mini Scarecrow, page 257

Paint a Fall Mural, page 261

bag. Or you can simply hand them a field guide and a pair of binoculars. Anything you see can be sketched or painted; gathered items can be made into crafts.

Take a hike. Grab a walking stick (see page 258), pick a favorite route, and walk it at least once each season. Encourage your kids to attend to the shifting landscape, the absent or reappearing wildlife, and which views become more or less prominent. Keep a nature journal (see our Beat-a-leaf Journal on page 284) to record your observations from season to season and year to year. Or make a seasonal photo album and use it to document the changing scenery — and your changing kids.

Grow a garden. There may be no better way to understand the rhythms of nature: bulbs planted in the fall will send up shoots in the spring; tomato seeds pushed deep into spring's chilly soil will bear heavy fruit come summertime. Even the winter offers indoor gardeners a crack at sprouting some greenery. In the dark days of winter, this bit of color can really invigorate the senses.

Seasonal Classics

Fall: Pick apples, plant bulbs, carve pumpkins, collect leaves, mull cider, dry gourds for rattles
Winter: Go sledding, play ice hockey, make a snow angel, drink hot cocoa, cook a giant pot of soup
Spring: Make mud pies, splash in puddles, plant seeds, visit baby animals, dig for worms, dye eggs
Summer: Build sand castles, freeze Popsicles, play Marco Polo, go to a fair, make a daisy chain, pick berries for jam

Spring

Whirly Bottles

106
Celebrate spring by planting a row of spinning wind catchers in your front yard.

MATERIALS

- **2-liter plastic soda bottle**
- **Colored marker, paper, and tape**
- **Craft knife**
- **Acrylic paints and paintbrushes**
- **Power drill, hammer, and a small nail**
- **3 feet of 1-inch-diameter wooden dowel**

First, remove the label from the bottle. This is easier if you fill the bottle with hot water and let it sit for 10 minutes. Then use soapy water and a vegetable scrubber to remove any glue. Drain the bottle and let it dry.

Ask your child to come up with a decorative image to paint on the bottle, then make a template by drawing the design on paper. If she chooses a symmetrical image, such as a butterfly or flower, have her draw a straight line down the center of her drawing and cut out one half of the image. If it's an animal, draw a profile of its head and neck.

Tape the template onto the inverted bottle. Use the marker to trace around its outer edge (do not trace the centerline or the base of the neck). Repeat this step a few times, keeping an equal amount of space between the outlines.

Use the craft knife to cut along the outlines (adults only). Fold the silhouettes forward at a 90-degree angle from the bottle. Now paint the images.

Once the paint dries, drill a small hole in the center of the bottle bottom (adults only). Insert the dowel into the bottle. Tap the nail through the hole in the bottom and into the top of the dowel so that the head extends ¼ inch above the plastic.

Run Like the Wind

107 With its breezy long tail, this toy will make any kid feel like he's flying. Cut the bottoms off two large plastic cups. Lay a large, clear trash bag flat and roll its bottom end around the outside of one cup. Tape in place about an inch below its rim. Feed the trash bag through the bottom of the second cup and nest this cup firmly over the first. Fringe the tail of the trash bag with scissors and punch opposing holes through both cups just below the rims. Push a dowel through the holes and secure it with a rubber band. Run like the wind!

Spring Scavenger Hunt

108 Clues of the season's arrival come in many forms. Give kids a list of spring signs to hunt for, including sounds (like peepers, the knocking of a woodpecker, a bird singing), plant life (a tree bud, a mushroom), critters (a salamander, a baby animal, a turtle on a log), or human hints (a baby out in a stroller, laundry hanging out to dry, someone on a skateboard), and send your kids out into the sun. Players get a point for every sign of spring they find. The winner is crowned Super Spring Sleuth.

Grow Something Big

109 Gardening, for many kids, would be a whole lot more exciting if growing things didn't take so darn long. The following four varieties, however, shoot up right away in your garden — and then they keep growing, and growing, and growing …

♦ **Atlantic giant pumpkin:** This pale, slightly lumpy pumpkin holds the current world weight record, topping 800 pounds. More typical are 50- and 100-pounders (115 days to maturity).

♦ **Mammoth Russian sunflower:** Flowers grow to 10 inches across on plants more than 10 feet tall (120 days).

♦ **Scarlett runner beans:** You can almost see this climbing vine grow (up to 12 feet), and the purple beans are as pretty as they are tasty (70 to 115 days).

♦ **Morning glory:** Here's another fast-growing vine that rewards gardeners with a show of magnificent blossoms. This one's invasive, so plant it solo (110 to 120 days).

FUN FACT You might be blown away to learn that the world's windiest place is Antarctica, where winds regularly gust at more than 60 mph.

Wind Bags

110 Throw your grocery bag to the wind with this kite-flying feat. First, tie together the handles of a plastic shopping bag with the end of a ball of string. Staple a few 2-foot lengths of ribbon to the bottom of the bag for kite tails. Now find a windy spot outdoors and start running. As the bag fills with air, slowly let out the string and the kite should begin to soar and dive.

Blow a Blade of Grass

111 Nothing heralds the arrival of summer quite like a blast from a blade of grass played between the thumbs. In the hands of one kid, it's a trumpet fanfare. In the hands of another, it's more like the honk of a man blowing his nose. No matter. The fun is more in the playing than the listening. With a blade of grass and a little know-how, anyone can grasp the technique.

First, find a nice, wide blade of grass at least 3 inches long. Lick the edge of one thumb from wrist to tip and stick the blade of grass where you've licked (it's gross, we know, but the moisture keeps the grass from falling off). Carefully press your two hands together, as if in prayer, lining up your thumbs so that

they sandwich the grass at the top knuckle and at the base of your palms, with a gap in between. Wiggle your thumbs until the grass bisects the gap, put your lips to your thumbs, and blow through the hole.

FUN FACT When you blow a blade of grass between your thumbs, you're using the same physics employed by modern reed instruments, such as clarinets. In each case, blown air causes a thin blade, or reed, to vibrate, creating sound.

Spring Picnic

112 Keep a "just add food" picnic basket packed, and you can lunch alfresco at the drop of a blanket. Simply stock a wicker basket with paper plates, plastic cups, forks, and spoons, napkins, a tablecloth, salt and pepper shakers, and a Frisbee. Then just add food and go!

Wind Dancer

113 The next time a warm breeze starts to stir, hang up one of these foam wind socks and watch the ribbon streamers start to dance. To assemble one, use a hole punch to make five holes along one shorter end of a 4^1/$_2$- by 12-inch piece of craft foam. Roll the foam into a tube, overlapping the edges, and punch matching holes in the other end. Lace the two ends together with ribbon. Next, punch a series of holes along the lower edge of the sock and tie a long ribbon from each one. Then make two holes in the top and tie on a ribbon for hanging. Lastly, lace on cutout foam flowers through holes punched in the sock.

The Four Seasons

Stuck in the Mud

114

After a long, cold winter, we don't warm to a game with a name like "freeze tag." Try this springtime variation on the classic.

What you need:

Three or more players

How to play: Choose someone to be "It." His name is Mud. To start, each player grabs hold of one of Mr. (or Ms.) Mud's fingers, and all chant, "What happened to you, Mr. Mud, while spring flowers, they did bud?!" Then, at an unpredictable speed — the point is to trick the players — Mr. Mud chants back, "I slipped into the crud! I got stuck in the ... mud!" At the sound of the word mud, all the players let go of Mr. Mud's fingers and scatter away while he gives chase. If Mr. Mud tags a player, that player is "stuck in the mud" (that is, frozen). The sole way to get unstuck is for an untagged player to crawl under the stuck player's legs. Players are safe only while they are in those crawling-under moments. You play until everyone is caught. Then name another Mud and begin again.

Prepare a Mud Parfait

115 Mired in mud? Let your children make the most of it with our elegant twist on the classic mud pie. Make the parfait glass (see below) several hours before heading for the mud, to allow the glue time to dry. Your mud chefs can collect parfait ingredients, such as leaves, twigs, or pebbles, while they wait.

MATERIALS

- Rubber band
- Clear 2-liter bottle with cap
- Craft knife or scissors
- Craft Goop (or other glue made for plastics)
- Mud, pebbles, leaves, and other ingredients

Using a rubber band around the bottle as a guide, cut around the bottle about 4 inches from the bottom (a parent's job).

Trim the base section again just above the molded ridges. Discard the center portion.

Turn the top and bottom parts upside down and glue the cap onto the center of the base.

When the glue's dry, your child can fill it trifle style — alternating layers of mud with pebbles, sand, dirt, leaves, and any other ingredients she likes. Top with a rock cherry and a leaf.

Enjoy a Pie à la Mud

116 To make an edible counterpart to the muddy creation above, spread a store-bought chocolate cookie piecrust with $\frac{1}{2}$ quart of softened chocolate ice cream. Dig eight holes in the ice cream and fill each with a tablespoon of fudge topping. Freeze until firm. Stir $\frac{1}{2}$ cup of chocolate chip rocks into $\frac{1}{2}$ quart of ice cream and spread over the pie. Top with chocolate whipped cream ($\frac{1}{4}$ cup of hot-cocoa mix beaten with 1 cup of heavy cream) and chocolate cookie crumb dirt. Freeze until serving time.

Gumdrop Garden

117 This spring, plant a row of candy tulips in a cake-and-cookie garden. First, ice the top and sides of a pound cake with chocolate frosting, then trim a row of ladyfingers to make a picket fence. Sprinkle on chocolate cookie crumbs for soil. Use kitchen scissors to snip flattened gumdrops into tulips. Trim flattened green gumdrops into leaves, and use toothpicks to attach the leaves and flowers to the cake. FInally, tint coconut with green food coloring to make yummy grass.

May Day Bouquets

118 Create a buzz by hanging these easy May Day baskets on all your neighbors' doorknobs.

MATERIALS

Construction paper

Tape or stapler

Pipe cleaners

Pom-poms

Glue

Googly eyes

Feathers

Hold a sheet of construction paper (black for the bee, yellow for the duck) with the shorter ends at the top and bottom. Starting at the lower right-hand corner, roll the sheet into a cone and tape or staple the overlap. Trim the top front to create a rounded head on the front side.

To make a bee, the next step is to form antennae. Fold a pipe cleaner in half, stapling the bend to the back of the head. Curl each tip around a black pom-pom.

Next, create stripes by wrapping strips of yellow paper around the cone and gluing them in place. Tape on paper wings and a heart-shaped paper face complete with a drawn mouth and glued-on pom-pom eyeballs topped with googly-eye pupils. For a hanger, make holes in opposite sides of the cone a half inch from the top. Thread a

length of ribbon through the holes and knot it.

To make the duck, cut out wings, a broad breast feather, and webbed feet from construction paper. Tape the pieces in place. Glue tail feathers to the tip of the cone and googly eyes to the head. Finally, cut out a bill from a folded piece of orange paper, using the fold for the top edge. Attach the bottom flap to the cone, then glue a pair of mini pom-pom nostrils to the top.

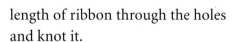

A Doorstep Garden

119 You don't need window boxes to spruce up your front yard with spring flowers. Just plant your favorite annuals in an old boot to set beside a welcome mat. Remove the lace from the boot and fill its bottom with a layer of pebbles or gravel to provide drainage, then pack in a 2-inch layer of potting soil. Now fit in the root base of a small flowering plant (pansies, marigolds, or impatiens work well), and gently pack more soil around and on top of the roots.

Pal Around

120 With warming temperatures, Little League games, and school vacation just weeks away, springtime puts friends in the mood to kick up their heels. Here are a few suggestions for ushering in a spring of good company:

Go into business (selling cookies and pink lemonade, delivering groceries, or dog walking) and design flyers to post in your neighborhood.

Pack a picnic lunch (see page 239), spread a blanket on the grass, then sit back and watch the clouds roll by.

Plant a friendship garden full of your favorite flowers. After they bloom, try drying them, then make cards to swap with friends.

Go strawberry picking at a local farm, then get help cooking the berries down into a thick syrup or jam to top your post-sleepover pancakes.

A Pick-and-eat Garden

121 A pick-and-eat garden is fast food at its healthiest, boredom-busting best. Look for varieties that can go from vine to table with just a quick wash.

Peas: Try compact varieties that don't require trellising, like Sugar Ann.

Pole beans: Kentucky Wonder and Kentucky Blue are both dependable varieties that produce long, tender beans. Create a tepee of bamboo stakes for them to climb.

Cherry tomatoes: We like Super Sweet 100 because it's easy for small hands to harvest. Plant in cages, or stake.

Radishes: Kids may find them too spicy to eat, but few crops grow faster. Plus, it's fun to yank them from the earth. We like the Easter Egg II variety.

Tin Man

122

Looking for a garden sentry that's worth crowing about? This one is well equipped to ruffle some feathers — particularly if they're about to light on your vegetable patch.

MATERIALS

- 7 feet of 2- by 3-inch wooden stud
- 4 feet of 3¼-inch dowel
- 4 large brass hooks
- Twine
- Assorted hardware, kitchen utensils, and
  clothing (see right)
- Glue

First, set one end of the wooden stud 18 inches into the ground. Next, cut two pieces of dowel to measure 3 feet long and 1 foot long. Screw hooks into the ends of both dowels.

With twine, securely tie the longer dowel to the stud about 10 inches from the top, as shown. Hang metal spatula forearms from the hooks and use safety pins to attach metal measuring-spoon fingers to the spatulas. Tie on the shorter dowel 18 inches below the top one. Then loop leg-length pieces of twine around the hooks on the short dowel.

Now dress the scarecrow in jeans, using suspenders to hang them from the shoulder dowel. Thread the twine through the legs and tie saucepan boots to the ends. Button on a flappy shirt.

For a head, fit an inverted metal coffeepot atop the stud and glue on washers for eyes. Tie a bandanna around the neck. To cap it all off, use wire to firmly fasten a metal colander hat to the coffeepot handle and then attach measuring spoons for hair.

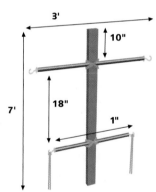

I Spy Salamanders

123

Spring showers trigger an annual parade of salamanders marching to ponds to lay their eggs. The following conditions lend themselves to amphibian-spotting: warm, wet weather; the muted light of dusk; roads that border wetlands. Ask your town conservation commission if it knows of a favorite salamander crossing.

FamilyFun BOREDOM BUSTERS

Visit a Farm

125 Even while your kids are waiting to shed their parkas, farms are coming to life with litters of newborns. Visit a farm in early spring, and you may get to bottle-feed a tiny pink piglet (one from a litter of more than a dozen!) or a snowy lamb. Goats butt their way into the world a little later in the season, and with any luck, calves, foals, chicks, and kittens may also be included in the spring mix. An added bonus: farms tend to be friendly and free! Look in your phone book for a farm associated with an agricultural college or a vocational school.

NATURE CRAFT

Sprout Necklace

124 Our all-natural necklace requires daily attention to thrive, but it rewards its caretaker with a real live sprout, suitable for transplanting to a pot and growing in a sunny window. The necklace itself, we should note, also serves as an attractive spring fashion accessory.

MATERIALS

- Small screw eye
- Small clear plastic jar with a cap (like those for spices, vitamins, or cake decorations)
- 3 one-yard lengths of colorful string
- 3 cotton balls
- 3 or 4 dried beans (like kidney, pinto, or lima)

Carefully twist the screw eye into the center of the jar lid (create a pilot hole with a pushpin if necessary).

Braid the colored string, thread it through the screw eye, and tie the ends, making sure the loop can fit over your head.

Moisten the cotton balls until they are wet but not dripping and place them in the jar. Press the beans down between the jar wall and the cotton so they are clearly visible from the outside. Screw on the cap.

Wear your sprout necklace during the day, keeping it out of direct sunlight to avoid overheating. Store it in a warm place at night. After about five days, the beans should begin to sprout. When they begin to crowd the jar, transplant them to a flowerpot, or discard them and start a new batch.

Tip: Under normal conditions, the cotton should not dry out, but check it periodically and add more water if it does.

The Four Seasons

Ants on a Log

126 These critters make a welcome addition to any picnic. First, scrape a flat spot on the bottoms of 12 chocolate malt balls. Melt $1/2$ cup of chocolate chips in a double boiler. Set four pretzel rods on a wire rack, drizzle on melted chocolate, then press three malt balls, flat sides down, on each pretzel. For legs, use six chow mein noodles dipped into the chocolate. Use chocolate to attach candy dot eyes and licorice antennae.

Bug Hotel

127 They show up every spring, flying into town and banging on our screens as if we owed them a room for the night. Well, here's hospitality everyone can live with. Our bug hotel is simple yet sturdy, with lots of observation windows for young entomologists. Guests check in, then you get to check 'em out.

MATERIALS

- **Oatmeal container**
- **Markers or poster paint and paintbrushes**
- **Craft knife**
- **2 feet of fiberglass screening (from a hardware store)**

Use markers or poster paint to decorate the outside of the oatmeal container, making sure you post the house rules!

Paint or draw the shutters, then use a craft knife (adults only) to cut them out with sideways H shapes.

Paint the door, then cut it out, making sure its bottom edge is at least ¼ inch above the floor inside (to keep your captured "guests" from checking out too early).

Roll the screening around the inside of the container so it fits snugly. Trim it so the top edge fits beneath the lid and leave a 1-inch overlap where the side edges meet.

Tip: Be sure to provide your guests with food (notice what they were eating when you found them) and water (a filled plastic bottle cap should meet their needs).

Terra-cotta Birdbath

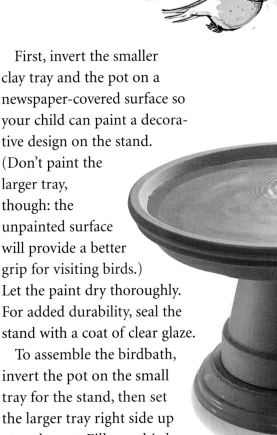

128 A fresh, clean source of water can be hard for birds to come by. That's why a birdbath is a great device for attracting all kinds of species, such as catbirds, wrens, waxwings, even screech owls. Here's one that couldn't be simpler to put together.

MATERIALS

- 2 unglazed pot trays, one 8¼ inches in diameter and one 12¼ inches in diameter
- Unglazed clay pot, 6 inches in diameter
- Permanent enamel satin-finish paint (we recommend Delta CeramDecor's PermEnamel air-drying nontoxic paint)
- Paintbrushes
- Clear satin-finish enamel glaze

First, invert the smaller clay tray and the pot on a newspaper-covered surface so your child can paint a decorative design on the stand. (Don't paint the larger tray, though: the unpainted surface will provide a better grip for visiting birds.) Let the paint dry thoroughly. For added durability, seal the stand with a coat of clear glaze.

To assemble the birdbath, invert the pot on the small tray for the stand, then set the larger tray right side up atop the pot. Fill your birdbath with no more than 3 inches of water.

Wrangle Some Worms

129 This see-through ranch allows kids to watch earthworms tunneling. Fill a 1-gallon clear glass or plastic jar with potting soil that you've mixed with about 6 cups of manure. Moisten the soil well with water. Now gather up about a half dozen worms (they're easiest to spot after a rain) and add them to your container. Cover the jar with a screen, or punch plenty of air-holes in its lid. Now tape black construction paper around the jar — worms like the dark — and set your ranch in a cool, shady place. Keep the soil moist. In a few days, remove the paper and look for worm tunnels down the side of the jar: the worms are hard at work digesting dirt! When you're all done spying on them, release the worms into your garden.

Early Bird Special

130 Even a child who usually pecks at her breakfast will find this tasty nest hard to resist. Grease a large muffin cup with butter. Let your child crush two Shredded Wheat biscuits and set them aside. Melt 1 tablespoon of butter in a small saucepan over medium heat. Add ¼ cup of Marshmallow Fluff. Continue to cook, stirring constantly. As soon as the mixture starts to bubble, remove it from the heat and stir in the crushed cereal until it is well coated. Press the mixture into the greased mold in a nest shape. Let it harden. Remove it from the mold and place it in a serving bowl. Fill with fresh berries and milk. Serves 1.

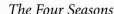

Summer

OUTDOOR ACTIVITIES

Fun in the Sun

131 Make the most of these long, warm days with a summertime-only activity:

- Race the sun by trying to eat a Popsicle before it melts
- Pick blueberries from a farm, then make a pie or a jar of jam
- Team up around the clothesline for an impromptu volleyball match
- Hose off the dog
- Stay up late and watch the stars come out

CRAFT FUN

Memory Box

132 One way your child can treasure her summer memories is by collecting all kinds of mementos in, and on, a special box.

MATERIALS

- Plain box, shoe box, or photo box with a cover
- Adhesives (a glue stick or double-sided tape for flat, lightweight objects; tacky glue or a low-temperature glue gun for heavier objects)
- Colored permanent markers

Throughout the summer school vacation, as she collects ticket stubs, postcards, trinkets, stickers, or any other paraphernalia, your child can either glue them to the outside of the box or store them inside. She can even add a note in colored marker about where or when she came by a certain item.

FUN FACT The phrase "dog days of summer" was coined 2,500 years ago after the Dog Star, Sirius, visible in the Northern Hemisphere by mid-July. The ancient Greeks believed its light caused temperatures to soar. Sirius does burn almost twice as hotly as our sun, but it's much too far away to have any effect on the earth's climate.

Sights of Summer

133 To savor your kids' sunny days of free play, compile a list of classic sights of summer and see how many they can scope out and photograph with a disposable camera. Here are some ideas: Black-eyed Susans ✦ Watermelons, tomatoes, beans, or other summer harvest fruits or vegetables ✦ Dragonfly, ladybug, or praying mantis ✦ Kids running through the sprinkler ✦ Starfish, sand castle, and seaweed ✦ Garter snake ✦ Fishing pole ✦ Tennis racket ✦ A favorite tree in full bloom ✦ Summer-reading book cover

Bake a Sunshine Cake

134 A summer birthday or dinner party calls for a dessert that's all sweetness and light — like this glittery sunburst cake.

INGREDIENTS

2   8- or 9-inch round baked cakes
Yellow frosting

7   to 9 sugar cones
Yellow crystallized sugar

Frost the top of one cake, then add the second layer and frost the entire cake. Ice the outside of one cone and roll it in the sugar. Push the open end into the side of the cake, using more frosting to hold it in place, if needed. Repeat with the other cones, positioning them around the cake like sunrays.

Sun Catchers

135 When you hang these translucent shapes in a window, the marker colors light up like stained glass. To begin, your child should use a black permanent marker to draw the outline of a picture or geometric shape on a soft, clear plastic lid, such as that from a coffee can. Cut out the shape with scissors (a parent's job), then have your child completely fill in the shape with colored permanent markers. Punch a hole in the top of the shape, tie on a loop of string or fishing line, and hang your sun catcher from the top of a window.

Backyard Camp-out

137 Sure, we like acres of land, flickering fireflies, and the howl of distant coyotes, but all the space you really need for a wild camp-out is a suburban backyard, a city rooftop, or a nearby grassy field.

WHAT YOU NEED

Tent

Sleeping bags

Flashlights and battery-
    operated lanterns

Kids and grown-ups can set up the campsite nice and early, then the grown-ups can order a pizza and scuttle away inside to let the kids go it alone in the great backyard — until s'more time! After dessert, the kids can make shadow puppets on the tent wall, turn off the lights for ghost stories, or lie outside on their backs and watch the constellations pass by. Come morning, greet your brave campers with hot chocolate and a hearty pancake breakfast.

KITCHEN FUN

Simple S'mores

136 Summer just wouldn't be complete if you didn't get your fill of the classic campfire dessert — a warm and gooey s'more. To sample this supersimple double-chocolate version, toast a marshmallow to golden perfection, sandwich it between chocolate-covered graham crackers, squish, and eat.

INSTANT FUN

Shadow Puppet Show

138 Hand shadows projected on the tent wall by flashlight add a spooky touch to your ghost stories. To create a dog's face, hold you hands in the shape shown at right. Move your fingers to make the dog look as if it's talking. For bigger shadows, move your hands closer to the light. Now make up a shadowy tale about a ghost dog that haunts the tent, the sleeping bags, and even the campers.

Ship Ahoy!

139

If landlocked boredom's got your kids walking the plank, let them turn a refrigerator box on its side and chill out on the salty waves of their imagination.

MATERIALS

- Blue tarp
- Large appliance box
- Clothesline and sheet
- Assorted props

Spread out the tarp and set the box on it, on its side, underneath a clothesline. Open up — or cut away — the top side of the box (only parents should use a craft knife). Now drape a sheet sail over the line, assemble some themed props, and it's anchors away!

Fishing trip: Bring a tackle box and wooden-dowel fishing rods, construction paper fish, snorkels, and worms!

Pirate ship: Grab bandannas, a stuffed parrot, eye patches, broom oars, striped leggings, and a black flag with a skull and crossbones.

Yacht: Have pretend pipes, sailing caps, blazers, fancy snacks, and juice in plastic wineglasses.

Tour Your Hometown

140

Who says you have to go away to have a special family vacation? With a little creativity and imagination (you do, after all, have to pretend you're a tourist), you can have a memorable getaway without ever leaving town.

- Call your chamber of commerce or visitors' bureau for local brochures and maps to area attractions.
- Take a nature walk at a local park, conservation area, or reservoir.
- Consider hopping aboard a local train, bus, trolley, or subway — for the pure fun of it.
- Ask the fire station, bakery, or a local factory if your family can have a tour.
- Visit a college campus. You'll find athletic fields for playing baseball and flying kites. You might also find museums, sporting events, theater, and arcades in the student centers (a treat to kids, at least).

FUN FACT

A typical beach pail holds nearly 3.5 billion grains of sand.

A Beachside Shower

141 Everybody loves spending a fun-packed day at the shore — until it's time to climb back into the car, still sticky and sandy, for the ride home. Here's a quick way for your backseat travelers to freshen up before hitting the road. Fill two or three clean plastic milk jugs with water and leave them in the car while you swim. When you're ready to leave, the water will be warm enough for a soothing rinse.

BEACH CRAFT

Ocean City

142 Your sandy architects can mold a whole seaside metropolis — and then play Godzilla (take a picture first).

MATERIALS

- Shallow, broad-bottomed container (like a bin or a baking pan)
- Cardboard milk carton, with the bottom removed
- Funnel

Use the container as a mold for the ground story of each skyscraper. Pack it with damp sand, invert it onto a flat section of beach, then lift it off.

To erect a second story, set the milk carton upright on the base, fill it halfway with sand, then slowly pour in enough water to dampen it. Repeat, filling to the top with sand, then remove the mold. Top off the building with a sand dome (mold with the funnel) or a stone roof. Finally, press on shell windows and driftwood doors, and arrange beach pebbles into a road.

Tide Pooling

143 You don't have to take your family scuba diving to catch a glimpse of undersea life. Those shallow saltwater pools that form along rocky coastlines are usually teeming with fascinating creatures.

Below you will find a few you're likely to encounter on both the East and West coasts. Remind your children to approach slowly and be very still, lest the animals sense your motion and dart under a rock for cover. And return every animal to its habitat.

Sea cucumbers: A knobby, oblong shape gives these critters their name. They range in color from gray to rose and tend to burrow under the sand.

Sea urchins: Algae are the favorite food of these porcupinelike creatures.

Sand dollars: These flat, disk-shaped animals sport star patterns on their centers and live at the bottom of tide pools.

Hermit crabs: If you

notice a head and claws poking out of a snail shell, it's probably a hermit crab. These crustaceans move into an empty shell (sometimes pulling out the original resident first) to protect their soft abdomens.

Barnacles: These crusty creatures rely on their feathery feet to kick food particles through the valved openings of their bodies.

Starfish: Five arms (and sometimes more) distinguish these creatures. They feed on clams, using the suction cups on their feet to pull open shells.

Sponges: Protruding from the floor and walls of tide pools, sponges are actually large colonies of minuscule animals that eat by sifting food from the ocean water that flows through them.

Art at the Beach

To make the most of your beachcombing finds, consider bringing these supplies:

+ Fishing line for stringing any shells that have holes
+ Glue and paper for sand painting
+ Paper, paint, and paintbrushes to make prints of found objects — seaweed, seashells, sea stars, and so on
+ Plaster of Paris and a bucket to make casts of footprints in hardpacked sand
+ Sieves for rinsing shells; bags for storing them

FUN FACT

Do fish sleep? Sort of. All that swimming might make them sleepy, but most fish have no eyelids to close. So they just rest by floating and daydreaming.

The Four Seasons

Hang a Hideout

144 Call it what you want — a tent, a hideout, a permanent-press playhouse — but a breezy, easy-to-make clothesline fort offers kids ample shade and privacy for tea parties, secret clubs, or just whiling away long afternoons. The construction of the tent is fairly free-form, with its design depending on the length of your clothesline, the size of your yard, and how many sheets you want to use. To make our tent, we strung three clotheslines between a tree and a tall fence (one clothesline runs higher to form the peaked ridgepole of the roof). Then we hung several sheets to form the walls and roof, clipping them in places with clothespins. If your kids like, you can furnish their tent wth kid-size chairs and an old rug — or, as we did, just stick with the original decor by Mother Nature.

Fold Up a Beach Umbrella

145 It's too windy on the beach to read the paper, so you might as well follow these easy directions, adapted from the book *Extra! Extra!: The Who, What, Where, When, and Why of Newspapers*, and recycle those flapping sheets into a shady parasol.

MATERIALS

10 full-size (double) newspaper sheets

Tape

Stapler

Decorative cutouts and fishing line

To make the handle, layer five sheets of newspaper and roll them up diagonally. Tape the roll closed.

To make the stop, roll a sheet of newspaper diagonally into a tube about 2 inches wide and tape the ends. Roll a second sheet the same as the first. Staple the two tubes together at one end and flatten them.

Tape one end of this long, flattened tube to the umbrella handle about 2 inches from the top. Wind the long strip around and around until it ends. Tape down the end.

For the canopy, make 1-inch pleats in a sheet of newspaper along its width, like an accordion.

Fold the accordion in half. Make two more accordions, fit the three folded accordions together like pieces of a pie, and staple them at all the seams.

To assemble, push the handle of the umbrella up through the center of the canopy. The stop will keep the umbrella top from sliding down or closing. Tape the top to the handle to hold it in place. We decorated ours with metallic fish and cutouts that we strung on with fishing line.

The Four Seasons

Ice Cream in a Bag

146 Forget endlessly cranking the handle of an ice-cream maker. After combining the ingredients, you can shake up your own pouch of soft serve — and it's done in just 5 minutes.

Combine 2 tablespoons of sugar with 1 cup of half and half and $\frac{1}{2}$ teaspoon of vanilla extract in a pint-size ziplock bag. Seal it tightly. Place $\frac{1}{2}$ cup of salt (kosher or rock salt works best, but table salt is fine) in a gallon-size ziplock bag, and add enough ice cubes to fill the bag halfway. Place the sealed smaller bag inside as well, then seal the larger bag. Now shake the bags until the mixture hardens (about 5 minutes). Feel the small bag to determine when it's done. Take the smaller bag out of the larger one, add mix-ins, and eat the ice cream right out of the bag. Cleanup is fast too! Serves 1.

Fall

Go on a Corn Stalk

147 A crisp autumn day practically begs for this corny contest. All you need is one ear of dried corn per player. Hide the corn around the yard in spots that are neither obvious nor too hard to find. Now round up everyone and explain that the object is for each player to retrieve an ear and remove all of its kernels (just rub them off). The first one to succeed is the winner. Once everybody in the group has accomplished the task, you can feed the kernels to the squirrels and birds.

Make a Mini Scarecrow

148 These toy sentries are just right for decorating a windowsill or autumn wreath.

MATERIALS

Corrugated cardboard

Fabric scraps

Yarn

Glue stick

Popsicle sticks

Fine-tipped pen

From cardboard, cut out individual shapes that resemble a miniature shirt, pants, and hat. Trace around each shape onto two contrasting fabric scraps (one to cover each side of the cardboard). Cut out the cloth tracings and set them aside.

For straw, snip yarn into short lengths and use a glue stick to affix several to both sides of your cardboard cutouts at the ends of the arms and legs and to the center of the hat brim. Then glue the fabric cutouts to the cardboard and atop the straw.

To assemble the scarecrow, insert a Popsicle stick through the corrugated center of the cardboard pieces (as shown at left), leaving a space between the shirt and hat for a face. Draw on eyes and a mouth with a fine-tipped pen.

Celebrate Fall

149 Relish the glory of an autumn day with one of these seasonal activities:

- Set up a row of pumpkins and try landing a hula hoop around each one.
- Visit a pick-your-own orchard, then make an apple pie.
- Iron brightly hued leaves between two sheets of waxed paper to make colorful window decorations.
- Turn your kids' outgrown clothes into a scarecrow to pose on your porch.

Pumpkin Smoothies

150 This easy-to-make treat offers a taste of pie in a glass — perfect when you're squashed for time.

In a blender, combine $1/2$ cup of canned pumpkin, $3/4$ cup of milk or vanilla yogurt, $1/4$ teaspoon of cinnamon, $1/8$ teaspoon of nutmeg, 2 teaspoons of brown sugar, and 4 ice cubes and puree until smooth. Pour the smoothies into small glasses (this drink is rich) and garnish each with a dollop of vanilla yogurt or whipped topping. For a fun touch, add a pinch of cinnamon or a few colored sprinkles. Serves 2 or 3.

FUN FACT Stand anywhere on earth with a compass in your hand, and the needle will point north. Why? Because our planet's core is magnetized. Although its pull is weak by the time it reaches the planet's surface, the magnetism is still sufficient to turn a compass's lightweight needle relatively in line with the earth's axis.

Fall Trail Mix

151 To keep your kids nourished trailside, gather some of their favorite berries and nuts and whip up a sweet and crunchy snack. In a large mixing bowl, stir together 2 cups of dry-roasted, unsalted peanuts, 2 cups of raw sunflower seeds, 1 cup of raw pumpkin seeds, 1 cup of raisins or dried sweetened cranberries, and 1 cup of mini chocolate chips. Store in an airtight container.

NATURE CRAFT

Stick Grip

152 Here's a way for kids to spruce up and personalize a favorite walking stick.

MATERIALS

Old T-shirt

Wooden beads

Walking stick

Tear or cut an old T-shirt into 1-inch-wide strips. Tie the strips end to end to create three strips roughly 2 yards long.

Thread a bead or two onto the end of each strip and tie a knot in the strip to hold the bead in place.

Tie all three strips together about 4 inches from the beads. Braid the strips.

Make a wrist strap with the end closest to the beads by tying off a loop big enough for a hand to fit through. Hold the loop against the walking stick and thread the other end of the braid through the middle of the loop, as shown. Pull it tight.

Tightly wrap the rest of the braid around the top 6 inches of the walking stick to form a grip. Tie off the braid by looping the end through the last few wraps.

Make a Paper Bag Head

153

Put a happy face on a plain paper bag — for handing out Halloween treats, or just for ferrying your lunch.

MATERIALS

- Colored markers
- Plain lunch-size paper bag
- White crayon or chalk
- Stapler
- Raffia

Use the markers to draw scarecrow-style facial features on the bag. Use the white crayon or chalk for eyes and teeth. Once the bag is filled — with goodies or lunch — staple the top closed and add a bundle of raffia for hair.

The Shape of Things to Fall

A tree can often be identified by the shape of its leaves. Can you make the match? (Answers below.)

A.

B.

C.

D.

E.

F.

1. **Scarlet oak:** Its leaves provide a natural litmus test — the brighter their fall coloring, the more acidic the surrounding soil.

2. **Sugar maple:** The amount of sugar these leaves contain determines the hue of the foliage, which ranges from deep red to orange to brilliant yellow.

3. **American beech:** After the leaves turn a rich yellow-bronze in fall, they often remain on the lower parts of the tree throughout the winter.

4. **Quaking aspen:** Its golden-yellow autumn leaves flutter in the slightest breeze.

5. **Sassafras:** In the fall, outer sassafras leaves turn red or orange, while inner leaves turn yellow; this makes the tree appear to glow.

6. **Ginkgo:** A tough survivor from the Triassic Period, it thrives even in an urban setting. Look for its gold leaves in autumn.

Answers: A-3, B-1, C-5, D-6, E-2, F-4

FUN FACT Leaves don't really change color in the fall. Rather, as daylight decreases, cells at the base of the leaves swell, cutting off the flow of fresh water and causing chlorophyll (which makes leaves look green) to disappear. Other pigments that have been there all along, such as red and orange, become visible.

Tom Thumb

154

With nontoxic ink pads, your child can make fall turkeys for Thanksgiving cards and pictures. Just use a thumb to print the turkey's body and fingertips to create a head and feathers. Use markers to add a beak, wattle, and feet.

BACKYARD CRAFT

Backyard Tepee

155 Like the Native American tepee that inspired it, this shelter can be assembled and dismantled in a jiffy. Best of all, it provides a fun play space on a sunny fall day.

MATERIALS

- 9- by 12-foot canvas tarp or drop cloth
- Measuring tape
- Colored marker
- White cotton rope
- Ten 8-foot-long white PVC pipes, ¾ inch in diameter (an adult can cut longer PVC pipes to length with a hacksaw)
- 2 chopsticks or similar strips of wood

Fold the tarp in half so that it forms a 9- by 6-foot rectangle. Measure in

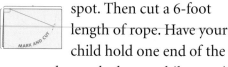

1 foot along the fold and mark the spot. Then cut a 6-foot length of rope. Have your child hold one end of the rope at the marked spot while you tie the opposite end around the colored marker. Step away from your child until the line is taut and move the rope in an arc, marking a line on the canvas as you go. Cut the tarp along the line and then cut out a 12- by 6-inch rectangle to the left of the marked spot at the top corner of the tepee.

Now you're ready to assemble the tepee. Loosely tie together three of the PVC pipes 2 feet down from the tops with a piece of rope, then stand them up like a tripod. Lean the remaining poles against the tripod so that they are evenly spaced.

Drape the cut canvas around the tepee frame, overlapping the top a bit. Make two sets of holes through both layers of the overlapped portion and thread the chopsticks through them to hold the canvas in place.

To secure the lower edge of the canvas to the frame, first snip a small hole about 1 inch in from one of the tarp's bottom corners. Loop a short length of rope through the hole, as shown, and tie the ends around the base of one pole (this pole will become part of the doorway). Now gently stretch the canvas around the PVC frame so that the canvas extends past the first pole to create a door flap. Snip a small hole near the lower edge of the canvas where it falls on the remaining poles and tie it in place using the same method as before.

Paint a Fall Mural

156 Hosting a harvest dinner or Halloween party? This activity lets all the guests have a hand in painting a decorative autumn mural. All it takes is a large sheet of white or brown nonglossy wrapping paper tacked to a family room wall or outdoor fence, tempera paints, and paintbrushes.

Start by painting a big yellow-leafed maple tree in the center or fence pickets across the bottom. If your group of artists needs further inspiration, try writing the names of different symbols of fall, such as a jack-o'-lantern, a scarecrow, or a harvest moon, on slips of paper and putting them in a paper bag. Then everyone can draw slips from the bag and paint those objects into the scene.

Stamp an Apple-picking Bag

157 You can make apple prints on T-shirts, on wrapping paper, on tablecloths, on backs and bellies. Heck, you can stamp them just about anywhere. Even the youngest children can make this aptly appley sack to use on your next excursion to a pick-your-own orchard.

MATERIALS

Newspaper

Fabric bag (cloth grocery sacks work well)

Fabric paint (brown, green, and red)

Paintbrush

Apples

Slip several layers of newspaper into the fabric bag so that the paint will not seep through. With a paintbrush, use brown paint to fashion a tree trunk. Let it dry. Then use a horizontally cut apple to make leaves by brushing a thin layer of green fabric paint onto the apple and pressing it around the top of the trunk. Repeat several times (make sure to look for the star in the print!). After the green paint dries, cut an apple in half vertically. Brush it with red fabric paint. Then "hang" juicy apples on the tree.

Winter

CRAFT FUN

There's Snow Place Like Home

158 A cheerfully chilly snow person is a true icon of winter, and we love the warmth of our parent-child pair. Just wait for perfect snow, get out your waterproof mittens, and start sculpting.

MATERIALS

Snow	Mittens
Charcoal briquettes	Scarf
Carrots	Child's snow pants,
Apple chunks	winter boots,
Toothpicks	mittens, and
Stones and sticks	hat

Start with a three-snowball body for the parent and add charcoal briquette eyes, a carrot nose, an apple-chunk mouth (secured with toothpicks), and stone buttons. Use sticks to support mittened hands, then wrap a scarf around the neck.

The snow child is formed from the bottom up, starting with snow pants stuffed with packed snow. His torso is a made from a single elongated snowball smooshed into the snow at the waist of the stuffed snow pants, then joined to the back of his parent's head.

Use a stick brace to support the child on his parent's shoulders, then stuff boots into his snow pants and use snow to hold his mittens in place. Form his snowy head with a point to support his hat, and make his face as you did his parent's.

CRAFT FUN

Marshmallow Snowman

159 Here's a sweet treat that's a piece of cake to make. Start with a wedge of angel food cake and spoon on whipped cream snow. Next, push thin pretzel sticks through the center of a stack of three marshmallows to create a snowman's body. Stick two more pretzels into the sides of the stack to form arms, and press on candy bits for facial features and buttons. Tie on a fruit leather scarf and fashion a hat out of gumdrops. Then place licorice stick skis on top of the snow and use a pretzel to anchor the snowman atop the skis.

A Slick Trick

160 Here's a cool feat your child can pull off — or up. Have him challenge his friends to pick up an ice cube with a piece of string. Once they've tried (and given up), he can sprinkle some salt on the cube and lay the end of the string on the salted area. The ice will melt and then quickly re-freeze, adhering to the string, which will allow him to pick up the cube with ease.

Snow Château

161 Forget summer's plain old sand castles. Winter means your kids can construct beautiful rainbow-colored ice castles.

MATERIALS

Plastic containers (pails, gelatin molds, plastic storage containers, cups)

Food coloring

Fill the containers with water. Add food coloring (we used about 20 drops of color per cup of water) and freeze outside overnight. When you're ready to build, bring the ice to room temperature. When the ice turns in its container, that means it's ready to slip out. Voilà! Crown yourself royal architect and build away.

Color Your World

162 Got a snowy fort to decorate? Or the blank slate of a snowbank? Go ahead and paint it. We fill spray bottles with food coloring and water (about six drops per bottle) and let the troops run wild. Thinking of a more precise look? If the surface is solid and smooth, try working with regular tempera paint and paintbrushes.

NATURE CRAFT

Ice Light

163 This crystal lantern may be as cold as ice, but it's guaranteed to cast a warm glow. To make one, you'll need a large metal mixing bowl, a plastic yogurt container, a cupful of coins, and, of course, freezing temperatures. Start by pouring a couple of inches of water into the mixing bowl. Place it outdoors to freeze. Fill the yogurt container with stones or coins, then center it on the ice in the bowl. Slowly pour more water into the bowl, so that it nearly reaches the rim of the smaller container, and let it freeze solid. To remove the lantern from its mold, run warm water around the outside of the bowl and the ice should slip out. Dump out the contents of the inner container and pour in warm water to loosen it. Remove the container and place a votive candle in the opening.

INSTANT FUN

Indoor Igloos

When it's just too chilly to go out, bring winter in. A few shovelfuls of snow in the tub will keep your kids busy till it melts. Or get out a bag of sugar cubes and a tub of frosting, and let your kids build mini igloos — good wintry fun, minus the frostbite factor.

SNOW GAME

Snowgusta National

164 Backyard golfers will enjoy the challenge of a course where the greens are always slick and the changing conditions — ice, slush, blizzards — keep the game exciting.

MATERIALS

- Food coloring and spray bottles
- Assorted obstacles and plastic containers
- Ski poles or dowels, tape, and felt
- Rubber ball and hockey stick

For a perfectly manicured green, stomp down an area around each hole (hard-packed snow holds color better than fluffy snow), mix water and green food coloring in a spray bottle, then spray the mix on the packed snow.

Once your green is set, add wacky obstacles like these: pool toy rings or a hula hoop sunk halfway in the snow, a toboggan or skateboard upside down, a trash can lid, or a tunnel through the bottom of a snowman. And don't forget to make holes. We used recycled plastic containers sunk in the snow. Top ski poles with taped-on felt flags.

It's a snow in one! Using a rubber ball and his hockey-stick nine iron, our pro sinks an ace.

The Four Seasons

It's a good thing sleds don't get speeding tickets. Fastest documented sled speed: 247.93 mph, set by Sammy Miller in 1981 on a rocket-powered sled on Lake George, New York. Fastest undocumented sled speed: 650 miles per second – set every year by Santa.

KITCHEN ART

Pasta Doodles

165 Even if it never gets cold where you live, your kids can still play in the "snow" — by turning pasta shapes into ornate flakes.

Working on waxed paper, arrange wagon wheels, bow ties, and other dried pastas into different geometric patterns. Once you've settled on a few that you like, use a toothpick dipped in glue to stick together the pieces of each one. Let the glue dry completely. Then peel away the waxed paper and hang your snowflakes from a window frame or the ceiling.

SNOW GAMES

A Flurry of Fun

166 One of the cool things about snow is that it only takes a few inches of the stuff to have a pile of fun. Try one of our favorite frosty games.

Rope Tow: Team up for a slip-sliding variation of tug-of-war. Tamp down a wide, shallow trench in the snow to serves as the midline. Then take up positions at the ends of a long, thick rope and let the tugging and towing begin.

Whichever team pulls the entire opposing group over to its side of the trench wins.

Hat Trick: Once you've built a plump snowman to stand sentry in your front yard, make a game of topping him off in style. Take turns trying to land a hat on his head by throwing it Frisbee style from about 10 feet away.

Snowballs

167 Your kids will be naturals at shaping and rolling these buttery snowball cookies. But don't expect these treats to last any longer than the real ones — they melt as soon as you pop them into your mouth.

INGREDIENTS

- 1 cup walnuts
- 1 cup margarine or butter, softened
- ½ cup confectioners' sugar, plus extra for rolling
- 1 teaspoon vanilla extract or maple syrup
- 2¼ cups all-purpose flour
- ¼ teaspoon salt

Finely chop the walnut meats in a blender or food processor, then set them aside. Cream together the margarine and the ½ cup of confectioners' sugar. Add the vanilla extract or maple syrup. Stir in the flour, salt, and nut meal.

Roll the dough into 1-inch balls and place them an inch apart on an ungreased cookie sheet. Bake in a preheated 400° oven until set but not brown (about 10 minutes).

Roll the cookies in confectioners' sugar while they're still warm and then again when they've cooled. Makes about 4 dozen.

FUN FACT Snow may look white, but the billions of tiny ice crystals that make up snow are really clear. Instead of reflecting a particular color (in the case of an apple, a shade of red), snow crystals reflect all the colors of the spectrum – a combination that appears white to the human eye.

They're Not Just a Bunch of Flakes

168 Snow is made up of strikingly beautiful crystals, falling singly or in the clumps we call flakes. See for yourself. Chill a sheet of black paper in your freezer, take it outside during the next storm, and as the flakes land, examine them with a magnifying glass. Can you find these six major crystal types? **Stellar crystals:** Look for these in a windless snowstorm (they break in rough weather). **Plates:** Is the snow sparkling? Light often reflects off these mirrorlike crystals. **Spatial dendrites:** Feathery and irregular, these crystals float down from the sky at 2 to 3½ mph. **Columns:** These dense crystals can act like small prisms, creating halos around the moon. **Capped columns:** These are also called tsuzumi crystals, after a similar-shaped Japanese drum. **Needles:** Although long and thin, these common crystals have six sides.

Nature T-shirt, page 290

CHAPTER SIX

Arts & Crafts

Presenting more than 40 projects to bring

out the artist in your child

OVER THE YEARS, we here at *FamilyFun* have written about thousands of crafts. As time passes, a few of them emerge as classics, members of what we call our Crafts Hall of Fame. To make it into this exclusive club of plaster beetles and aquarium-tube bracelets, a craft not only must be easy, inexpensive, and made from readily available materials, but also must have that elusive "wow" factor. It has to be so cool that when you and your kids spy it in our pages, you don't just say, "We could do that," but "We can't *wait* to do that."

Well, we've selected dozens of great crafts for this chapter, from bright ideas for dressing up your kids' clothes to simple projects that turn beach finds into keepsake treasures. And they all embody that boredom-shattering wow factor we prize. Take our geodesic dome (page 274). What makes it a classic Crafts Hall of Famer? For one thing, you can create it with just a stack of newspaper and a stapler. For another, its ingenious design is easy, yet absorbing enough to take up the better part of a rainy day. Plus, your kids can play with (and in) it for days or weeks, and then recycle it when they're done!

As you skim through the following pages, you'll find a range of craft ideas. Some can be made quickly and easily by an unassisted child; others can busy a family for an entire afternoon. Many are crowd-pleasers — simple, mass-producible, and inexpensive enough to be created en masse by a large group of glue-stick-wielding crafters. We offer you this wealth of projects, and a few helpful tips.

Gather materials before you begin. There's nothing worse than realizing halfway through a project that you're out of tempera paint or construction paper. Read all the way through the directions and amass the necessary supplies before you start a project — or decide in advance that you'll be happy to improvise where necessary.

Beach Butterflies, page 287

Trash Treasures, page 278

Emphasize the process. It's fine to have an end result in mind, but make sure you aren't so determined to follow directions that your child can't add her own flair. The end result, after all, is no more important than the steps that lead up to it. So, when you're trying a new project, always ask yourself, "Can my child be creative with what we're doing here, or am I running an assembly line?"

Encourage respect. The happiest artists have a healthy respect for themselves and their own projects, and for the artwork of their peers. Teach them to appreciate the unique quirks of each artist, and to use descriptive, nonjudgmental language with one another ("Wow! You've really used a lot of blue in that painting!"). While you're at it, it's not a bad idea to teach respect for the materials themselves, setting basic ground rules for capping pens and glue, washing out paintbrushes, and protecting surfaces and clothing.

Make cleanup part of the project. Cleaning up as you go will help preserve order in your workspace, and it may

also save art supplies from an early demise. Start this habit early, and it will become a part of your child's regular craft ritual. And why not make it fun? Try putting on an upbeat song and cleaning up as much and as quickly as you can before the music ends.

The Craft Supply Closet

There is probably nothing more crucial to your child's artistic happiness and independence than having a well stocked store of supplies. Get the best ones you can afford and keep them easily accessible. Consider keeping

- Paper (white, construction and a large roll of newsprint)
- Paints (tempera, watercolor, finger, and acrylic) and paintbrushes
- Scissors
- Glue (glue sticks, white glue, tacky glue, and a glue gun)
- Markers
- Crayons and colored chalk
- Pencils, colored pencils, and a sharpener
- Tape (clear, masking, and double-sided)
- Paper clips and a stapler
- Clay (modeling and polymer)
- Sewing supplies
- Recyclables (toilet paper tubes, newspaper, egg cartons, and so on)
- Fun extras like glitter, sequins, pipe cleaners, beads, craft foam, yarn, ribbons, tissue paper, and googly eyes

Paper

EASY CRAFT

Collage Quilts

169 A quilt is, perhaps, the quintessential American craft, combining industry with beauty and thrift. With this paper collage activity, you can host a scaled-down version of an old-style quilting bee for your child and a pal.

To start, you'll need several sheets of colored paper, a ruler, a pencil, scissors, a 4-inch white poster board square for each child, and a glue stick. Cut the colored paper into 6- by 1-inch strips. Then cut each strip into six 1-inch squares. Next, snip most of the squares in half diagonally to create triangles.

Now your child can experiment with various quilting patterns by arranging the pieces on top of the poster board square. She can even customize her design with a larger colored shape or a border. Once she decides on a particular design, help her glue the pieces in place.

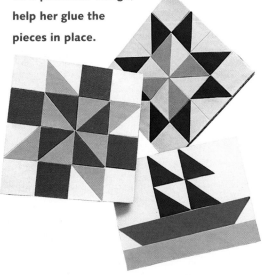

HOMEMADE NECKLACE

Paper Leis

170 A trademark of Hawaiian hospitality, leis are typically made from fragrant flowers. Our paper ones are unscented, but they make a festive birthday craft or a cheering rainy-day play activity.

MATERIALS

Muffin pan liners

Embroidery needle

Yarn

To make each flower, flatten one or two muffin pan liners and trim the edge of each to create petal shapes. Then cut a round flower center from the bottom of another liner and leaves from green liners or tissue paper, if desired.

Once you have a dozen or so flowers, thread the embroidery needle with a strand of yarn long enough to form a loop that fits loosely over your child's head. String on each flower, starting with the leaves and followed by the petals and a center, spacing them evenly along the strand. Tie the yarn ends together, and you've got a pretty paper lei.

Fashion Plates

Dinner Plate Portraits

"My daughter, Amanda, age ten, enjoys making her own paper dolls from discontinued pattern books, which usually sell for $1 to $3 at fabric stores. She cuts out the figures, then glues them onto pieces of cardboard. Amanda also cuts out pictures of clothing from the books, leaving tabs at the edges to help the outfits stay on the dolls. Not only are these paper dolls inexpensive, but the pattern books offer an extensive variety of people and outfits."

— Peggy Schulten, Elgin, Illinois

171 Whether your kids are preschoolers or preteens, this mask-making project is a real crowd-pleaser. The kids can cut out pictures of favorite rock stars, clothing, and accessories from magazines to create plates that are part mask, part instant autobiography.

MATERIALS

Paint stirrers

Heavy-duty paper dinner plates

White glue and glue sticks

Old magazines and catalogs

Markers and crayons

Colored construction paper or card stock

Yarn and/or fun fur

Scissors

Attach a wooden paint stirrer as a handle to the bottom of each plate. To help the handle lie flat over the plate rim, cut a tab in the plate that's the same width as the stirrer. Then use white glue to attach the handle to the tab and to the back of the mask.

Set out magazines, markers, crayons, construction paper, yarn, fun fur, and other decorating supplies, along with glue sticks and scissors. Hand each child a mask and ask her to pair up with a pal. Have the paired-up kids sit face-to-face so they can do portraits of each other,

using the supplies set out to create hair, eyes, lips, noses, freckles, and other features. If your crowd isn't big enough to pair everyone up, let them make self-portraits. And be ready with some sharp scissors to make eyeholes for those artists desiring real "vision" in their portraits.

Set Up House

172 If you've got stacks of magazines and holiday catalogs hanging around, let your kids fill an afternoon, or more, with this fun and endless 2-D project.

MATERIALS

- Poster-size piece of paper
- Catalogs
- Scissors
- Glue sticks
- Paper and markers
- Clear Con-Tact paper
- Double-sided tape

For each child, draw a house shape on a poster-size piece of paper, then set out catalogs, scissors, glue sticks, paper, and markers and let the decorating begin. Each person can custom-design her own house — filling it with everything from furniture to teapots to fishbowls. Encourage kids to add fantasy touches: What would make houses more fun? Bunk beds five high? A system of pulleys and chutes? To make their creations more durable, you can help attach the "permanent" fixtures (couches, tables) to the house by covering them with Con-Tact paper. Objects that might need to be moved around (pet dogs or people) can be covered front and back with Con-Tact paper and cut out (double-sided tape on the back will help them stick in place). Still have catalogs left? Challenge your kids to make a whole town.

Mosaic Mural

174 In ancient Rome, artisans pieced together small stone squares to create exquisite floors that were both a feast for the eyes and a cool treat for the feet on days when temperatures soared. Using the same method, your child can create mosaic art of his own.

First, sketch a basic design on poster board and cut or tear colored paper into a bunch of small squares. Working in sections, apply glue to the poster board and press on paper squares, spacing them slightly apart just like a stone mosaic.

Sandpaper Bookmarks

173 Your child can dress up the books she reads with these place holders made from scratch. To make one, first cut out two matching bookmark shapes, one from white construction paper and one from fine-grained sandpaper. Pressing down firmly, use crayons to create a design on the sandpaper. Lay the white paper squarely atop the drawing and set them both on top of several sheets of newspaper. With an iron on medium heat (adults only), iron over the white paper, then carefully lift it away (it will be hot!). When it has cooled, cover the bookmark with clear Con-Tact paper.

Arts & Crafts

273

Build a Geodesic Dome

175 Who would ever believe that the Sunday paper and a stapler would be all you need to create a life-size structure big enough to hold a bevy of children? Black and white and fun all over, our dome is, at turns, a fort, a gingerbread house, a cave, and a camping tent. And after the fun, it is easily turned back into plain old recyclable newspaper.

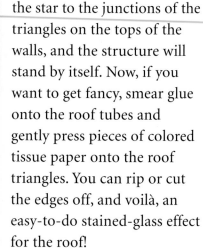

MATERIALS

- **100 sheets of newspaper (choose a paper with large-size pages — tabloid size is too small — and use the full square spread)**
- **Pencil**
- **Masking tape**
- **Yardstick**
- **Stapler**
- **Glue stick (optional)**
- **Colored tissue paper (optional)**

You'll need four sheets to make each newspaper log. Spread the sheets open flat, one on top of the other. Set the pencil in the corner and roll across the diagonal (see step 1, below). Use the pencil as a general guide to help you roll evenly; don't try to roll the newspaper as thin as the pencil! When you get to the other end of the paper, you'll have a tube. Slip the pencil out and tape the tube shut. Repeat this process until you have 25 tubes. Then trim the ends, using a yard-stick to make sure all the tubes are the same length. Ours were each about 30 inches long.

At this point, you'll need a big, open space to construct the dome in. Staple three tubes together to create a triangle. Repeat the process until you've constructed five triangles like the one shown in step 2.

Staple the five triangles to each other at their bottom

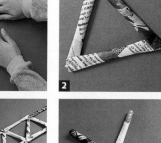

corners. Add five connecting tubes across the top (see step 3). Then raise the triangles, or walls, off the floor and staple the ends together to form a pentagonal structure. It helps to have a few kids hold up the walls while you staple.

Take the remaining five tubes and staple their ends together at the center to make a star (see step 4). Staple the free ends of the star to the junctions of the triangles on the tops of the walls, and the structure will stand by itself. Now, if you want to get fancy, smear glue onto the roof tubes and gently press pieces of colored tissue paper onto the roof triangles. You can rip or cut the edges off, and voilà, an easy-to-do stained-glass effect for the roof!

Life-size Paper Dolls

176
This paper alter ego is easy to fashion and a blast to outfit. Just trace around your child's body on brown paper and cut out the form. Brush the entire body with a thin layer of white glue and stick it, back to back, to another piece of paper (this will keep the doll from curling up).

Cut out the doubled shape and let the glue dry. Your child can use construction paper to decorate the doll and make hair. Have your child trace around the doll to fashion clothes from wrapping or construction paper, felt, or anything that strikes her fancy. Cut out the clothes and use paper clips to dress the doll in its new wardrobe.

Newspaper Sandals

177
Read all about it! Then roll it up and hit the town in these spiffy sandals, adapted from *The Anti-Boredom Book.*

MATERIALS FOR A PAIR
About 30 newspaper sheets (half of a full double-page)
Masking tape and craft glue

Roll each sheet of newspaper lengthwise into a tight tube and tape it. Press each tube hard along its length to flatten it into a 1-inch-wide strip. For each sandal, begin by making a 2-inch fold at one end of a strip and then coiling the strip tightly around the folded section. Tape the next strip to the end of the first and continue winding and taping until the oval is half the length of your foot. For a stronger sandal, wind a strip tightly across the width of the oval and tape it. Wind more strips around the outside of the sandal until it is big enough for your foot, then tightly tape around the entire perimeter (see Figure A).

For a strap, thread one end of a strip between two outer strips, then thread the other end through the other side (B). Position the strap so it fits your foot, then trim the ends and secure them with lots of glue or tape or both.

To finish the sandal, trace your foot on a colored sheet of newspaper (try the funnies!), cut out the shape, and glue it to the foot bed of the sandal. Finally, cut two 1-inch-wide strips from the same decorative newspaper and glue them around the edge and the strap of the sandal. Let dry, and strut!

A

B

Swirl Postcard

179 Based on the age-old principle that oil and water don't mix, this marbleized paper is one of those projects that looks difficult but is easy enough for a six-year-old.

MATERIALS

- Tupperware container, or aluminum foil or plastic takeout containers
- Small plastic eyedroppers
- Two or more colors of enamel paint (the kind used for models)
- Toothpicks or sticks
- A pack of white watercolor postcards or index cards

Fill your container halfway with water. Using an eyedropper, add a few drops of paint in different colors to the water. Swirl the colors with a toothpick or stick. Drop a blank card on the water. After a second or two, carefully lift the card straight up and set it aside to dry on newspaper or paper towels. When it's completely dry, if the card curls, place it beneath a heavy book for a couple of days to flatten the edges. **Tip:** You may want to clear the water between card dips by dragging a toothpick through the water.

Let's Paint!

178 Nothing celebrates color like paint. Get your child into a smock, mix up one of our fun recipes, and let her color her world. **Decorate your windows** with these easy-to-clean-up hues: mix 1 part powdered tempera paint with 2 parts clear dishwashing liquid and apply with paintbrushes. The dried paint wipes away easily with a dry paper towel. Make your own **puffy paint** by mixing drops of food coloring with 1 part each of flour, salt, and water. Use a squeeze bottle to paint designs on paper, which will dry puffy and textured. **For mess-free "finger painting,"** sandwich globs of tempera paint between two sheets of waxed paper, then press and squish to swirl the colors. To make prints of the resulting designs, remove the top sheet of waxed paper and lay a piece of plain paper atop the paint.

FamilyFun BOREDOM BUSTERS

Eric Carle Collage

Spread out the newspapers. Using a large paintbrush, completely paint a piece of paper one color. Paint contrasting dots with a small paintbrush or squiggles with a medium brush. For a funky, textured look, dip one of the found objects — say, the sneaker sole — into another paint color and press it all over the paper. Continue until you have enough papers to create your collage (about ten should do). Spread out the papers to dry completely.

On scrap paper, sketch an outline of the collage you'd like to create. We've chosen a bird, but the possibilities are endless: try a sailboat, a garden of flowers, even your own version of Carle's famously lonely firefly. Using this sketch as a guide, cut out the shapes from the painted papers.

Arrange the cutouts on white paper. Using the glue stick, glue down the large central piece of the picture first. Glue down the rest of the picture around it, according to the blueprint sketch you've created. Finally, draw in finishing touches such as eyes and feet with crayons or colored pencils.

180 Nobody can transform scraps into art like Eric Carle, beloved author of *The Very Hungry Caterpillar*. But his step-by-step instructions will bring out the collage master in your child.

MATERIALS

- **Newspapers**
- **Acrylic or tempera paints and paintbrushes**
- **White paper**
- **Found objects such as a carpet scrap, an old sneaker, sponges, a plastic comb, a slice of potato cut into a star**
- **Glue stick**
- **Crayons or colored pencils**

Quick Draw

"When my sons, Justin, now age 15, and Joshua, 12, were younger, I discovered an easy way to keep them amused while waiting for our order at a restaurant or while on a trip. I would keep a small pad of paper in my handbag, and whenever we found ourselves with a few extra minutes, I would draw random squiggles or shapes on pieces of paper and let them fill in the rest. At first, I drew shapes that resembled something specific (like a fish or a turtle). As they got older, I began making the squiggles more complex and encouraged them to turn the sheets upside down and sideways to look for other possibilities. In the beginning, they just drew faces, but before long they had created spaceships, aliens, monsters — even new animal species."

— Susan Michalczak, Orlando, Florida

Recycled Crafts

Sew Happy

"My four-year-old daughter, Tessa, and I thought it was wasteful to throw away all the colorful greeting cards she receives on her birthdays and holidays, so we created a way to recycle them: we make sewing cards. First we remove the back of the card, and then, on the front, we punch out a design using a standard hole punch. Tessa uses a darning needle and yarn (with a bit of clear tape on the end to keep it from unraveling) to weave in and out of the punched pattern. She gets to enjoy her cards again and again!"

— Terri Delzer,
Bismarck,
North Dakota

CRAFT SUPPLIES

Trash Treasures

181 Creative crafters can make something beautiful out of even the most unlikely materials. For example:

Crushed eggshells. Parents can dye them with a mixture of food coloring paste (a dab) and rubbing alcohol (3 tablespoons); kids can glue them onto paper to make mosaics. Store the extras in ziplock bags.

Packing material. The biodegradable packing peanuts made from cornstarch can be assembled into fascinating sculptures by moistening one end of each piece with a damp cotton swab to make them stick together.

Berry baskets. Use them as weaving boards for yarn, grass, or strips of paper; cover them with construction paper for buildings; add a string handle for a carry-along treasure basket; or print with them by painting the bottoms and pressing them onto paper.

Bubble Wrap. Assuming you can stop the kids from popping it all, paint a section and use it to make polka-dot prints that look like snakeskin.

Old socks. Turn mateless socks into beanbags (cut one at the ankle, fill with beans, then sew or glue it closed) or zany puppets, like the one shown above, using whatever recyclables you have on hand.

Craft scraps. Scoop those leftover sequins, pieces of felt, and pipe cleaners into a ziplock bag. When it's full, challenge your kids to use the contents of your Rainy-day Grab Bag to make something new, such as a collage or free-form sculpture. Larger pieces of unwanted artwork can be cut into strips or squares and used to make collage cards or quilted wrapping paper.

FamilyFun BOREDOM BUSTERS

The Paper Bag Neighborhood

182 This project illustrates two of the basic rules of boredom busting: it has a simple design that requires almost no instruction, and each child can put his own creative twist on the idea. The buildings can be purely imaginative — a fantasy house, say — or based on your actual town or neighborhood (making it a fun project for a classroom, troop, or church group).

MATERIALS

Large paper grocery bags (2 per building)

Markers and crayons

Newspaper

Glue stick and/or double-sided tape

Colored construction paper and
poster board

Old magazines and catalogs for cutting
out images

Toilet paper tubes

Give each child two flattened grocery bags. (If your bags have logos printed on the sides, you can create a plain surface by taping a brown paper sheet over the housefront or by carefully cutting apart the bag, turning it inside out, and taping it back together.) Have the kids decorate one of their bags with markers and crayons, drawing windows and doors, coloring in bricks or clapboards, and adding distinctive touches like cutout flower boxes and creeping ivy.

When the basic drawing and coloring are complete, stuff the second grocery bag with crumpled newspaper. Now open the decorated bag and slide it on top to create a six-sided block.

Help the crafters cut out, fold, and glue or tape in place shutters, doors, and stairs from colored paper. Add pictures of people, pets, and other images cut from magazines. Top off the house by cutting out a poster-board roof and gluing or taping it in place. For a crowning touch, add a chimney fashioned out of construction paper or a toilet paper tube.

WACKY FUN
Bottle Beings

183 They look like they're out of this world, but the fact is, you'll probably find everything you need to fashion these futuristic figures right in your recycling bin — which makes them the perfect project the next time rainy weather has your family housebound.

Fill your bottle bodies with plastic beads, pinto beans, pennies, or colored sand — anything you can pack in a plastic bottle.

For each head, use a craft knife (adults only) to cut a hole in a small ball. Make the opening just large enough to fit over the cap of the bottle body. If you're using a ball that's not hollow, such as a mini sponge ball, pull out some of the inner foam once you cut the opening (a foam football works especially well). Add facial features with acrylic paints, or use tacky glue to attach bottle cap or button eyes and milk-jug-cap ears. For hair, make holes in the ball and insert golf tees or plastic forks (trim the fork handles first).

Attach curled pipe cleaner or craft wire arms with packing tape, and tape on felt or craft foam hands.

HOMEMADE TOY
Glitter Globes

184 These mini aquariums make great boredom busters on a day when your kids are waiting for the sun to come out.

MATERIALS

- Baby food or jelly jar with a tight-fitting lid
- Polymer clay (such as Fimo)
- Small plastic or rubber toys and plants
- Water, glycerin, and glitter
- Small shells or aquarium gravel

Place the jar lid on a flat surface and use a small lump of clay to stick the bottom of each plastic item to the inside of the lid. Fill the jar almost to the top with water and stir in a few drops of glycerin and ½ teaspoon of glitter. Add shells and aquarium gravel. Finally, tightly screw the lid onto the jar. Then invert the globe and enjoy the glittery show.

FamilyFun

Bobbing Bird

185

With its comical waddle and tuxedolike coat, a penguin is always good for a laugh. Roll a ball at this toy bird, and he'll do a bouncy jig sure to put a smile on your child's face.

To make one, use a craft knife (adults only) to cut a flap in one side of a 1-liter plastic soda bottle. Place a fist-size ball of clay inside the bottle (this keeps it from toppling too easily), then pull a white athletic sock up over the bottle from the bottom. Twist a rubber band around the bottle neck to secure the sock and use the handle of a wooden spoon to tuck the sock top into the bottle. From black craft foam, cut a rectangle that wraps three quarters of the way around the bottle and extends about two thirds of the way up from the bottom. Trim the edges to resemble penguin wings and attach them to the sock with mounting tape. Next, cut out colored-foam eyes, a beak, a bow tie, and feet and tape them in place. Top off your bird with a detergent bottle–cap hat.

To make the penguin waddle, roll a rubber ball so that it knocks the bottle smartly without tipping it over.

Tin Man

186

This is our take on a popular spud-based toy: stored under his wig lid are magnetic features your child can use to create funny expressions on his tin can face.

MATERIALS

- Felt or craft foam
- Glue
- Permanent markers
- Magnetic tape
- Yarn and a rubber band
- Tin can, label removed
- Plastic lid that fits the can
- Craft knife

From the felt or foam, cut at least three different sets of eyes and ears, noses, and mouths. For details, such as teeth and eyelashes, try gluing together layered shapes or draw them on with markers. Stick magnetic tape to the back of each feature.

To make a wig, bind together a thick bunch of yarn with a rubber band. With the craft knife, cut two holes in the plastic lid (adults only). Thread the ends of the yarn up through the holes, as shown.

Milkmen

"My kids and I came up with a cute, inexpensive craft using 'chugs' (single-serving milk jugs) — we turn them into snowmen. First, we paint the lids to look like hats and add pom-poms to the tops. Then we glue buttons down the front of the white containers, attach beads and googly eyes for a face, and tie a fabric scrap around the neck for a scarf. They are so fun and easy to make that last year, my son's second grade class made them at a party and then filled them with candies to take home."

—Amy King, Roscoe, Illinois

Box Turtle

187 To make this boxy slowpoke, start with an empty gelatin box. For the head, cut a slit in the closed end and slide in the handle of a wooden ice-cream spoon. For the legs, cut two sets of slits in the skinny sides of the box and slide in two wooden craft sticks. Tape the head and legs in place inside the box.

For the tail, poke a doubled piece of pipe cleaner into the end flap, securing it inside the flap with tape.

Paint the turtle with green acrylic paint, let it dry, then sponge-paint the box with slightly darker paint. Glue tiny pompoms and googly eyes to the head and use a marker to draw the nostrils and toes.

HOMEMADE TOY

Dolled Up

188 Although they're made of common household materials, these dolls have personalities you can't keep bottled up.

Begin by turning a cotton sock inside out and stuffing the toe into the top of a dishwashing-liquid bottle. Turn the protruding portion of the sock right side out, pulling it down over the bottle in the process.

For the doll's face and neck, fold a piece of construction paper over the bowl of a short-handled wooden spoon. Trim the paper around the sides of the bowl and partway down the handle. Wrap a rubber band around the paper at the base of the handle to hold it in place.

Cut out and glue on a paper wig and ears. Use colored markers to draw on eyes and a mouth, or cut them from magazines. Then your child can accessorize her doll with real jewelry, hair ribbons, or a scrunchy shawl.

WATER FUN

The S.S. *Juice Box*

189 Hot weather invariably leads to two things: piles of empty juice boxes and thoughts of water. This craft lets you combine the two, as your young shipwrights head out to chart the depths of the backyard kiddie pool.

MATERIALS

Scrap plastic (like an old report cover or milk jug)

Permanent markers or stickers

Hole punch

Drinking straws

Scissors or craft knife

Empty juice box

Cut a rectangular sail from the scrap plastic and decorate it with markers or stickers. Punch a hole at each end and thread the straw through.

With the scissors or craft knife (a parent's job), cut a small X in the center of the empty juice box and insert the straw and sail. Float your boat in the wading pool, and blow through another straw to send it sailing.

Nature Crafts

WOODLAND CRAFT

Stick Vase

190 It's a natural fact that kids love gathering stuff outdoors. To put that stocking impulse to good use, save all their sticks for decorating this woodsy vase that even young children can make in minutes.

MATERIALS

Sticks (about 1/4 inch in
    diameter)
Clippers
Empty plastic peanut
    butter jar
2 thick rubber bands
Raffia or ribbon
Glue
Pinecones (optional)

Break or snip your sticks to about an inch longer than the jar. Put two rubber bands around the jar, an inch from the top and bottom. Now begin tucking the sticks under both rubber bands, placing them as close as possible to each other. Once you've surrounded the jar with sticks, slide the rubber bands together at the jar's middle and cover them with a decorative bow. Glue on a few pinecones, then fill the vase with flowers. For kids uninterested in flower arrangements, this vessel also makes a fine pencil holder.

Mushroom Magic

191 **To make a mushroom-spore print on paper, carefully trim the stem and lower edge of the cap of a store-bought mushroom to expose the gills. Set the cap on paper and cover it with an inverted glass. A few hours later, lift the glass and the mushroom to reveal a distinctive spore print.**

Beat-a-leaf Journal

192 This project combines your kids' most primal gathering instincts with another activity they love: banging rocks. Put the finished print on the cover of a blank notebook, and your kids will have a journal for recording their outdoor adventures.

MATERIALS

- **Green leaves**
- **Wooden board**
- **Small square of muslin**
- **Thumbtacks**
- **Flat, smooth, palm-size rock or hammer**
- **Blank journal**
- **Glue**
- **Twine, ribbon, or colored paper**

After selecting a leaf or two, lay them on the board (put a piece of paper on the board first if you don't want to stain it). Place the piece of muslin on top, tacking down the fabric at the corners so it won't shift. Using the rock or hammer, beat the fabric carefully but with consistent, even force. Lift up the fabric, and the leaf will have left its image in green. Glue the muslin square to the front cover of the blank journal. To cover the fabric's edges, glue on a border of twine, flat ribbon, or colored paper.

Nest Guests

193

After a brief foray for pinecones, you and your child can rustle up a happy family of owls.

MATERIALS

- Pinecones
- Tacky glue
- Googly eyes
- Brown and yellow felt
- Cardboard
- Shredded paper or fine wood packing material (sometimes called excelsior, and also sold at many craft stores)

First, you'll need to collect two large pinecones for the parents and a few small ones for the owlets. (If you can't find any outdoors, you can buy them at most craft stores.) Snip off a small portion from the bottom of each large cone so that it is flat enough to stand the cone on end.

Make eyes for all of the owls by glu-

ing googly eyes onto felt circles. Then glue the eyes to the cone. Glue on triangular felt ears and beaks as well.

For the owls' nest, cut out a cardboard circle (large enough to fit all the pinecones on). Glue on shredded paper or fine wood packing material in the shape of a nest. Allow the glue to dry. Lastly, apply glue to the bottom of each owl and carefully stick them all in place in the nest.

Pet Snake

195

Many snakes hibernate in the winter, but this colorful reptile can contentedly bask on a sunny windowsill all year. To make one, remove the bark from a small, curvy stick and have your child paint the wood with tempera or acrylic paints. For a tongue, use a pushpin to make a small hole in one end of the stick and insert a length of twisted craft wire, setting it in place with a dab of tacky glue.

Roll a Coaster

194

To make these leaf-imprinted coasters, just take a scavenging stroll outside: leaves and pine needles make lovely lasting impressions. Begin by cutting a 4-inch square cardboard template. Cover your work area with a piece of waxed paper and use a rolling pin to flatten a 2$\frac{1}{2}$-inch ball of self-hardening pottery clay to a $\frac{1}{4}$-inch thickness for each coaster. Arrange a pattern of leaves or pine needles atop the clay and gently press them into the clay with the rolling pin, leaving distinct but fairly shallow impressions. Remove the foliage and position the template on top of the clay. Use a butter knife to cut around the cardboard, then lift away the excess clay. Set the coasters aside to dry on a clean piece of waxed paper (this takes a day or so). Cover the dry coasters with a thin layer of matte acrylic varnish. Let it dry for 45 minutes, then accent your designs using a damp sponge and white paint. Let the paint dry thoroughly before adding a last coat of varnish.

Memory Stones

196
This stepping-stone path offers a concrete method of preserving your most precious harvest: happy memories.

MATERIALS

- 12-inch-diameter cardboard building form and small handsaw (optional)
- Spade
- Small stones or gravel
- Concrete mortar mix such as Quikrete (a 60-pound bag will yield 3 stones)
- Mixing tub or bucket, hoe, and trowel
- Scrap of wood
- Mementos (shells, pet rocks, broken china, small toys)
- Craft knife

Make the molds. For round stepping-stones, use the handsaw (adults only) to cut a 2½-inch-wide section from the building form. In the area where you'll be setting the path, dig a hole just large enough to accommodate the form and set it into the ground, firming the soil around it. Alternatively, you can create a free-form stone by digging a hole in the shape you desire, roughly 2½ inches deep. Once the mold is ready, place a 1-inch layer of small stones or gravel in the bottom.

Mix the concrete. Following the directions on the bag, combine the concrete with water in a mixing tub, stirring it with a hoe (parents only). It's ready to pour when it doesn't fall off a hoe held nearly parallel to the ground. Use the hoe and a trowel, if necessary, to scoop the concrete into each form. Smooth the surface with a scrap of wood.

Add mementos. When your fingertip leaves a lasting impression in the mixture (usually after one to two hours), you can start customizing. Using a stick or pebbles, write your name and the date, make impressions (of your hand, a favorite toy, a prize begonia), and add your mementos. Let the stones cure for several days — covering the stones with a cloth and misting them with water several times a day for three or four days will keep them from cracking in a severe winter. Remove the cardboard forms with a craft knife (adults only).

Beach Lights

197
A day at the beach means mayonnaise jars full of salty treasures. Why not put them to beautiful use? Your kids can sift through the day's loot and festoon these sparkling candleholders. They'll be ready just in time to light at the table.

Use tacky glue to stick assorted shells and sea glass

onto a glass votive-candleholder (these cost less than a dollar at craft stores). Allow it to dry, add a votive candle, and light! For immediate gratification (no drying time), a parent can use a hot-glue gun to affix the treasures.

SHELL CRAFT
Beach Butterflies

198 Before summer flies by, turn your family's beach finds into colorful keepsakes like the ones shown here. For each butterfly, you'll need a matching pair of small or medium-size clean, dry mussel, clam, or oyster shells. Arrange the pair side by side with the insides facedown and the hinged edges flush. Hot-glue the hinged edges together (a parent's job), creating a strong bond. Then bend a 6-inch length of pipe cleaner into a V and curl the tips to create antennae. Hot-glue the base of the V to the top of the glued joint. Now flip over the butterfly, and your child can use acrylic or puffy paint to adorn the insides of the shells with a distinctive wing pattern.

MUSIC TIME
Chime Bracelets

199 Made with shells or lightweight trinkets, these bracelets are fun to wear because they jingle when you move.

MATERIALS

Felt

Self-adhesive Velcro fastener

Large-eyed needle and yarn

Shells or charms

Cut out a strip of felt that will fit around your child's wrist or ankle with a half-inch overlap. Stick the parts of the Velcro fastener to the ends.

With the needle, individually thread short lengths of yarn through the felt along the lower edge and knot the tops to keep them from slipping back through. Glue shells or other charms to the strands, as shown.

HOMEMADE GAME
Nature Bingo

200 Try out this homemade beach-themed matching game. Trim index cards to fit inside a small metal box with a hinged lid (we used Altoids boxes). Use a ruler and pencil to mark each card into nine equal squares. Inside each square, use crayons or colored pencils to draw and label common nature sights, consulting a field guide as needed: we've chosen tide pools for a topic, but you could use any theme.

Put the finished cards inside the box, along with nine small, round magnets. Each player selects a card and places it inside the lid of the open tin. Every time you see a creature or plant from your card, mark it with a magnet. Three in a row — horizontal, vertical, or diagonal — wins. Or play to fill the whole card.

Ready to Wear

Friendly Face T-shirts

201 Perfect for a birthday party, sports team event, or family reunion, this project lets guests create their own favor — wearable mementos featuring the names and faces of their friends.

MATERIALS

- **Prewashed cotton or cotton-mix T-shirts (one for each person)**
- **Sheets of cardboard**
- **Potato and knife**
- **Fabric paints**
- **Stiff paper plates**
- **Fabric paint tubes and markers**

Before the party, prepare the shirts for decorating by stamping blank faces on them with your child. Begin by inserting a piece of cardboard inside each shirt. Chop a potato in half (adults only) to create an oval or circular stamp. Spread thin layers of fabric paint onto the plates and press in the potato stamp. Test the stamp on newspaper first, then on each shirt have your child stamp as many ovals as you'll have guests. Let the paint dry.

At the party, set out the prestamped shirts (with the cardboard inserts still inside), paint tubes, and markers. Guests can move from one shirt to the next, using the supplies to create a self-portrait on one of the faces and to autograph it beneath. Let the paint dry and heat-set according to the package directions.

Sleepytime Slippers

202 To make a pair of jungle slippers, place flip-flops on the back of a piece of fake fur and trace around the bottoms. Cut out the shapes, then make three slits where the foot straps join the insoles. Cover each insole with double-sided cloth carpet tape and roll the fur cutout onto the insole, adjusting it around the toe straps. Firmly press down on the fur, and slip on your slippers!

Psychedelic Tie-dye Shoelaces

203 This colorful project is sure to be a shoe-in with your kids! Just tie knots in white shoelaces about 1¹⁄₂ inches apart. Now prepare each color of dye in its own bowl by mixing equal parts fabric paint (we used Scribblers brand) and water (we started with a tablespoon of each). If needed, add a few drops of paint (to deepen) or water (to lighten) the color. Mix with a paintbrush or stick. Dip each

knot or loop into a different color. Remove the lace from the dye after a few seconds unless you want a very dark color. Keep in mind that the colors will bleed slightly. Dry the laces flat on a plastic bag. Undo the knots when the laces are dry.

Designer Flip-flops

204 Here's a fun project that will have your kids stepping out in the latest fashions.

MATERIALS

- Cloth ribbon, fringe, or similar trim
- Flip-flops with foam soles and foam or fabric straps
- Low-temperature glue gun

Cut a length of trim to fit around each flip-flop sole with a half-inch overlap. Cut separate pieces of trim for the left and right sides of the foot strap. To attach the trim to the sole, evenly apply a line of hot glue to a 2-inch section of the foam, using the glue gun tip to spread it if necessary. Firmly press the end of the trim onto the glued portion so that it sticks well, then smooth it toward the unglued section. Continue gluing and pressing until you've fully circled the sole. Use the same method to attach the strap trim. Let dry for 1 hour.

For a matching summer hat, you can attach trim with a nontoxic fabric glue.

Nature T-shirt

205 This method of capturing

the shapes of natural objects works best with shirts in bright hues of pink, blue, and green. Lay a solid-color shirt outdoors on a hard, flat surface, such as cement, away from anything that might be damaged by bleach. Arrange leaves, flowers, and other objects in a simple design on the shirt. Only the silhouettes will show, so objects with distinctive shapes work best. If there's a breeze, set stones on the objects to hold them in place. Wearing rubber gloves, use a spray bottle to spray the shirt lightly with bleach around all the edges of the design (adults only). Let the shirt set until you see the color start to change, about a minute or so. Carefully remove and dispose of the flowers and leaves. Submerge the shirt in a bucket of water and thoroughly rinse it. Put it through the washer and dryer, and it's ready to wear. Note: Be sure to label the spray bottle or empty and rinse it immediately.

Paper Bag Hats

206 Go shopping for a hat — at the

grocery store! With this wacky group activity, kids can create fashion in a bag.

MATERIALS

Paper bags, standard grocery size or slightly smaller
Tape (double-sided and clear)
Pom-poms, googly eyes, pipe cleaners, feathers, and other craft supplies
Construction paper
Hole punch
Green curling ribbon

Help each child gently roll down the top of a bag until it reaches the size hat he wants to wear. Have him try it on for size; if it slips over his eyes, pinch the brim to adjust the size, then tape.

Now set out craft materials for decorating the hat. Kids can make their hats as simple or as elaborate as they like. They can use double-sided tape to attach pom-poms, googly eyes, and feathers. For antennae, coil a pipe cleaner around a pencil, then tape on large pom-poms. Poke the end of the pipe cleaner through the hat and tape the inside to secure.

To make a flower, cut a flower shape out of construction paper. Punch two holes in its center and thread a 3-foot-long piece of green curling ribbon through the holes. Use scissors to curl the ribbon, then stick the flower to the hat with a piece of double-sided tape.

Fleece Hat

207 This cozy cap is just the thing to keep your child's noggin warm in brisk winter weather. In fact, it's so easy to put together — there's just one seam — she could even fashion some for chilly-headed siblings and friends!

MATERIALS

- Tape measure
- ¹/₂ yard fleece fabric
- Needle and thread
- Buttons, appliqués, or felt pieces for decoration
- 1 yard decorative cord

First, determine the size of the hat by measuring around your child's head with a tape measure. Now cut a piece of fleece that's 16 inches wide and as long as the measurement you took plus 2 inches.

Fold the fleece in half, right side in, so the 16-inch edges match up. Sew a ¹/₂-inch-wide seam along this edge, stopping 5 inches from the bottom (see Figure A). Just below the last stitch, make a ¹/₂-inch cut in from the side. Turn the material right side out. Now sew a seam along the last 5 inches of unsewn fleece (B).

Roll the bottom of the hat up two turns, so the cuff conceals the bottom part of the seam. To keep the cuff from unrolling, sew on a decorative button, an appliqué, or a felt cutout.

Finally, gather the top 3 inches of the hat and tie a colorful cord around it.

Glad Hatters

208 These decorated hats give new meaning to the expression "wearing a grin from ear to ear." All it takes to make one is a flat-top cotton hat, cardboard, fabric paints, and paintbrushes.

Start by trimming the cardboard to fit into the top of the hat; this will keep the fabric flat while you decorate it. Then paint the hat top to create a colored face (it's a good idea to mix whatever tint you choose with a bit of white to make the paint more opaque). Use two coats if needed, allowing the paint to dry after each application.

Next, lightly pencil on facial features and use different shades of paint to fill them in. Some features may need to be done in layers. To create a toothy grin, for example, first paint on white teeth only. When they dry, you can outline them with thin black lines or enclose them in bright pink lips. Once the last layer of paint dries, remove the cardboard from the hat, and it's ready to wear.

Felt fashion: For a quick decorating alternative, cut eyes, a nose, and a mouth out of adhesive-backed felt and firmly press them onto the hat.

Jewelry

BEAD CRAFT

Crystal Clear

209 It only takes a handful of translucent beads and some fishing line to make a necklace that's sure to reel in compliments.

MATERIALS

- Monofilament or fishing line
- Translucent glass or plastic beads
- 2 clamshell bead tips
- Needle-nose pliers
- Barrel clasp

Start with a piece of monofilament or fishing line that's twice the desired length of your necklace. String a bead onto the line, then loop the line back around and through the bead, as shown at right (this keeps the bead in place). Using the same method, add on the remaining beads, spacing them evenly. Insert each monofilament end into a clamshell bead tip and double-knot the line to keep the bead tips from slipping off. Use the pliers to pinch the bead tips, then attach the barrel clasp.

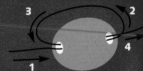

Hand Painted

210 Here's a handful of designs to inspire your young manicurist.

Starry Nights: Top a dark undercoat with a glittery gold star.

Tiger Stripes: Apply orange polish, then top with irregular black stripes.

Checkerboard: Apply a red base coat, then add staggered rows of black squares.

Cow: Paint the nail white. Top with black patches.

Pot of Gold: Paint a mini rainbow at the tip of the nail.

HOMEMADE GIFT

Hydro Bracelets

211 *Hydro* means water, and that's just what makes the beads and glitter in these bracelets float and sparkle.

MATERIALS

- **2 feet of clear plastic tubing with a ¼-inch inner diameter and 3 inches of clear plastic tubing with a ⅜-inch inner diameter (sold in most hardware stores)**
- **Ruler**
- **Tiny beads or glitter and water**

To create each bracelet (these materials make three), cut an 8-inch-long piece from the ¼-inch tubing and a 1-inch length from the ⅜-inch tubing (for a fastener). Slide both ends of the 8-inch tube into the fastener, as shown, and have your child try on the bracelet for fit. If it's too big, take it apart and trim it to size, remembering that it will need to slip over her hand. Remove one end of the bracelet from the fastener. Use a finger to stopper one end and drop in tiny beads or pieces of glitter. Now slowly fill the tube with water, leaving several inches of air so it has room to move. Carefully slide the free end into the fastener as far as it will go.

CLUTTER BUSTER

Cancan Girl

212 Although she looks like she's ready to kick up her heels, this gal is perfectly content to sit still and keep your child's stuff organized. Begin with a clean, empty can (for safety, cover the cut edge with tape). Glue pink paper around the outside of the can and create a skirt by gluing two lengths of crepe paper streamer around the can, one above the other, gathering and gluing a few inches at a time. Add a pipe cleaner waistband. Now glue on a pipe cleaner and feather headdress, hair made from strips of construction paper (curl it around a toothpick first), felt arms and hands (add pipe cleaner jewelry and fabric paint nails), and purple felt legs (use black fabric paint to create shoes and fishnet stockings). Finally, add facial features such as googly eyes, paper cheeks and lips, and curled paper lashes.

CHAPTER SEVEN

Brain Boosters

Inspiring activities that bring out

your child's natural curiosity

WHEN IT COMES to cheering up a rainy afternoon, multiplication tables are unlikely, we know, to be first on your child's list of activities. Baking cookies, on the other hand, just might be. What do the two have in common? Math skills, of course! But while straight-up arithmetic smacks of homework, cookie baking sneaks in skills deliciously. It's what we call stealth learning — a fun, casual way to encourage kids' curiosity about the world around them.

While helping to measure ingredients for a favorite recipe, your child starts to get the scoop on fractions. As she watches the backyard bird feeder, she peers into the secret lives of robins and wrens and discovers the thrill of scientific observation. These everyday learning moments often seem to come about by chance, but there are ways to make sure they happen more regularly.

What works best? Keep learning playful. You've probably noticed that some of the most memorable learning experiences take place when you and your children are just enjoying each other's company. The biggest hits don't have the feel of homework (for child or parent) but are simply new ways to have a good time together. Here are some of our favorite ideas — inspiration, we hope, to make learning fun in your home.

Encourage your kids' passions. Whenever you can, blur the boundaries between learning and pleasure. Does your child love writing stories? Help your budding author decorate a special journal and create a nest of pillows for him to write in. Got a kid who's wild for dinosaurs? Take a road trip to the nearest natural history museum or visit the library for some books on Jurassic life.

Show your own love of learning. Modeling enthusiastic learning habits is probably the best way to inspire a child. Get out the dictionary when your novel presents you with a word you don't know. Pore over the atlas to

Learning Activity Bingo

Want to keep your kids energized about learning? Try this activity-based version of bingo. Just set up a game board that includes all of your child's school subjects and write an activity in each square. The squares in the science category, for example, might ask your child to do a fun experiment, identify a new wildflower, or find an unfamiliar constellation. Mark every completed activity with a sticker and determine a prize for each bingo. Why not keep stealth learning in mind when you reward your winning contestant? Try a trip to a discovery museum.

Invent units of measure, page 306

further your understanding of international news. Bring along a field guide when you set out for a hike. Stay curious, and your child will inevitably follow suit.

Get involved at school. Volunteer in the library once a week, teach the class a family recipe, or tag along on field trips — the students will benefit from your skills and interests. In addition, a regular visit to the classroom will give you important information about what, and how, your child is learning.

Make your home a classroom. Think about organizing your house so that a variety of learning materials are readily accessible to your kids. Besides stocking your child's bookshelves with fiction and nonfiction, keep a telescope and an astronomy guide by the window, a box of utensils and containers earmarked for science experiments in the pantry, an up-to-date globe in the family room, and a good encyclopedia CD-ROM near the computer.

Science Experiments

Penciled In

213 Poke a hole in a plastic bag filled with water, and you're sure to spring a leak, right? Not necessarily. Try this!

MATERIALS

Plastic bag

Water

Sharpened pencils

Fill the bag three quarters of the way with water and then knot the top. With one hand, hold the bag over a sink. In one swift motion, push a pencil, point first, straight through one side of the bag and out the other. No water should leak out. See how many more pencils you can poke through without causing a leak.

The explanation behind this mysterious feat involves the elasticity of the plastic. When you pierce the bag, the plastic stretches and then breaks open just enough for the pencil to fit through. The glovelike fit leaves no room for the water to pass through.

Trick Your Buds

214 Without taste buds on our tongues (and a sense of smell), we couldn't tell jelly beans from lima beans. Most scientists think the tongue "specializes" in four tastes: sweet, salty, sour, and bitter. Slice some citrus fruit and touch different parts of your tongue with it. Is the taste most distinct on the sour sections? Now rinse your mouth and try again with a bit of banana. Does it taste best on the sweet section?

er
ty
eet
Sour

Raisin Races

215 This wacky game demonstrates some fascinating science — and refreshes your kids with a cold drink. Carefully fill glasses with equal amounts of a clear carbonated beverage, trying to minimize the fizzing. On cue, everyone drops in a raisin, which should sink to

the bottom, then — as the carbon dioxide bubbles gather on the raisin's surface, increasing its buoyancy — quickly rise to the surface. First raisin to the top wins.

SCIENCE TRICK

A Glass of Air

216 This trick offers graphic proof of how much air and water don't like each other: they won't even share the same glass.

First, wedge a paper napkin tightly in the bottom of a clear plastic glass or cup. Now turn the glass so its rim is down and sink it straight into the water, being careful not to tilt the rim. If the trick is done right, the trapped air will prevent the water from entering the glass, and the napkin will stay high and dry. **Note:** The diving bells of old operated on the same principle. In essence, they were huge metal cups that held a bubble of air for the divers to breathe.

FASCINATING PHYSICS

Amazing Eggs-periment

217 You'd think that forcing a hard-boiled egg through the neck of a bottle would be near impossible. But here's how you can use physics to make it happen.

MATERIALS

- Peeled hard-boiled egg
- Glass returnable milk bottle (ask at natural food stores)
- Bowl of cold water
- Hot tap water
- Dish gloves

First, try it yourself: set the egg on the mouth of the bottle and try to push it inside without smooshing the egg. Give up? Now place the egg in a bowl of cold water. Meanwhile, place the milk bottle under hot tap water for a minute or so, letting it fill. Then, wearing dish gloves to protect your hands, empty the water down the drain (a parent's job). Quickly place the egg, tapered end down, on the mouth of the bottle and watch carefully. The egg slowly gets sucked into the bottle with a satisfying *thunk*. That's because the hot air inside the bottle is less dense (and thus at a lower pressure) than the cooler outside air. The difference creates a suction that pulls the squishy egg through the bottle neck.

Lava Lite

218

This seventies-style retro-vention uses the principles of immiscible liquids (fluids that just won't mix) and density to create the Lava Lite, a homemade version of that classic mind-expanding device, the Lava lamp.

MATERIALS

Glass jar

Water with food coloring added

$1/3$ cup vegetable oil

Shaker filled with salt

Fill the jar with 3 inches of the colored water. Add the oil and let the layers settle. Shake in salt while you count to five. The oil and salt should form a glob and sink to the bottom of the jar, but after a short while, the oil should float back to the top. Add salt again to watch the action repeat.

Here's what's going on: At first, the oil floats on top because it's less dense than water. The salt, however, is denser than the water. When you shake it onto the oil, it drags a glob to the jar bottom. There, the salt dissolves in the water and can no longer hold down the oil blob, which rises back to the surface.

Rubber Blubber

219 Invite your young scientists to see what happens when glue molecules interact with a borax solution – you end up with a rubbery substance that actually bounces!

Directions: Combine 1 quart of water and 1 tablespoon of borax in a large jar. Stir well and let the mix stand for a few minutes. Next, fill a disposable cup three quarters of the way with the borax solution. Stir in a few drops of food coloring. Add white glue (in a thin, steady stream), stirring continuously. Keep adding glue until a large stringy mass wraps around the spoon. Pull the mass off the spoon and drop it into a container of cold water. Then remove the Rubber Blubber and, with dry hands, squeeze it for a minute or so to get rid of the air bubbles. Now roll it into a ball and see how high it will bounce. Store the Rubber Blubber in a plastic bag.

Brain Boosters

Rocket Balloons

220 This activity, which turns balloons into rockets, is great for teaching kids about Isaac Newton's Third Law of Motion (for every action, there is an equal and opposite reaction). That's because the balloon gets its lifting thrust from air rushing out of the neck. For each rocket, securely tape one end of a long string to the ceiling. Thread a drinking straw onto the string, then stretch the string taut to the floor and tie it to a weight or tape it down. Have each kid inflate a long, torpedo-shaped balloon and keep the neck pinched shut while you tape it to the straw. While the kids hold their balloons near the floor, count down to takeoff and see whose rocket goes fastest and highest.

KITCHEN EXPERIMENT

Volcano in a Bottle

221 More than 2,000 square miles of Hawaii's Big Island have been covered with the lava flows of Mauna Loa, the world's biggest volcano. Here's a vivid way to show your child how and why a volcano erupts.

MATERIALS

- **Small plastic water bottle**
- **Warm water**
- **Red food coloring**
- **¼ cup vinegar**
- **Heaping teaspoon baking soda**

Set the bottle in your sink and fill it three quarters of the way with warm water. Add a few drops of red food coloring and the vinegar. Now, using a kitchen funnel held just above the bottle top, quickly add the baking soda. The mixture will instantly fizz and overflow from the bottle.

Inform your child that vinegar and baking soda together produce carbon dioxide — the very gas that makes hot liquid rock beneath the earth's surface erupt from Mauna Loa and other volcanoes.

MAGNET FUN

Magnetic Attractions

222 Here are a couple of simple experiments that will let your kids explore the world of magnet magic.

Compass in a Bowl: Magnetize a needle by repeatedly stroking it in one direction with the end of a magnet. Cut a slice of cork, set it in a bowl of water, and place the needle on top. The needle will slowly turn to align itself with the lines of force of the earth's magnetic field.

Flying Fish: Cut a fish shape from lightweight paper and affix a paper clip. Tie a length of thread to the clip. Tape the opposite end of the thread to the inner bottom of a glass jar (one that has a metal lid), adjusting the thread length so that the clip almost (but not quite) reaches the rim. Screw on the lid and place a magnet on top of it. Then invert the jar so that the clip is caught in the magnetic field. Finally, turn the jar upright again, and your fish will be flying.

Eyewitnessed

223 Pictures, written words, and other things we see account for two thirds of the information we store in our brains. But sometimes what we think we see isn't real. Here are a few ways our eyes play tricks on us.

Seeing Spots: Color a nickel-size red dot on white paper. Place this sheet atop another blank sheet, then set them under a bright light and stare at the dot for 30 seconds. Remove the top sheet and stare at the blank paper. A green spot will appear. Staring at the dot fatigues the cone cells on your retina that see red. Look away, and the ones that see green (a complementary color to red) briefly overcompensate, so you see a "ghost" image.

Missing Money: Place a quarter on a table and set an empty glass jar on top of it. Looking through the side of the jar, focus on the coin while you pour in enough water to nearly fill the jar. The coin will seemingly disappear. Here's why: the empty jar lets light bounce straight from the coin to your eyes. When the jar is filled, the water refracts light, bending it away from your eyes and making the coin invisible.

Now You See It: Form a circle with your thumb and index finger and

hold it at arm's length. Looking through the circle, focus on an object. Without moving, close one eye and then the other. One eye will see the object through the circle; the other won't. That's because one eye is dominant and does the job of focusing your gaze.

Stir Up an Incredible Edible Lens

224 Next time you're making a light-colored batch of gelatin dessert, fill the bottom of a wineglass with about an inch of the liquid. Refrigerate the gelatin for at least 4 hours. When it is completely set, run hot water over the outside of the glass and use a warm, wet knife to gently loosen the gelatin. Now invert the gelatin, flat side down, onto a piece of damp, clear plastic wrap — and look before you eat! Try moving your jiggly lens different distances from a newspaper or other objects you want to magnify.

Brain Boosters

Reading

QUICK CRAFT

Page Savers

Reading can be lots of fun — until you lose your page! These clip-on place keepers come in handy.

Bead Bangles: Tie thin cording to a paper clip. String on beads or charms. Then double-knot the loose end to keep the beads from slipping off.

Fuzzy Braid: Bend three different-colored pipe cleaners in half and hook them over one end of a paper clip. Pair up and braid the like-colored ends and pinch together the bottoms.

NEIGHBORHOOD FUN

Start a Book Club

225 A kids' book club can relieve boredom on two fronts. First, it offers a fun weekly (or monthly) occasion to look forward to, and second, it is a great incentive to read stories that jump-start the imagination.

To make lighter work, partner up with a friend, then send out invitations that include the title of the first book (ask your librarian for a recommendation) and a weekly time to meet. Before each club meeting, have all the kids read the same book (or specified chapters).

Then, when members get together, they can share their thoughts — and some snacks too.

To get things started, the host child might want to make a list of five or so discussion questions (What was your favorite part? Who was the best character?). Or, if the readers are younger, you can read aloud while they listen or draw along to the story. If the kids like, you might consider choosing a loose theme for the books — for example, all wintertime stories or books from everyone's favorite series of the moment.

WORD GAME

Play Dictionary

226 Words rule in this bluffing game. One person reads a word from the dictionary that he thinks no one knows. While he writes down the real definition, the other players write fakes that sound wacky enough to be true. Next, he reads out all of the definitions. Whoever picks the real one gets 1 point. If no one does, the chooser gets 2 points. Now it's someone else's turn to pick a word.

Late-night Reading

227 Bookworms and night owls unite in this special literary treat. Give your kids a flashlight and let them stay awake later than usual to read in the dark. They'll start looking forward to bedtime, plus they'll get in some extra reading time. Try ten minutes on weeknights and a longer (or unlimited) time on weekends.

Home Library

"My daughter, Cailin, wanted to start her own library, so I scoured yard sales and used-book sales and found about 50 books (the average price per book was 25 cents). Then I bought a date stamp and ink pad, and with the help of our school librarian, I got book pockets and book cards. Cailin, her sister, Erin, and their friends have spent hours checking out books and hosting story-time at our new neighborhood library."

— Connie Lowry
Gastonia, North Carolina

Bring Books to Life

228 A great book doesn't have to end when you've read the last page. As the following examples show, the simplest activity is often all it takes to keep the story alive in a child's imagination.

Cook a storybook recipe: Make chocolate sauce after reading *Charlie and the Chocolate Factory,* bake old-fashioned breads or cookies from *The Little House on the Prairie,* or serve a tiny buffet — an apple, a tea sandwich, an oatmeal cookie — à la *The Very Hungry Caterpillar.*

Put on a teddy bear picnic: Read *Winnie-the-Pooh, Paddington Bear,* or *Corduroy* books and have everyone bring their bears to a picnic in the park.

Grow a garden: Be inspired by *The Lorax* and plant a tree to take care of the earth and beautify your yard. Or follow Mary Lenox's lead in *The Secret Garden* and bring new life to an old flowerbed.

Go on a treasure hunt: Design a map according to the storybook: a deserted island from *Treasure Island* or Neverland from *Peter Pan.*

Make a craft: Fashion a small raft out of sticks after reading *The Adventures of Tom Sawyer* or make Harry Potteresque wizard hats with poster board and sticker stars.

Brain Boosters

Writing Games

WORD GAME

Snip a Silly Sentence

230 Even kids who think they don't like to write will enjoy this playful word game. Give everyone a pair of scissors, blank paper, a glue stick, and a part of the newspaper. Tell them they have to construct a silly sentence using any words or phrases they see in the headlines. The punnier and funnier, the better! Don't forget to read your snippy sentences aloud and post them on the fridge or family bulletin board.

He loves his steady progress in **making** students just take the day off

Honoring a celebrated brother is The ultimate victory

Swamp Bat may help kids to get money

ACTIVITY KIT

Writing Basket

229 This stationery supply station will come in handy whenever your kids want to write a letter or send a thank-you note.

MATERIALS

Stationery supplies
Wire mesh or
    plastic desk
    organizer

First, let your kids help pick out a cool assortment of postcards, notecards, stickers, stamps, pencils, and pens. Then fill out a personal calendar book together, recording important addresses, birthdays, anniversaries, and any other significant dates. Put all the write stuff in a tidy organizer and keep it in an accessible place. You might even set aside a special time each week and call it "Write a Note Night."

FAMILYFUN READER IDEA

The Alphabet Museum

"Nicolas, my kindergartner, needed an entertaining way to learn his letters and start recognizing words, so we hit upon the idea of setting up an Alphabet Museum. We gathered all the boxes we could find, then went looking through his toy chest for things whose names started with different letters. I wrote 'Aa' on the first box, and Nicolas found a toy airplane to put inside. I added the word airplane to the top of the box. It took clever thinking to find an item for every box (such as a yak Beanie Baby for Y!). But when we finished, we held a grand opening and invited the rest of the family to guess what was in each box before Nicolas 'read' the word and showed us."

— *Pat McGough-Wujcik*

In-house Mailbox

231 Getting her own mail can be really exciting for a child. A note from a friend, a card from Grandma, even junk mail is quickly opened and (here's why we're telling you this) eagerly read. The experience can be all the more special if the mail is delivered to a personalized indoor mailbox. On days when there's no real mail, you can surprise your child with a short letter or postcard you wrote yourself.

MATERIALS

Shoe box

Decorative supplies (construction paper, glitter, paint, stamps, photographs)

Red poster board

Paper fastener

Scissors

Have your child decorate a shoe box using construction paper, glitter, paint, stamps, photographs, and other supplies of her liking. Cut a flag out of poster board and attach to the box with the paper fastener so it can be raised when someone leaves a letter. You can cut a delivery slot in the box top or merely remove the cover to deposit and retrieve mail.

Put the finished mailbox in a prominent spot and keep a pad of paper and a pencil near it. Then try to keep the mail flowing by encouraging other family members and visitors to post a friendly note whenever the mood strikes.

Words on the Fridge

232 Turn your kitchen into a learning zone. Gather your alphabet magnets, grab the dictionary, and spell out words your family doesn't ordinarily use. Now challenge everyone to incorporate them into your daily conversations.

Cooking Lessons

233 In Colonial days, when children learned the alphabet, their families celebrated by making gingerbread letters. Try it yourself by rolling out your favorite gingerbread or sugar cookie dough and cutting out a tasty batch of letters. Roll the dough flat to a ¼-inch thickness and let your kids cut out large letters with a butter knife (if you're lucky enough to have them, you could use alphabet cookie cutters). With a spatula, set the letters on a lightly greased baking sheet and bake them according to your recipe's directions. Once the cookies cool, your kids can spell words before they eat them. (Y-u-m would make a nice-size snack; w-o-n-d-e-r-f-u-l might be a two- or three-person job!)

Math Magic

Invent Your Own Units of Measure

234 Young kids get practice counting, and learn that numbers have meaning, when you teach them how to measure. But instead of employing a ruler or measuring tape, show them how to use their own hand or foot as a sizing-up device. Attaching your child's name to this new custom unit — calling it a Joshua foot or a Jenna hand — adds to the fun. How many Joshua feet does it take to cross the parking lot? How many Jenna hands long is the cat? With his own custom unit, your child is always equipped to "measure up"!

Par 20: Card Game

235 This game is great for improving a child's math skills. Plus, it poses an interesting challenge: scoring as few points as possible.

WHAT YOU NEED

A deck of cards (remove the jacks and kings)

Paper and a pencil

Deal five cards to each player and place the rest of the deck facedown. Starting left of the dealer, players try to make a mathematical equation totaling 20 from any three of their five cards (aces equal 1, and queens equal 0). If you have, say, 6, 3, 7, 8, and 2, one answer would be $6 \times 3 + 2 = 20$. If you succeed, you get zero points. If your equation doesn't equal exactly 20, your score for that round is the difference (higher or lower) between your total and 20. A total of 18 or 22, for example, saddles you with 2 points. After recording your equation and score, discard your used cards and draw new ones. Whoever has the lowest score after five rounds wins.

Go on a Treasure Hunt

Maribeth Knierim of Mokena, Illinois, knows few things appeal to a kid's sense of adventure more than a treasure hunt — an allure she uses to teach math to her two sons, Austin, age nine, and Max, five. The list of clues for one of her hunts might read: A. Start at the porch facing north. B. Take 4×5 steps. C. Turn left and jump $8 + 46$ times. D. Face west and skip 6×2 times. E. Look under the rock marked X. Sometimes the boys discover chocolate coins, but mostly, Maribeth says, they have a good time learning to add, multiply, and follow directions.

FamilyFun BOREDOM BUSTERS

Tricky Triangles

236 Sometimes the key to answering a tricky math problem has everything to do with how you look at it. Take this cheesy pyramid puzzle. How many triangles can you find? One? Sixteen? More? To come up with the total number, you'll need to look at the big and little picture.

(For the answer, see page 313.)

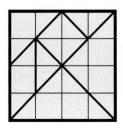

GEOMETRIC PUZZLE

Tangram

237 The Chinese call this classic game *Qi Qiao Ban*, which translates as "seven clever pieces." To make it, repeatedly fold a square of paper in half to create 16 smaller squares, then cut the open sheet along the bold lines, as shown below, to make a square, a rhomboid, and five triangles. With the cutout shapes, you can make hundreds of designs. For starters, see if you and your kids can piece together the long-eared rabbit shown above.

GEOMETRY PROJECT

Triangular Construction

238 Sometimes more is less. Take a triangle. It only has three sides, but when used in construction, it's stronger than a square. That's because a triangle spreads the force equally over its sides, which keeps it from collapsing under pressure. (That's why a pitched roof is supported by a series of wooden triangles — to keep it from caving in under heavy rain or snow.) Here's a fun — and flavorful — way your child can test the strength of triangular construction.

MATERIALS

Toothpicks

Lots of gumdrops

Push the tips of three toothpicks into three gumdrops to create a basic triangle.

With two more toothpicks and another gumdrop, attach an adjoining triangle.

Add more and more toothpick triangles to build a bridge or a tower — then test its strength by seeing how many CDs it can hold.

The Natural World

Great Gizzards

239 This activity demonstrates how birds digest their insect meals. First, explain to your child that birds swallow their food whole, then th[e] stomach's digestive juices break it into smaller pieces. These bits the[n] pass into a muscular organ called a gizzard, which grinds the food. [Fill?] a sturdy plastic bag (for a gizzard) with a half cup of uncooked rolle[d] oats. Drop in 15 marbles to simulate the small stones that birds swallow t[o] aid digestion and seal the bag. Have your child knead the bag to mimic the contracting walls of a gizzard. Shortly, the oats will be ground into fine bits.

The Buzz on Hummingbirds

240 The world's smallest birds are tall on talent. The buzz that a hummingbird makes comes from the incredible speed of its beating wings — up to 80 beats a second. To help your child gauge just how fast that is, ask her to clap her hands as many times as possible for one minute. Divide that number by 60 to get the number of "beats" per second. How'd she do?

Set Up a Birding Basket

241 The sudden arrival of a colorful new visitor at a backyard bird feeder can be just the thrill that turns on a kid to the wonders of the natural world. Put together a birding basket — equipped with binoculars, guidebooks, and a birding log — and she'll be ready for bird-watching at the drop of a feather.

The National Audubon Society suggests that you furnish your basket with compact, rubber-coated binoculars; a good guidebook, such as the group's own *First Field Guide: Birds* by Scott Weidensaul; and a blank journal, pen, and coloring pencils. The journal can be used for sketching and keeping track of the birds you see — their shapes, colors, and sizes, whether they chirp or sing, or any other interesting trait.

Backyard Bug Safari

242 You may think that only humans can garden, but the truth is, certain insects lend a hand in helping vegetables grow. Here are a few you and your child can try to spy.

Dragonfly: Also called a sewing needle or snake dragon, this long-bodied, four-winged insect has been around for about 300 million years and likes to eat pesky mosquitoes.

Ladybug: These ladies (or gents) are usually red with black spots, but can be yellow, orange, or black. They're great at polishing off aphids, which feed on roses and broccoli.

Praying mantis: A master of disguise, this critter can blend in with its environment and is adept at catching flies and moths.

Walk in a Spider's Shoes

244 To catch its dinner, a spider spins a sticky silk web for unsuspecting insects to land on. So why doesn't the spider itself get stuck? One theory is that it covers its feet with an oily liquid. To see how this works, have your child rub a bit of shortening on his fingertips. Place a long strip of tape (sticky side up) on a table. Use shorter pieces to tape down the ends. Now your child can easily walk his fingers the length of the strip.

Brain Boosters

Ant Farm

243 An ant farm gives you a chance to see how hard ants work to dig tunnels and get food. We like this design (adapted from one in *Do Bees Sneeze?* by James K. Wangberg), which is made with things from your recycling bin.

MATERIALS

2 widemouthed plastic jars that fit fairly closely one inside the other (we used 1-quart and ½-gallon jars)

Sandy soil

Sponge, bottle cap, corn syrup, and string

Scrap paper and black paper

Plastic wrap, rubber bands, and a pin

Place the smaller jar inside the larger one and fill the gap between the two with soil. Wet the sponge and place it in the smaller jar, along with a capful of corn syrup. Dangle several lengths of string from the soil in the larger jar to the bottom of the small jar so the ants can reach their food and water.

Now look around your neighborhood for ants (under parental supervision, as ants can bite). When you find an area with lots of ants, put down a sheet of paper with a bit of corn syrup on it. When several dozen ants have gathered on the paper, quickly transfer them to the jar. Cover the mouth of the jar with plastic wrap, secure it with a rubber band, and use a pin to poke airholes (smaller than the ants!) through the plastic. Wrap black paper around the jar (secure it with another rubber band) to keep the ant farm in the dark. When you remove the paper in a day or two, you should see the beginnings of a network of tunnels. Add more syrup and water, as needed. When you're done observing, release the ants where you found them.

Index

Eggheads,
141

Answer Key

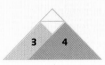

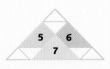

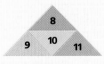

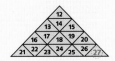

Art & Photography Credits

Special thanks to the following *FamilyFun* magazine photographers, illustrators, and stylists for their excellent work:

Photographers

Susan Barr: *224, 225 top right and left)*

Robert Benson: *44, 151, 216 (top), 294*

Robert Bossi: *Front Cover (bottom left), 236 (bottom), 262, 263 (top), 264 (top, bottom), 265 (bottom)*

Paul Berg: *63 (bottom right), 156, 157 (middle)*

John Burke: *80*

Michael Carroll: *25 (bottom left), 99, 150*

Susie Cushner: *62, 101 (top)*

Ron Dahlquist: *74 (right three), 75, 77*

Peter N. Fox: *Front Cover (top center), 20 (top left), 68, 76 (bottom left), 93 (bottom), 101 (bottom), 104 (left), 107 (bottom right), 121 (top left and bottom left), 128-129, 134 (top left and bottom left), 135, 143 (bottom right), 144, 160, 161 (right), 162 (top and bottom middle), 168, 170 (bottom left), 173 (bottom left), 176, 181, 184 (left), 185, 190 (top, bottom left), 191 (top), 198-200, 201 (bottom), 202 (bottom), 203 (top), 206 (top right), 205 (bottom), 206-207, 208 (top right and bottom), 209 (top, middle) 227 (top right), 237 (bottom right), 239 (bottom left), 240-241, 244 (bottom), 245 (top, middle), 246 (top, bottom), 251, 252, 254-255, 258 (bottom), 259, 260 (top), 268, 272 (right) 276 (right), 275, 276 (bottom), 279, 282 (bottom), 288, 289 (top right, bottom), 291 (bottom), 292-293, 297 (bottom right), Back Cover (top right and top left)*

Jim Gipe: *78 (top left), 146*

Andrew Greto: *173 (bottom right), 201 (top), 226, 277*

Jacqueline Hopkins: *154 (top left and bottom right)*

Tom Hopkins: *27 (top)*

Ed Judice: *Front Cover (top left, top, middle, lower right, middle center, middle left, bottom center)16-18, 20 (top right and bottom right), 21(bottom), 22, 24, 28, 31, 33 (top left), 34, 35, 38, 45, 47 (bottom) 48, 49 (bottom), 50-53, 55, 56 (bottom right), 59 (top left and bottom left), 64, 65 (bottom), 70, 72-73, 76 (top left and middle), 82, 84, 85, (top and bottom left), 87-88, 89 (top left), 94, 96 (top left) 100, 106, 107 (top left, middle left and bottom left), 108, 109 (top), 110, 112-113, 115 (bottom), 117 (top left, top middle, and botttom), 118, 121 (bottom right), 123 (top and bottom left), 125 (top right), 127, 133, 134 (top right and bottom right), 136, 137 (bottom left and bottom middle), 138 (bottom left) 139-140, 141 (top middle and middle left) 145, 148, 152 (bottom right), 155 (top left and bottom left), 157 (bottom right), 158, 161 (left), 163 (top left and bottom left), 169, 171 (top, bottom left, and right), 172, 173 (top and bottom middle), 175 (bottom), 177-179, 180 (middle), 182 (top), 183, 184 (top and bottom right), 186-189, 190 (bottom right), 191 (bottom), 192 (right), 193, 205 (top), 210-211, 213-215, 217-221, 222 (right), 223, 225 (bottom), 227 (bottom), 228-229, 230 (top, and middle), 232 (top), 233-235, 236 (top), 237 (top and bottom left), 239 (bottom right), 242 (right), 243 (right), 244 (top), 246 (middle), 248 (bottom), 249 (top), 250 (middle), 256-257, 258 (top), 260 (bottom), 261 (top), 263 (bottom), 264 (middle), 265 (top), 266 (top), 269-271, 273-274, 276 (top), 280-281, 282 (top and middle), 283-285, 286 (top), 287 (left), 289 (top left), 290, 295-296, 297 (top and bottom left), 298 (bottom), 299 (bottom), 304, 301 (top), 302, 303 (top left), 304, 305 (top and bottom), 306-309, Back Cover (bottom left and bottom right)*

Al Karevy: *238 (top and middle)*

Brian Leatart: *131, 132, 142, 239 (top)*

Lightworks Photographic: *8-9, 19 (top), 21 (top), 23 (top* right), 26 (top right and middle), 29, 33 (bottom), 36, 37, 39 , 40, 41, 42 (bottom), 43, 46 (bottom right), 47 (top left), 54, 56 (top left), 57-58, 59 (right), 60-61, 63 (top left), 67, 71, 79 (top), 81, 83, 85 (bottom right), 86, 89 (bottom right), 90, 91-92, 93 (middle), 95, 96 (top right and bottom), 103 (bottom), 105, 109 (middle and bottom), 111, 114, 115 (top), 116, 117 (right), 120, 121 (middle right), 123 (bottom right), 125 (top left), 126, 137 (top), 141 (bottom right), 143 (top), 149, 152 (top), 153, 154 (bottom left), 159 (top right and bottom, 162 (bottom right), 195 (top)

Marcy Maloy: 69, 104 (top middle and bottom), 194, 195 (bottom)

Robert Manella: 192 (left)

David Martinez: 286 (bottom), 287 (right)

Todd Powell: 78 (middle left and bottom)

Jim Scherer: 122 (bottom)

Joanne Schmaltz: 231 (right), 242 (left), 247 (right), 266 (bottom left), 271 (top), 305 (middle)

Shaffer/Smith Photography: 10-15, 26 (middle right and bottom [crayon shades]), 30, 97, 147, 155 (bottom right), 170 (top right), 171 (bottom middle), 174, 197, 202 (top and middle), 209 (bottom), 232, (bottom), 249 (bottom), 261 (bottom), 278 (top), 298 (top), 299 (top), 301 (bottom)

Steve Smith: 98, 102, 119, 124, 125 (bottom), 130, 138 (top left and middle), 163 (top right and bottom right)

Team Russell: 32, 66, 76 (bottom right), 79 (bottom right), 93 (top), 212, 231 (left), 243 (left), 245 (bottom), 250 (top), 253, 266 (bottom right)

Illustrators

Douglas Bantz: 180, 219, 244, 250, 260, 275, 292

Eldon Doty: 222, 313

John Hart: 40, 259, 271

Sandy Littrell: 150, 151

Bruce Macpherson: 303

Jeff Moores: 182, 194, 238, 252, 300, 301

Debbie Palen: 186, 193, 229

Kevin Rechin: 247, 258

Donna Ruff: 44, 126, 146, 216 (top)

Maryellen Sullivan: 103

John Ursino: 113

Stylists

Fazia Ali, Bonnie Anderson/Team, Grace Arias, Bonnie Aunchman-Goudreau, Laurie Baer, Suzanne Boucher/Ennis, Melissa Boudreau/Team, Margo, Brumme, Catherine Callahan, D.J. Carey, Carol Case, Mary Cates, Pamela Courtleigh, Bill Doggett, Katia Echivard, Erica Ell/Team, Susan Fox, Ron Garnica, Harriet E. Granthen, Scott Gordon/Ennis, Anastasia Hagerstrom/Koko Represents, Karin Lidbeck, Jacqueline Lemieux-Bokor, Karin Lidbeck, Barbar Jo Metcalfe, Amy Malkin Pearl, Marie Piraino, Karen Quatsoe, Jilliam Rahm, HIlda Shum, Lisa Smith/Ennis, Edwina Stevenson, Karen Uzell, Stacey Webb, Nan Whitney/Ennis, Lynn Zimmerman

Geodesic dome, page 274

Also from FamilyFun magazine

✳ FamilyFun magazine: a creative guide to all the great things families can do together. Call 800-289-4849 for a subscription.

✳ FamilyFun Cookbook: a collection of more than 250 irresistible recipes for you and your kids, from healthy snacks to birthday cakes to dinners everyone in the family can enjoy (Disney Editions, $24.95).

✳ FamilyFun Home: a handbook of 200 creative projects and practical tips to make your home truly family-friendly (Disney Editions, $24.95).

✳ FamilyFun Parties: a complete party planner featuring 100 celebrations for birthdays, holidays, and every day (Disney Editions, $24.95).

✳ FamilyFun Cookies for Christmas: a batch of 50 recipes for creative holiday treats (Disney Editions, $9.95).

✳ FamilyFun Tricks and Treats: a collection of wickedly easy crafts, costumes, party plans, and recipes for Halloween (Disney Editions, $14.95).

✳ FamilyFun.com: visit us at www.familyfun.com and search our extensive archives for games, crafts, recipes, and other boredom-busting activities.